Super-State

Also by Stephen Haseler

The Gaitskellites
The Death of British Democracy
Eurocommunism
Battle For Britain: Thatcher and the New Liberals
Anti-Americanism
The Politics of Giving
The End of the House of Windsor
The English Tribe
The Super-Rich

Super-State

The New Europe and Its Challenge to America

Stephen Haseler

I.B. TAURIS

LONDON · NEW YORK

Reprinted 2005
Published in 2004 by I.B.Tauris & Co Ltd
6 Salem Road, London W2 4BU
175 Fifth Avenue, New York NY 10010
www.ibtauris.com

In the United States of America and in Canada distributed by
Palgrave Macmillan, a division of St Martin's Press
175 Fifth Avenue, New York NY 10010

ISBN 1 86064 843 6
EAN 978 1 86064 843 4

A full CIP record for this book is available from the British Library
A full CIP record for this book is available from the Library
of Congress

Library of Congress catalog card: available

Typeset in Ehrhardt MT by Steve Tribe, Andover
Printed and bound in Great Britain by TJ International Ltd, Padstow, Cornwall

Contents

Preface

This is a book about Europe's future. But, as my life on both sides of the Atlantic has taught me, any book about Europe must also be a book about America. *Super-State* has been in the making for two decades. For me, as a young Englishman living and working in cold-war London and Washington during the 1970s and 1980s, America was the answer to all Europe's problems. She was the saviour in 1945, and was now, during the cold war, the defender. Like many Europeans of my generation, I readily accepted the full Atlanticist outlook (and the 'hands across the sea' sentiment which drove it). During these years I saw, I still believe rightly, Europe and America (certainly Britain and America) as possessing identical, or near-identical, interests – above all, the joint need to deter Soviet influence in Europe.

And in the 1970s and 1980s, in Reagan's America, I had a superb and privileged vantage-point – in the influential Washington think-tanks and in US universities. There I met the impressive breed of conservative, and more specifically, neo-conservative, thinkers and strategists, who were beginning to influence the Republican Party, and who now, after the Clinton interregnum, dominate the strategic and political thinking of the Bush White House. Intriguingly, many of them, like me, were social democrats (and in the late 1970s they were working for Democratic Senators Scoop Jackson and Daniel Patrick Moynihan and other Democrats), and I still count them – I hope even after this book – as my friends.

The sudden collapse of the Soviet Union brought this cold-war world to an abrupt end. For many Europeans, the fall of the Berlin Wall in 1989 is still the great historical watershed (as important for Europe as '9/11' is for the USA). And Europe without the Wall ushered in more than just a new future for Europe. It changed the character of the Atlantic world. For, with the Soviet threat removed, Europe, suddenly, was no longer dependent upon the USA and US-led NATO for its security. Europeans could now bring to an end the unhealthy dependence on the USA which was the root cause of growing anti-Americanism. The continent was now free to unite, and to develop towards a federal future and eventually become a power in the world, equal partners with the USA. And European unity had been a long-proclaimed goal of Washington as well – ever since John F. Kennedy's call for the creation of 'twin pillars' for the West.

But on visits to post-cold-war Washington during the 1990s I noticed a perceptible change in attitude – not just from conservatives in the Heritage Foundation and neo-conservatives in the American Enterprise Institute and advisors to both Bush senior and junior, but even amongst some moderate Democrats around Clinton. As I describe in this book, a surprising hubris had taken hold of the American capital long before 11 September 2001 – surprising because, to me, one of the attractive features of Americans during the cold war had been that for all their power, Americans possessed a humility – and égalité – in their outlook and manners (not a noted feature of Europe's political grandees). But, America's 'victory' in the cold war had changed the atmosphere, and, amongst conservatives at least, it had gone to their heads. By the late 1990s, harsh terms like 'hegemony' and phrases like 'global dominance' were being bandied around in an extraordinary triumphalist atmosphere. Some amongst Washington's foreign policy elites were actually coming to believe that in the post-cold war era American power could police and even dominate the world. It was an outlandish viewpoint, but one which was to lead to the Bush presidency's fateful decision to invade a country which in no way threatened it.

And there was also a decided cooling towards Europe and Europeans and a growing resistance to moves towards European unity, particularly in the defence and security field. In the new world view of Washington, Germany vacillated between being a pacifist 'Euro-wimp' and a potentially resurgent power rival. France was intensely irritating, but in a more edgy way than during the cold war and, following the Iraq war, has become something of an American obsession, a 'bête noir'. And Britain, or 'the Brits', were simply less noticed, and during the Iraq crisis almost taken for granted, seen as always available for support (although the more knowledgeable Washingtonians knew that such support was somewhat unreliable).

And all the time Europe was moving towards ever-closer union – particularly with the arrival of the euro on the world economic stage in 1999, a truly seminal moment in European unity. But the final pillar needed to construct the superpower (true unity on defence and foreign policy) still eluded the Europeans. It is here, though, that the fall-out from the great transatlantic crisis over Iraq may yet prove decisive. For, first the Germans, and then the French, by saying their historic 'no' to Washington during the high-profile 2002 UN diplomatic 'shoot-out' over the Iraq invasion, have reshaped Atlantic relations. And, together with what looks like a developing new strategic alliance with Moscow, they may well have, literally, begun to reshape world politics. The Iraq crisis has also reinvigorated the Franco-German 'European core' (that I call 'Charlemagna'), which, acting like a magnet for other EU countries (even including Britain), can now drive Europe towards a common defence and foreign policy, and, thus, full superpower-hood.

The Iraq crisis may have caused yet another fateful twist in Atlantic relations, for the USA, no matter the administration, can be expected to look unfavourably on any further strategic unification of Europe and to play off 'New Europe' against 'Old Europe' at every opportunity. As European and American interests, although similar in many areas, are now significantly diverging, Europe and America are now competing as much as cooperating around the world, particularly so in energy-rich Eurasia, which, I argue, is a coming battleground between the EU and the USA.

In Europe's domestic debate about its own future, advocates of European unity now have a major new argument on their side. For, following 9/11, the War on Terrorism and the Iraq imbroglio, US power in the world has become highly contentious; indeed, as many polls show, Europe's peoples no longer trust American global leadership. They are also increasingly fearful of the kind of Americanized or 'globalized' (often the same thing) future world order often nowadays sketched out by thinkers in Washington. And it is now abundantly clear that in the medium-term future, the only power centre that has the potential to balance and to check US power in the world is the EU (and then only if it finally creates a foreign and defence policy). Such a new European superpower can also serve to help forward a new global order very distinct from a world of 'American primacy' or 'American hegemony' being offered by US neo-conservatives in Washington.

In an ideal world, Europe would act to further a future world order based upon international law, and would attempt to create a world governance within the framework of the UN. However, as I argue in this book, although there is no future for American dominance in the world, and American power will in the future be checked and balanced, the USA (even should she retrench) can hardly be written out of the future of global politics. And as long as Washington feels that it cannot accept multilateral governance, the UN will remain hobbled, with world government a hope only. What though is possible, and is now emerging, is a multi-polar, multi-superpower world in which the USA, Europe, Japan and, later, probably China and India (and maybe Russia) compete, negotiate and compromise with each other, hopefully within the framework of the UN.

This book is unabashedly federalist – democratic federalist – in its approach to the future of Europe. And it draws heavily on what I consider to be a highly relevant American federal history. Some enthusiasts for Europe believe that today's European Union has little to learn from US history – that great differences between the EU and the USA, not least Europe's language divisions and cultural variety, rule out drawing sensible lessons and comparisons with the nineteenth and early twentieth-century USA. I cannot agree. For the basic similarities are too striking to be set aside. The basic proportions are the same: a continent-wide system, similar issues of federal-state relations, similar population size, similar level of economic and cultural development, similar ethnic divisions and, notwithstanding recent divergences (which I highlight in this book), similar ideology and values.

Europe is not special or *sui generis*; in my view, Europeans should put provincial conceits aside, and should, instead, be prepared to learn the lessons from the rich American federal experience, and from its role as a superpower. We should take the best, abandon the worst and move on.

I have had the great good fortune over the years to be able to hone my analysis on both sides of the Atlantic in the company of some real experts. Mark Falcoff, Elliot Abrams (now White House special advisor), Richard Perle, Herb Levine, Edwin J. Feulner (President of the Heritage Foundation), Peter Rodman (now Deputy Assistant Secretary of State), Bill Schneider (Member of the Defence Policy Board), Bruce Weinrod, Charles Horner, Ben Wattenberg, Sven Kraemer, Michael Ledeen, former Ambassador Robert Hunter and former National Security Advisor Richard Allen (now of the CSIS, where, in the 1980s, whilst it was the Georgetown Centre for Strategic and International Studies, I was a fellow), John O'Sullivan (editor of the influential Washington journal *The National Interest*) and Kendall Myers (of the US State Department).

In Europe, I have been privileged to work alongside leading federalists in the Federal Union, most notably John Pinder and Ernest Wistrich, and, as a Senior Research Fellow at the Federal Trust, with the trust's Director, and the former MEP, Brendon Donnelly. My friend John Stevens, a former Member of the European Parliament for Thames Valley and a Vice Chairman of the Monetary Affairs Committee of the European Parliament, has helped forward my understanding of the political significance of the euro; another friend, and university colleague, Jacques Reland, has given me a real insight into much contemporary French thinking on Europe; and numerous friends in Hamburg, Berlin and the University of Trier (including Masters and Doctoral students of mine) have helped me understand recent, and I believe potentially momentous, changes in Germany. I have also been aided in my thinking by my own university's conference held in early 2003 in Trier, Germany (on the SPD and British New Labour) and two excellent conferences on contemporary Europe arranged in late 2003 by the London and Paris branches of the Konrad Adenauer Stiftung.

My own university and the researchers at the policy think-tank, the Federal Trust, in London, have been invaluable to me in both in time and research.

Introduction

Europe's Hour

It was in Tokyo, of all places, that Europe's great symbol, the flag with the circle of gold stars on the deep blue background, was first unfurled. Jacques Delors, the President of the Commission, had fussed over the design and the colours for months, and had kept it a secret, even from Europe's top leaders: three of them there that day – Kohl of Germany, Thatcher of Britain and Mitterrand of France – for the G7 summit. And as they gathered in public with the other world leaders for a photo opportunity, and saw the unfamiliar gold circle fluttering next to the stars and stripes and the red sun on white, both Kohl and Mitterrand registered mild surprise. Thatcher's countenance was stiff. The flag changed little. But 15 years later, when, in the German financial capital of Frankfurt, that other great symbol of European unity, the euro, was unveiled, Europe was quietly changing world history.

Europe is already a great civilian power. With the euro successfully launched, with over 370 million people in the world's largest economy and with EU expansion to the east, the old continent is back. From the rubble of war, division and poverty, Europeans not only live in the most stable, peaceful and prosperous region of the world, but also possess a quality of life that surpasses that of any other continent, including North America. They live in what amounts to 'a paradise' of modern convenience and cultural tradition.[1]

But in order to emerge as a fully fledged superpower, Europe needs to be able to 'act as one'. In December 2003, the European Union proved how 'acting as one' (as it does on trade questions) has already made it an economic power to be reckoned with. Having gone head-to-head with the US administration in a serious trade war over US steel tariffs (the EU had threatened to retaliate with politically targeted tariffs of its own), even the unilateralist-leaning Bush presidency was forced publicly to back down. This victory for Europe over steel tariffs allowed the EU Trade Commissioner, Pascal Lamy, to argue that 'when Europe is united… it can play a role in world affairs that corresponds to its weight.'[2] And it led other Europeans to speculate that had the EU shown the same unity during the lead-up to the Iraq war, then European pressure on Washington may even have been able to stop the war.

With Europe united over trade, protected by the world's largest single market and, potentially, its most powerful currency, Europe greets the new century as a great civilian superpower (the dimensions of which are outlined in Chapter 3). And, in the early years of the new century, it is moving towards creating the economic government of a super-state (described in Chapter 4). At the time of writing, tough negotiations – between big and small states, but also between big states themselves (principally Germany, Poland and Spain – about the power balances within the new superpower were forging the written constitution of a decentralized super-state. This constitution had as its centrepiece a European executive built around a new dual presidency. The two presidents suggested by the draft constitution could well evolve, either through competition, or by future design, into one elected presidency, which would resemble that of the 'President of the United States of America'. And, by the second quarter of the century, such a 'President of the European Union' may well find himself or herself as the political head of a new superpower on the world stage, speaking on equal terms to the US President and the Chinese Chairman.

By early 2004, France and Germany, by threatening to go it alone, had finally secured Britain's support for the building of a serious defence arm for the new superpower. And, in an ironic twist, Europe's defining and uniting issue may turn out to be the US invasion of Iraq, which initially divided the EU. For the Iraq war produced a real, truer unity at the very heart of Europe. The decision of Germany and France in 2002 to say 'no' to the US war, and to the new US global doctrine of the Bush administration, was a huge gamble. But, only months after President Bush declared major combat operations over, it was a course that by the New Year of 2004 was looking increasingly vindicated as Washington's post-war Iraqi troubles piled up. And the subsequent unity between the two heartland European nations – forged in the heat of transatlantic battle at the UN – was deepened to embrace the new realm of security and defence that, later, with the addition of Britain, may change the geopolitical map of the world.

Whether through the mechanism of a deepening EU or through Franco-German Core Europe, the 'inevitability of Europe', of 'superpower Europe', remained a powerful idea. And it was grounded in another powerful idea: that a union of 400 million relatively well-off, well-educated people cannot for long remain dependent for their security on the leadership of another state (with only the same GDP and with less than 300 million people) 3,000 miles and an ocean away. Also, as I argue in Chapter 6, events themselves will help forge European unity and drive hesitant Europeans together. Already, opposition to the American-led war on Iraq in 2003 has united Europeans (if not their governments) in a common cause. More than by policies and constitutions coming out of Brussels or Strasbourg, a new European superpower will be built in the crucible of global rivalry and conflict, in global economic crises, in future conflicts along Europe's long borders and, above all, in Europe's response to American economic and military power.

What's more, continental Europeans are finally regaining that intangible confidence needed to gain public support behind creating a superpower. Europe's view of itself was severely damaged during the twentieth century. At the root of this European defensiveness about itself is both its history of imperialism (primarily down to Britain, France and Holland) and, more profoundly, the recent legacy of fascism – in Italy and Spain but, above all, in the aggressive and genocidal German state of the 1930s and 1940s. Indeed, so grim was Nazi Germany's record, and so central to European popular history has Hitler's time become, that, for some Europeans, even the 'idea of Europe' is considered reactionary and racist. But Hitler's dark shadow is beginning to lift, and memories of Europe's imperial past are also fading. Soon, Europeans will be able to see their own history less ruefully – in a longer, clearer and more balanced historical context. Then they can regain a sense of the importance, indeed glory, of their civilization, not just of Europe's art and science, but also of its historic economic dynamism and political institutions – a civilization that has spread throughout the world. Indeed, in the twenty-first century, the 'idea of Europe' may even become as alluring to Europeans as 'the American dream' was to Americans in the twentieth. After all, today's Western Europe, the heart of which is today's EU, can, without bombast, lay claim to being the historic heartland and homeland of the western world, of what we now call western civilization. From its crucible in post-medieval Western Europe in the seventeenth century and its rapid growth in the eighteenth and nineteenth centuries, Europe's commercial, scientific, individualistic, liberal civilization is now a culture that stretches from Hawaii in the west through to Moscow and beyond in the east, with outposts in Australasia and increasing influence worldwide, particularly in Latin America and Southeast Asia.

Europe is back at a propitious time. For, as will be suggested in Chapter 1, only a decade or so after its triumph in the cold war, and even after its 'victory' in Iraq, superpower America shows real signs of faltering. Its historically spectacular economy – much hyped during the late 1990s as a 'new paradigm' or 'new economy' – is now sputtering under corporate and accounting scandals, huge current account deficits and serious private debt levels; and the world's 'one remaining superpower' is frighteningly dependent upon foreign investment. Predictions are always tricky things, but this book is based upon the thesis that, because of the USA's unbalanced economy (its debts and deficits) and its over-stretched empire, the coming century will not be another 'American century'.

Unfortunately, this weakening America coincided with a US political leadership which seemed unsure of its global posture. And the events of 11 September 2001 played into the hands of conservatives with disturbing views, derived from the US triumph in the cold war, about American 'primacy' and 'hegemony'. This new aggressiveness (including an attack upon an Arab country that in no way threatened it) led, in response, to a worldwide anti-Americanism not seen ever before, even during the Vietnam conflict.

Since the end of the cold war, many of Washington's assumptions have become imperial – as US policy, often unconsciously, attempts to remake the world in its American image through a strategy of 'globalization', while consciously seeking to remake the Middle East through a process of 'democratization' and 'markets'. This future life in an Americanized world has been elegantly set out by former White House National Security official Phillip Bobbit.[3] Like many strategists in turn-of-the-century Washington, he sees a future homogenized 'market world' – 'a society of market states' – in which markets rule, and governments are weak and compete with each other for corporate capital. But, just like Francis Fukuyama's future world, Bobbit's world is really the world of America writ large. Or, rather, 'market America' writ large. In reality, though universal and liberal in its vision, this new Americanized world is a uni-polar world in which the USA remains the only superpower and polices the world alone.[4]

From Europe's perspective, though, the global reality differs significantly from this 'uni-polar' picture. Rather than one power centre, the world is evolving multiple power centres, as nascent superpowers (like the European Union itself) are arising from out of the existing trading blocs. The US elite, though, are still trying to run this multi-polar world – from Washington and New York in the image of market America – as though it were a single system.

A European superpower, serving to balance the USA in the world, would provide a different western approach to the world, one that would be more enduring. It would recognize, not obliterate, differences. Decisions would be made by negotiations between superpowers through multilateral organizations. And, normally at least, the peace would be kept by deterrence and containment, rather than 'pre-emptive attacks' by the strong on the weak.

A European superpower would also offer a different western model for both the economy and society. Europe's so-called 'sclerotic' welfare societies, so criticized by Wall Street during the great American boom, are proving more stable than the gyrating, raw, free-market American model. And Europe's 'social model – of capitalism with a social vision – could become the basis for a continent-wide ideology, a kind of 'European dream' every bit as successful in inspiring future Europeans as was the more individualist 'American dream' in inspiring Americans.

And such a Europe, as one of the twin pillars of 'the West', may well be able to act as a more effective bridge from western to non-western societies and civilizations. Seeking neither to remake the world in its own image nor to police it on its own, a new united

Europe on the world stage might start by trying to dramatically improve western relations with its 'border civilization' in the Middle East and the arc of Islam. This new strategy would mean that Europe would pursue and sustain, if necessarily separately from the USA, an independent European Israel-Palestine peace policy.

Europe's Choice

By the summer of 2004, the European Union stretched from the Atlantic Ocean to Russia's Ukrainian border, adding to its 370 million another 100 million people. It could now begin to form a strategic 'markets-for-energy' alliance with Russia, an alliance that, logically, could develop a security dimension (and complement or replace NATO). This alliance would stand at the crossroads between the West and Islam, China and India and would become a dominant power in Eurasia – the key to world power in the next few decades.[5]

Such a European superpower would inevitably, as I argue in Chapter 7, become seriously competitive with the USA. It would develop its separate interests around the world and inevitably challenge any notions of American primacy held in Washington. These interests would sometimes collide, as can be seen in the coming struggle for influence in Eurasia.

What's more, in the short run, Europe is America's only potential superpower competitor. It has the population, the skills, the potential technological and military resources and, above all, the economy to create and sustain a serious challenge to US primacy.

Such a challenge, though, raises fears about Europe becoming a 'rival' to the USA. During the 2003 Iraq crisis, the British Prime Minister, Tony Blair, openly warned his fellow European leaders against creating such a 'rival': he preferred a 'partnership'. But the 'partnership' he had in mind was not of the 'equal' kind. Inevitably, it would mean continuing with the present unbalanced transatlantic system, in which the USA could 'divide and rule' through a series of bilateral 'partnerships' with various European states, in which each European state remained a junior partner. It would remain a hub and spokes system in which Washington is the hub and the separate European states the spokes. European unity would replace the hub and spokes with two hubs.[6]

I argue in the final chapter that, in order to successfully balance (and challenge or rival) the USA, Europeans will need to overcome the 'great civilian temptation'. The EU will certainly be less reliant on military 'hard power' than are administrations in Washington. But 'soft power' alone does not an independent superpower make! Europe will need increased military and intelligence resources to provide against threats to its own security and to project power. But whatever the nature of future threats, now that the Soviet threat has ended, the old lynchpin of Europe's security, NATO, is now essentially redundant (even though 'NATO-think' still suffuses some European, particularly British, foreign policy establishments).

The stark truth is that Europe no longer needs America as it did in the cold war. Indeed, today, Europe needs America less than America needs Europe. From Washington's vantage point, its ambitious global mission, with its emphasis on power projection, will need support from NATO, both in the form of launching pads and in the aftermath of conflict; whereas Europe, not seeking a global mission in the same way, hardly needs NATO at all. All that Europe needs is a re-jigged 'Atlantic Community', able to secure good trading relations and cultural contacts between the peoples of Europe and North America. And should a global emergency arise in which joint action is needed, then there is nothing at all to stop Europe and America coming together to act.

That Europe can now stand on its own feet became clear during the 2002–2003 transatlantic crisis over an Iraq policy. Germany led the way in what may yet become a turning-point in Atlantic history. For Chancellor Gerhard Schroeder's decision in the late summer of 2002 to say 'no' to the USA on a vital matter of policy proved that today's Europeans can walk a separate path to that of America without the heavens caving in. In the short run, the Iraq crisis divided Europe, but in the long run Germany's decision to break with its erstwhile 'America before France' security policy, and to align with Paris, seriously eroded America's position in Europe.

The USA starts the new century – in decline or not – with a keen sense of its powerful world role, and Washington will not easily accept Europe as a rival, or even a complementary, superpower. If it sticks to the objectives of its 2002 National Security Strategy – to block rival power centres – Washington can be relied upon to play political hardball with Europe: to play one EU nation off against another and thus 'divide and rule'. A foretaste of such a strategy was on display during the Iraq dispute when Washington encouraged separatist tendencies throughout the continent, particularly in

Britain and Eastern Europe, specifically in Poland. US Secretary of Defense, Donald Rumsfeld, with his famous 'Old Europe' and 'New Europe' quip, set the scene. And later, after the war, the US decided to 'dis-aggregate' its relations with Europe (that is, lessen its dealings with the union and enhance its dealings with each country separately).

For Europe the prospect of such a 'divide and rule' strategy is ungainly; for it amounts to a future in which provincialized European prime ministers and presidents constantly bicker one with another, each seeking short-term national advantage, and 'one-up' each other by courting Washington's favour ever more assiduously. It is a future in which Europeans will remain divided between those (led by France) who, resenting American power, can only criticize the superpower from the sidelines (a criticism which will increasingly lapse into little more than elegant geopolitical whining); and those (led by Britain) who are content to remain junior partners and openly accept satellite, even colonial, status.

Yet, by early 2004, Europe remained well along the road to becoming the world's second superpower. An underlying dynamic was already in place. This dynamic was one in which the single market demands a single currency, which in turn demands a single government. And it was one in which this single European government, whether formed through the existing union or Core Europe, will, sooner or later, take control of Europe's security and defence as the sheer pressure of events – whether Washington's foreign policy, or terrorism, or a crisis on Europe's borders, or an environmental catastrophe – forges the final structure of unity.

But, of course, nothing in this world is certain. And one of the greatest uncertainties of all remains US global policy. Yet, whatever happens in the USA, Europe has now arrived. Should America remain unilateralist and aggressive, then Core Europe, in reaction, will increasingly play a separate role. On the other hand, should a new US administration begin to seriously retrench American power, then a united Europe is likely to fill the resultant vacuum.

1

Europe and
the American Empire

From Ascendancy to Subordination

When US troops landed in France during the First World War – becoming the first 'foreign' troops on European soil since the Turkish army besieged Vienna in the seventeenth century – the full significance of this seminal event went largely unnoticed. For these GIs were arriving in a Europe that, though tearing itself apart, was still the unrivalled centre of global power. At the outbreak of the war, Europe's empires stretched right around the world (including into North and South America). Not even the Romans at their height – when they shared the planet with the Han Dynasty of China, the Sasanians in Iran and the Indian empires – could compare with Europe's global power and reach. And although, on the eve of war in 1913, European global power was becoming somewhat over-stretched, the industrial and manufacturing base of Europe's three leading nations was still higher than that of the USA.[1]

Even 25 years later, after the ravages of the First World War and on the eve of the Second World War, Western Europe was still clinging on as the world's centre of power – and the globe was still very Euro-centred. During the inter-war period, the Western European economies had made something of a comeback against the USA: Western Europe's share of world manufacturing output had risen slightly, that of the USA had fallen significantly; Western Europe had also overtaken the USA's iron and steel production.[2] Additionally, the Western European empires were still intact, and the joint military might of Western Europe's four large nations was a striking nine times larger than that of the non-mobilized USA.[3]

This early twentieth-century European global primacy was the culmination of a remarkable 500-year story. In 1500, Western Europe was still little more than a marginal corner of Eurasia, considerably less developed than the other civilizations – the Safavid, Ottoman and Uzbek empires, and the Ming Dynasty in China – at the other end of the continent.[4] But by the mid eighteenth century, Europe had fully emerged as a defined area of the world and had become the undisputed risen star amongst the world's civilizations; and over the next hundred years – both economically and culturally – it pulled away from the rest, sharply and dramatically so. During the nineteenth century, the leading historian of Europe, Norman Davies, argues, there was a dynamism about Europe that 'far exceeds anything previously known'.[5]

By the turn of the century, after their long ascendancy in the nineteenth century, Europeans, certainly Europe's elites, were increasingly conscious of inhabiting a uniquely productive and powerful civilization – the most advanced and sophisticated that history had yet seen. Europe and Europeans were brimming with optimism and confidence, and an overweening pride, which, as Europe's empires spread around the world through European conquest, often flowed over into notions of superiority. Conservatives propounded ideas about innate European superiority – that of the 'white race'. And nineteenth-century liberals and progressives saw Europe's democratic advances as the key attribute of its 'superior' civilization – a view controversially expressed even a century or so later by Italian Prime Minister Silvio Berlusconi.[6]

A powerful Euro-centrism took hold, in which other world civilizations were largely ignored and, for Europeans (and others too), Europe became the unrivalled centre of the world, the base from which future great leaps in humankind would be launched – the only model for the future. During the last half of the nineteenth century, though, Europeans were beginning to recognize the growing USA as a rising power and potential competitor, but this advancing 'new world' only reinforced European Euro-centrism. The growing power of America, seen in Europe as an outgrowth of European civilization, was yet further proof of Europe's success story.

The key foundation under this exceptional Euro-centric confidence was Europe's inordinate wealth. Western Europeans had achieved extraordinary economic 'lift-off' by a ruthless capital accumulation derived from the Atlantic Ocean trading system. They extracted unprecedented wealth – primarily textile raw materials and gold and silver – from Atlantic trade in Europe and North America; and, in a clever two-way trade, used this wealth to penetrate and dominate the Indian Ocean economy.[7] Spanish, British, Portuguese and Dutch traders and businessmen underpinned this Atlantic trade with the slave trade and the slave plantation economies, which kept costs low and led directly to undreamt-of levels of capital accumulation.

This capital accumulation, when allied to advancing technology, had momentous consequences. It both allowed Europe's industrial revolution – which swept away the agricultural societies that had existed for 10,000 years – and, just as crucially, consolidated a military one. The late middle ages saw Europeans develop the new battle-fighting weapon of gunpowder (originally invented in China) which, when linked to changes in naval technology, produced the long-range armed sailing ship. These ships made Europe's armies and navies fearsome fighting machines, which – literally – conquered the world.

Yet this European revolution was about more than power and global reach. It was also about radical, even revolutionary, social change at home, as agricultural societies gave way to cities. Big cities existed before Europe's great rise – Peking, Cairo, Constantinople and Delhi were amongst the largest – but Europe pioneered the development of urban (and, later, suburban) *societies*, particularly in Britain where, by the 1830s, London had become the largest city in the world. And by the late nineteenth century, Europeans were the first people to create a society of mass affluence (even amidst considerable urban and rural poverty). Age-old class structures of agricultural and peasant life were replaced; and a sizeable middle class of big and small urban capitalists, shopkeepers and professionals (workers like doctors, teachers and managers) became a dynamic force, and a skilled urban proletariat began to join these middle classes in creating the growing mass consumer society later perfected in North America in the 1960s. No civilization in the history of the world had seen anything like this before.

Just as fundamental a change in world history was the European revolution in governance and political ideas. Europe's break with feudalism – in the English Civil War, in the creation of the Dutch Republic, in the American and French Revolutions – all set Europeans on a wholly new path of governance, one fundamentally different from their own past and from anything seen before in the rest of the world. This European revolution introduced the epoch-making political idea of consent into a world of emirs, sultans, shahs, Chinese emperor dynasties, Indian princes, African tribal chiefs and European kings and queens – all established by force and often divinely ordained.

Yet, in the twentieth century, Europeans – in Europe and North America – have pioneered a further transition in human living. The Europe which dominated the world in 1900 was built by elites, but the liberal world they created for themselves later and, inevitably, widened out – again uniquely amongst the civilizations – to usher in modern mass society with its mass markets and mass media.

This remarkable European story of capitalism and democracy (and mass affluence) – of modernity itself – was part, though, of an even deeper change. In what was the most significant European revolution of all, perhaps its most enduring contribution to world history, the western continent went through a radical change in the life of the mind. Known as 'the Enlightenment', Europe entered a period of unprecedented intellectual ferment stretching from the middle of the seventeenth century well into the eighteenth. This great intellectual awakening was captured by Emmanuel Kant as the era when 'mankind grew out of its self-inflicted immaturity.'[8] It was a period which saw the evocation of human reason and rationalism, of curiosity and experiment, and enabled a quantum leap in scientific development and technological change.

These ideas were swirling around Europe as the peninsula came out of the middle ages and rediscovered the classical civilizations of Greece and Rome during 'the Renaissance'; and they were fermenting too during the revolt against the church known as 'the Reformation'. This ideological turmoil was also to change for all time Europe's relationship with both its established church elites and its established Christian religion – a revolution which possessed the seeds of Europe's secular future.[9]

This European revolt against unreconstructed Christianity helped forge the core idea of modern European liberalism – that of the centrality of the individual (an idea derived from the reformation and North European Protestantism). And the idea that this individual was *rational* provided the seed for today's moderate secular humanism and the scientific rejection of the Christian supernatural story. So powerful is this liberal, secular idea that it has become today's European ideology.

Many of these brand new European ideas spread across the ocean to North America as Europeans settled the new continent. And they also fuelled a transatlantic 'quantum leap' in governance. During the eighteenth and nineteenth centuries, Europeans and Euro-Americans completely reformulated their relationship with their rulers. In Britain, parliamentary government gradually established itself; in Spain and Portugal, long struggles between and within church and state led to constitutional limits to church-backed monarchy in Spain and a republic in Portugal in 1910; a revolution in France, based upon universalist ideas of freedom and equality, overthrew a whole state structure; while the USA's colonial status was replaced by its republican written constitution with a presidency and congress and, later, its entrenched Bill of Rights.

Even though the political ideas of the English Civil War and the French Revolution were to 'ring around the world', it was in the USA that liberal revolutionary constitutional change – certainly after Lincoln's victory in the American civil war – was to run its course more fully. In Europe, the advance of constitutional liberalism was uneven. Aristocrats held sway even into the mid twentieth-century, some even co-opted liberal ideas, and there were real set backs, like the failed liberal revolutions of 1848 and 1930s fascism. And in the process, the USA, not Europe, assumed the mantle of 'the land of the free' – 'freedom's home'. And, as time went by, American independence came to be seen not as a European rebellion, but as a specifically American revolt against reactionary 'old-world' Europe.

One, often misunderstood, aspect of Europe's liberal awakening was the progressive character of the European nation state. In England and France, but also in Spain and Portugal and in Holland and Scandinavia and later in Germany and Italy, nation states were slowly wrought from a no man's land of princes and chieftains. During the seventeenth century, as local markets expanded into national ones, and the Hapsburgs had been overcome, they became unstoppable. They organized the transition from agriculture to industry and commerce by taking over the political functions of localities and, crucially, the church. Strange though it may sound to modern ears, the European nation states became the agents for the advance of liberal, democratic society. As they imposed their own taxes, they broke the medieval feudal bonds and the random and arbitrary power of Europe's chieftains and warlords and, over time, they became the focus for political and democratic expression. Some of these states would certainly suppress the individual; but some of them became the protector of citizen's rights through the rule of law.[10] The European nation states' most profound gift to the world, and to civilized life, may well have been the reintroduction – from Roman times – of the rule of law. It was, for its time, the work of liberty.

The Dark Side of Europe

By the time American troops returned a second time to Europe, in 1942 (this time to war-torn Britain), these seemingly confident European nations were unleashing the darkest and most destructive era in Europe's history. The two great wars – the long European civil war stretching from 1914 to 1945 – saw a cost in human life and wealth that not only shattered European power, but also brought European global primacy to a sudden and dramatic end.

From an unchallenged position of independent global primacy, Europe was about to sink into a devastated, divided and contested zone over which two completely new superpowers, the USA and USSR, were to fight a cold war and establish separate and competing spheres of influence. In 1950, after five years of peace and rebuilding, the three largest Western European nations combined (Britain, France and West Germany) had only 45% of the GNP of the USA; and Washington's defence expenditure was over three times the size of the top three in Western Europe (Britain, France and Italy – West Germany being completely disarmed).[11]

But, it was not only the power of Europe that was shattered by the world wars. It was also the confidence of its peoples and elites, especially their widely held view, developed during the Victorian era in the nineteenth century, that Europe was a unique force for human progress and moral good. Pride in history is a huge component of idealism and confidence, and as post-1945 Europeans looked back to try to explain the causes of the carnage of the wars, they saw things they would have preferred to forget. They saw the dark side of European thought and action. They saw extreme nationalism and xenophobia unleashed throughout the whole of Europe, and they saw a primary European nation, Germany, lapse into organized ruthless barbarism. Post-1945 Germans in particular had a huge cross of shame to bear. Fairly or not, Hitler's shadow fell over every post-war German, and every German leader from Adenauer to Kohl. So sensitive about their past are today's Germans that as recently as November 1998, when the President of the Bundestag and friend of Helmut Kohl, Rhinelander Philipp Jenninger, simply tried to explain the appeal of Hitler to inter-war Germans, large numbers of parliamentarians, including those in his own Christian Democrat party, left the hall and 'shrunk in shame'.[12]

From the late 1960s onwards, West Germany became Europe's largest economy and, after its re-unification, it reasserted its position as Europe's heartland nation. But Germany was hobbled by its history, and in the process it also hobbled post-war Europe's self-image. Germany's aggressive war and the genocide against the Jews still haunt the post-war German conscience, but as the years rolled by German guilt spilt over into European guilt. Even though many Europeans (in particular the British and their leader Winston Churchill) came out of the war with a strengthened moral position, able to hold their heads up high, seen from the outside (not least in Russia and the USA) all of Europe came to be implicated in the awesome tragedy – as either appeasers or collaborators.

Even by the time of the celebrations of the new millennium in 2000, every single EU nation was still living within the shadow of a war that had ended in 1945. And many of the older citizens of continental Europe still had direct experience of living under dictatorial regimes. Of the 15 members of the EU at the turn of the millennium, six – Germany, Spain, Italy, Austria, Portugal and Greece – have all experienced either fascist or neo-fascist regimes; five – France, Luxembourg, Belgium, Holland and Denmark – have been occupied by fascist regimes; two – Sweden and Ireland – were in the ungainly position of neutrality between fascism and the allies; and one – Finland – lived under a communist regime during the cold war.

As post-1945 Europeans looked back on their past they also took a new look at Europe's imperial history. By the late 1960s, almost all of Europe's colonies had been dismantled, and as these empires became a thing of the past their earlier glow dimmed sharply. Previously seen as a largely positive – meaning a Christian and a civilizing – force, they soon became another source of shame and guilt. For many younger Europeans growing up in the 1950s, 1960s and 1970s, for German youth rebelling against their parents, but for young French and English people too, Europe's history lost its progressive colouring and became instead an altogether darker imperial story – one of racist domination of subject peoples. Many post-war Europeans saw Europe's imperial history as inherently racist, either of the mild kind of the 'white man's burden' exhibited by many of their elders (people like General De Gaulle or Winston Churchill or Queen Elizabeth the Queen Mother) or of the 'scientific' type propagated by the anti-Semite ideologue Houston Chamberlain and the Nazis. Both sides of post-war political Europe found the European past distasteful. Socialist intellectuals saw Europe's history of empire and recent history of fascism as melded into one dreadful European capitalist story; post-war continental conservatives, finding their traditional nationalist ideas now discredited by fascism and anti-Semitism, were forced to re-make themselves in a new image, as Christian Democrats.

This loss of European confidence about the past took its toll on Europe's unity. The supporters of the European movement – from Jean Monnet and Robert Schuman in the 1950s right through to German Chancellor Helmut Kohl in the 1990s – could hardly summon up idealism in the idea of Europe by evoking the past; all they could do was to argue that unity would 'put the past to rest' and make sure that 'it never happened again'.

Compared with most Europeans, the new American superpower saw its history very differently. They saw an America which had just 'saved the world for democracy' and, untainted by Europe's history of imperialism, fascism and conflict, represented 'all that was noble and good', 'the last, best hope for mankind'. Their own dark mark of slavery and genocide was a long way back in the dim and distant past, and most Americans could, anyway, blame these horrors on the now minority Anglo-Saxons. So, modern Americans can wholeheartedly agree with Woodrow Wilson that 'America is the only idealistic nation in the world.'[13] This simple assuredness about the unique moral goodness of their country was not a belief contemporary Europeans could share about their own nations.

The American Empire in Europe: 'The Free World'

In post-war Europe, with the continent's power and confidence seriously eroded, the USA moved swiftly to fill the vacuum. Although the GIs went home in late 1945, Washington retained its wartime primacy in Western Europe – a position given real force, following Los Alamos, Hiroshima and Nagasaki, by its nuclear monopoly. Already, during the Second World War, the key strategic decisions of the western allies had been taken by the American leadership in Washington (Winston Churchill was effectively sidelined); and with the collapse of the Third Reich, the devastation of Europe and the rise of Soviet power in Eastern Europe, Washington quickly replaced Germany as the dominant power in Western Europe. By the early 1950s, following the Marshall Plan and the creation of NATO, all the major nations of Western Europe had fallen, largely willingly, into an American sphere of influence. So much so that Washington was in effective control of Western Europe's destiny.

As the cold war intensified, Western Europe became increasingly dependent on the American military guarantee (and its territory and territorial waters became populated with US bases, both conventional and nuclear). In this environment, most Europeans were willing to accept Washington's leadership of Western Europe – even when it was exercised robustly and bluntly, as it was during the Anglo-French invasion of Suez in 1956. But in the process, what was now an obvious US 'sphere of influence' in Western Europe began to take on, in the minds of European conservatives and socialists alike, the hallmarks of an informal 'empire'.

This mid twentieth-century transfer of power across the Atlantic – from Europe to the USA – was not, as some myths would have it, forced on a reluctant America by events outside its control. For, the GIs arriving in Britain in 1942 were not just coming as disinterested liberators, but also as conquerors with a political mission. The fact was that wartime and post-war Washington was no bosom friend of Europe; the USA, unsurprisingly, was acting in its own interests and was seeking a post-war settlement in which Britain and France (and their empires) would be much reduced.

President Roosevelt had played his hand skilfully during the 1930s and the Second World War. His strategic aim was to manoeuvre the USA into post-war supremacy by undermining the European empires, particularly the USA's main competitor, Britain. His tough attitude towards Britain whilst the country was fighting for its life in 1941 set the scene. The 'destroyers for bases' agreement in 1941 – in which the British handed over to Washington, rent free, bases in Newfoundland, the Bahamas, Jamaica and British Guyana in return for some old destroyers – revealed Roosevelt's lack of sentiment. As did his successor's abrupt ending of lend-lease, which fell on the deluded British 'like a V2 rocket in Whitehall' in 1945, and the subsequent very hard US terms for a loan.[14] Indeed, US strategy, from its entry into the war in 1941 right through to the onset of the cold war in 1947, sought, whilst accommodating Soviet power, to weaken post-war Britain and France. It succeeded spectacularly.

In this sense, the USA was fighting not one but two wars between 1941 and 1945: one war was against the axis powers but the other, more subtly, was against the European imperial powers, particularly Britain and France. It was Roosevelt's wisdom to enter the war at such a time as to maximize US influence in the post-war European peace settlements, and it was his huge legacy to leave the USA as the undisputed leader of the former imperial nations of Western Europe. Only a couple of years after the Anglo-American wartime alliance had got underway, Britain's Foreign Secretary, Anthony Eden, asked Churchill plaintively: 'Can't we really have a foreign policy of our own?'[15] And a decade later, when President Eisenhower and Secretary of State Dulles finally broke British and French – and Anthony Eden's – imperial illusions during their invasion of the Suez Canal, it was clear that the United States of America would be prepared to act like any other nation state and pursue its own interests with strength and resolve.

America's unexceptional resolve to act in its own interests – and when necessary lay down the law to the subordinate Western Europeans – was accepted in Western Europe because of the exigencies of the cold war and the fear of Soviet Russia. But, this new European subservience was rarely acknowledged, and, instead, many Europeans preferred to see the USA not as the dominant nation in an alliance, but rather as a cousin offering a helping hand in a joint and noble cause. Post-war Britain was awash with this romantic Atlanticism. Fine sentiments about 'hands across the water', about common European and American background and values, about a 'special relationship' became standard fare – and echoed forth from the Anglo-American Pilgrim's dinner long after the end of Hitler's war and the collapse of British power; and they set the thinking of a generation of Britain's elites.[16] And the idea that America was uniquely generous and benign was given life by the new superpower's post-1947 massive investment in post-war Europe through Marshall Aid and, later, NATO.

In the late 1940s, the US government – no longer leading just a nation, but now beginning to guide a western 'system' of nations – acclimatized itself swiftly to its new role as leader of the western world. It had come out of the world war in an unchallenged position in Western Europe: by 1950, it had more than twice the GNP of Western Europe's four largest countries put together and it had developed a strategic nuclear system which acted as the only serious deterrent to Soviet power.[17] And one of its first decisions as leader of the West was soon upon it: what to do about the devastated peoples and nations in its sphere of influence in the Western European continent.

Post-1945 Washington was completely free of triumphalism and hubris – unlike the post-cold-war capital some 50 years later. The US foreign policy establishment, comprising, amongst others, James Byrnes, George Marshall and Dean Acheson, were conscious, in Dean Acheson's famous words, of being 'in at the creation' of a new world order.[18] But they saw that a languishing Europe was in no one's interest and, as a matter of US national interest, decided on a strategy of reviving the western continent. The idea was to rebuild the transatlantic trading system and, through Europe's economic growth, provide a growing market for America's corporations. This was to be accomplished by pump priming with US taxpayers' money – an exercise later known as the 'Marshall Aid Plan'. This huge economic commitment to Western Europe was followed by an historic security guarantee through the NATO alliance formally signed in 1949.

Washington's strategic objective of a strong European economy led to a benign approach to Western European economic unity. Will Clayton, the US Under-Secretary of State at the time of the Marshall European Recovery Program, made clear the American desire to see a more united Europe, even if it meant no 'special relationship' with the UK. Special treatment for the British, he suggested, 'would violate the principle that no piecemeal approach to the European problem would be undertaken'.[19] Later, President John Kennedy would talk glowingly of a united Europe as one of the 'twin pillars of the West'. And even Euro-sceptic Britain's closest friends in Washington – from the 'Anglos' in the State Department through, later, to President George Bush Senior – would often urge the UK to get more involved in the process of European integration. Bush Senior's outgoing US Ambassador to Britain, Raymond Seitz, famously shocked the stately ranks of the Anglo-American establishment at a Pilgrim's dinner by suggesting politely to his British hosts that Britain alone carried little weight in Washington, and could only regain it as part of a single European voice.[20]

But the essential proof of American backing for European unity lies in the simple fact that all the great historic moves towards economic unity, such as the creation of the single market and the single currency, went ahead without American objection. Washington may sometimes have been *tempted* by a 'divide and rule' approach to post-1945 Western Europe, but such a strategy was never really necessary, for, during the cold war, with the exception of France, Western Europeans readily accepted American leadership through NATO. Europeans may have toyed with some *initial* alternatives to NATO. For a few years after 1945, the European left saw Europe as a potential 'third force' between American capitalism and Soviet communism. And Ernest Bevin, Britain's post-war Foreign Secretary, even tried to organize a 'third force' European bloc which would bring together Western Europe and their African and Middle Eastern colonies and which would be independent of and equal to America, yet part of the wider framework of an anti-Soviet alliance.[21]

This vision of a late 1940s European superpower fell foul, though, not of American opposition, but rather to the realities of the Eurasian scene at the time. Europeans realized that the looming power of the Soviet Union could only be deterred by the countervailing power of the USA (with its nuclear monopoly). For Europe's post-war elites, American leadership could not be avoided, and would have to be accepted. And a lopsided and unequal American-European pattern of relations was set. Until, that is, the abrupt and surprising end of the cold war when, with the Soviet threat removed, America's security guarantee was no longer needed.

Yet, needed or not, America's role in devastated post-war Europe was, in the end, good for everyone; everyone, that is, except Stalin's Soviet Union. It was good for the USA as it provided the US corporations with the extra market that fed the huge post-war boom. It was good, too, for Europe. By reviving Europe's battered economy and securing Western Europe against Soviet pressure, it built the platform for Europe's subsequent post-war economic 'lift off', and later unity.

By the mid to late 1950s, it was clear that American grand strategy in Europe during the 1940s had been a resounding triumph. Roosevelt's break from isolationism in December 1941, and his massive commitment to defeating Germany, had paid off. The American military and economic presence in Europe had been a huge success story, for it saw victory in two wars, one hot (over Germany) and one cold (the containment of the Soviet Union), and it had solidified the USA's emergence as a world power and the undisputed leader of the West.

It had also been a success for Western Europeans. Europe's long and bloody civil war from 1914 to 1945 could easily have destroyed Europe, turning the continent into a wasteland. Instead, viewed from the vantage point of the mid 1950s, the American presence in Europe had helped destroy Nazism, had kept Soviet Communism at bay and, through Marshall Aid and transatlantic trade, had induced an economic boom throughout the continent. (Also, during the 1950s, American pressure pushed Britain and France into shedding their empires.)

The effects of this great post-war transatlantic economic boom – the growth of a consumer society, which was both democratic and stable – were felt equally in the USA and Western Europe and, together with the joint NATO enterprise, created a sense, certainly amongst elites, of common endeavour across the Atlantic, indeed of a single Euro-Atlantic civilization spanning the ocean. And it was out of this idea that the contemporary notion of 'the West' was born. This 'West' – or 'the Western World' – encompassed the peoples on both sides of the Atlantic (and in some outposts, like Australia) that shared common cultural, ethnic, religious and political roots (in other words, European roots) and possessed advanced economies (and advanced science and technology). This 'Western World' – and the allied notion of 'the Free World' – saw itself as the engine of 'democracy and freedom', and increasingly defined itself against 'the East', which it saw as 'totalitarian', and the Third World, which it considered backward. And the concrete institution of the NATO alliance increasingly gave this 'Euro-Atlantic civilization' real political expression.

The notion of a 'single civilization' – a Euro-American civilization – spanning the Atlantic and defending shared goals of freedom and democracy was an idea and an image that continued to resonate for European publics and leaders. As Prime Minister, Margaret Thatcher once intrigued an audience by referring to the USA as a 'European' country; and German Chancellor Gerhard Schroeder used the term 'Euro-Atlantic community' at the 2001 Labour Party Conference.

But in the 1950s and 1960s this 'Western' or 'Free' world – whether conceived as a single or a plural transatlantic civilization or community – had an undisputed single leader: the President of the United States of America. And Washington, not London, Paris, Berlin or Brussels, led and guided the NATO alliance. Indeed, as it was the USA that provided the security guarantee for Europe during the cold war, and not the other way round, and as Western Europe remained politically divided, American leadership of 'the West' was both natural and – outside of Gaullist France – widely accepted throughout the Atlantic world.

In the 1950s, American leadership of Western Europe was also expressing itself in less formal ways. Post-war Europe was flooded with American movies, television programmes, mass catering, clothes and, above all, popular music. Whilst Europe was slowly getting back on its feet, the 'American dream' met European post-war drabness – and, amongst the newly aspirant European publics, the American dream won hands down! Mass consumer society was democratic; and unlike old Europe's old hierarchical societies, it was open to all, based on the egalitarian force of the new consumer.

'Euro-Fascists' and 'Euro-Wimps'

This US leadership of 'the West' slowly changed the way that Americans (and many Europeans) thought about Europe. For Americans, the USA remained, patently, a 'European' country, settled and constructed by Europeans coming in waves from all over the old continent. But this view of America as but a secondary branch of European civilization – as in some sense Europe's most successful colony – was being revised. To Americans (and to some Europeans), America began to appear as something altogether new, representing a quantum leap into a new, qualitatively distinct, civilization – breeding a new type of man and woman – which, at some point, seemed to develop a life of its own and now represented the best, and the future, of the human race.

Indeed, seeing the USA as an 'offshoot of Europe' was becoming controversial, often bitterly so, amongst Americans. During the 1960s and 1970s, an era dominated by the black civil rights movement and by the growth of feminism, serious objections arose to 'Eurocentric' thinking. To see the history of the USA only in European terms, as the history of 'dead, white males', was to undervalue the contributions of women and of the non-European peoples, of the Native Americans and the black Americans. And Eurocentrism did not help in the building of a new, multicultural American future in which 'minorities' – including the rapidly growing Hispanics and Asians – would eventually become a majority.

Many of those Americans who saw America as a multicultural nation with a multicultural future also saw the need to distinguish it from its European history and the European experience (which, then at least, was seen as 'monocultural', if not racist).[22] And many Americans of European descent also had reasons to distrust Europe. Anti-European sentiments going back to the founding of the nation and to the isolationist past still resonated. Nineteenth-century immigrant groups, such as the Germans and Irish, saw Europe as oppressive. Italians, Poles and East Europeans retained images of a continent that was fascist or communist. Many American Jews saw Europe through the lens of the German genocide, and the appeasement of the Nazis. Only the white, Anglo-Saxon Protestants (the WASPs) were essentially at home with their European forebears. And they, like most Americans, saw Europe as having been 'saved by the GIs' and then 'bailed out by American taxes' – images and themes developed and promoted by post-war Hollywood.

Anti-European sentiment was also stoked up during the very early cold war years by the battle between successive US administrations and Britain and France for influence in the Third World and in the oil regions. The USA, as it courted Third World leaders, sold itself as an anti-imperialist power. Americans had, after all, thrown off the colonial yoke themselves, whereas the European powers were still suspected of harbouring colonial ambitions. Later, as the cold war deepened, the growth of American anti-communism also took an anti-European turn. There was a nativist, nationalist aspect to American anti-communism in the McCarthy era – the junior Senator from Wisconsin, Joe McCarthy, himself called McCarthyism 'Americanism with its sleeves rolled up' – and in its world view Europeans were regularly depicted as 'soft on communism' and as 'pink' socialist fellow travellers. The succession of high-profile

Soviet spies exposed in the 1960s and 1970s in Europe did nothing to help Europe's image.

Americans turned somewhat introspective during the Vietnam era and the subsequent Watergate crisis, and Jimmy Carter famously pronounced that American society was suffering from a 'malaise'. But during Reagan's presidency it became, in his own upbeat phrase, 'Morning in America Again' and a new confidence was engendered. In Reagan's cold-war Washington, the Soviet Union needed to be 'opposed not appeased' and a patriotic Americanism was born again – it was no longer so acceptable to feel guilty about the American war in Vietnam, or about race relations. This assertive patriotism had a decidedly anti-European tinge to it. Traditional American conservatives, including Reagan himself, William Buckley, editor of *National Review*, Senator Jesse Helms and neo-isolationist Pat Buchanan, had fallen out with Nixon and Kissinger in the early 1970s over the US strategy of détente with the Soviet Union, and many of them saw 'leftist' European leaders, like Helmut Schmidt with his 'Ostpolitik' and Harold Wilson, as instrumental in pushing forward the strategy. In the 1980s, after they had overthrown détente, the underlying charge – Britain's Margaret Thatcher excepted – was that Western Europeans were not pulling their weight in NATO.

During the Reagan era, this developing anti-Europeanism was honed by new recruits to the conservative cause – influential neo-conservatives such as Irving Kristol, Norman Podhoretz, Midge Decter, Richard Perle, Elliot Abrams, Michael Ledeen, Paul Wolfowitz, Charles Horner and Kenneth Adelman. These neo-conservatives were so named because many of them came into politics as liberals and Democrats (some even as socialists and Trotskyites). They brought an extra dimension to the Reagan cold-war coalition in the 1980s. They were bright and fresh compared to the traditional conservatives (who came to be called 'paleo-conservatives'). They sharpened the 'freedom versus communism' (or 'with us or against us') rhetoric of the American right and depicted Europe as 'weak sisters' in the great cold-war struggle.

They also coined the arresting term 'Finlandization' to highlight their fears that much of Europe might be about to go the way of cold-war Finland and, in return for domestic freedom, allow their foreign policies to be controlled by Moscow.[23] And – in a neo-conservative theme to be echoed later during the 2003 Iraq controversy – they portrayed Europe as insufficiently democratic. They saw their old friends on the European left, socialists and social democrats alike, as lacking 'moral clarity' and inhabiting a sort of halfway house between capitalist democracy and communism; European conservatives were seen as no better – world-weary types trying to appease Soviet power and too accepting of abuses of Soviet tyranny (such as the treatment of Soviet Jews). Above all, the neo-conservative critique of Europe during the Reagan cold war amounted to a charge that Europeans were hypocritical. They were 'free riders' because many – particularly the French as well as the neutral Swedes – criticized America whilst 'living in luxury behind an American shield'.[24]

The most influential of the Reaganite neo-conservatives in 1980s Washington was Richard Perle, who was later to become world famous as a leading architect of the 2003 American war on Iraq and regular TV proponent of the war. Perle is a charming, soft-spoken gourmand (who adores French food and France) but is also a shrewd and tough political-cum-bureaucratic operator.

As a young man, and like many other neo-conservatives, Perle was a disciple of Albert Wohlstetter, a professor at the University of Chicago and later at the University of California. Wohlstetter was a cold warrior who believed that Soviet military power was underrated; it was Wohlstetter who introduced Perle to another cold warrior, Democratic Senator Henry 'Scoop' Jackson. Jackson was the archetypal American liberal cold warrior, leftist on domestic policy but in favour of a large defence budget. He was also a great champion of Israel's cause in the USA, the result of his witnessing the liberation of one of Hitler's concentration camps in 1945. It was during his years in the 1970s, as aide to Jackson, that Perle became the most influential non-elected person on Capitol Hill – dubbed the 101st Senator – when he helped to stop ratification of the SALT 11 Arms Control Treaty and secured passage of the Jackson-Vanik amendment which limited trade with the Soviet Union whilst it continued to restrict the emigration of Jews and other minorities. Later, as Reagan's Assistant Secretary of State, Perle continued his anti-Soviet campaign and gained the sobriquet in Europe of 'the Prince of Darkness' because of his opposition to arms control.

During the late 1970s, Perle's views on defence were also supported by that other cold-war liberal, New York Democratic Senator Daniel Patrick Moynihan and his two influential neo-conservative staffers, Elliot Abrams and Charles Horner. On all of these defence issues, Perle and the neo-conservatives met considerable opposition from

European leaders; and these disputes with Europe remained a source of resentment that turned over the years into a mild contempt for what many neo-conservatives believed to be the appeasing political culture of Europe (a charge also levelled at Europeans during the 2003 Iraq war crisis).

Some neo-conservatives were, though, to take this critique of Europe much further. Ever since the EEC's Venice Declaration of 1980, many neo-conservatives saw Europe as biased towards the Palestinians in the Middle East conflict. They also believed that European leaders, with their links to the largely European-derived Israeli Labour party, were constantly undermining Likud party prime ministers (from Begin to Sharon) whose hardline policies in the Middle East the neo-conservatives were increasingly supporting. Some saw Europe, and particularly the French, as mildly but inherently anti-Semitic, a charge that emerged during the transatlantic Iraq crisis when European commentators criticized the Israeli lobby in the USA.

The chief intellectual force behind this growing neo-conservative suspicion of Europe was Norman Podhoretz, editor of the highly influential magazine *Commentary*. Podhoretz and his wife, Midge Decter, were the central figures in the influential New York liberal intellectual movement, which broke ranks and supported Reagan's anti-communism. Podhoretz took few prisoners as he launched campaigns against Europeans for being soft on communism and 'Finlandized' in the great struggle underway between America and the Soviet Union. For a while, in the late 1970s, these neo-conservative cold warriors in New York, alongside their friends in Washington, remained hesitant about 'crossing the floor' and joining the Republicans (for, as they argued, 'country club Republicans' had traditionally shunned Jews and other minorities, and many neo-conservatives were Jewish). But, once welcomed by Reagan's team, they went from strength to strength. Later, Podhoretz then led another move, as during the 1980s the neo-conservatives dropped their domestic liberalism and embraced the American right's social agenda, including on gay and minority issues. It was an early sign of the later alliance between the neo-conservatives and the 'born again' Christian right that was to govern much of the thinking of the future presidency of George W. Bush.

By the late 1980s, the American conservative view of America's role in the world beyond its shores had changed. Nixon's geopolitics, based on the idea of national interest (and typified by détente and his overture to China), had given way to a far more ideological approach. Conservatives – both the Christian right and the neo-conservatives – saw the world as a struggle: 'democracy versus communism', 'freedom versus tyranny', and 'good versus evil'. In this struggle, Europe was a continent not to be trusted. The Soviets were enemies, Germany was riddled with Greens and pacifists (the term 'Euro-wimp' came into fashion), and France was guileful and anti-American. Only Margaret Thatcher stood out as a good soldier.

In the 1990s, the negative images of Europe held in Washington became primarily economic in nature: 'Euro-wimps' became 'Euro-sclerotics', inhabiting economies which, in comparison with the open and dynamic US model, were hobbled by labour market rigidities and by unfair subsidies. Europeans were regularly upbraided for continuing with unaffordable welfare systems in a global economy that demanded competitive low tax regimes. The charge was of being laggardly in following US leadership.

The USA lived through the most triumphalist phase of its whole history during the 1990s: it 'won the cold war'; it unleashed a revolution in economic thinking (of neo-liberal supply side free enterprise); it sat in the pilot's seat and engine room of the great new vehicle of economic globalization; and it won the Gulf War. America was the centre of the world; New York was the hub of global capitalism, the dispenser of culture and the setter of fashion. It was an era in which large numbers of Americans – in Main Street as much as in Wall Street – shared in Francis Fukuyama's American triumphal march in his world bestselling book *The End of History*. Some years before the Twin Towers were attacked, the collapse of communism had turned Washington's head. American strategists saw the world as a 'unipolar moment' and the talk was all about the USA's global role as the 'only superpower', or 'the hyperpower', and, unabashedly, of US 'hegemony'.[25]

In this heady environment, Europe was seen as a backwater. Viewed from Washington during the last 20 years of the century, the continent looked hopelessly divided and unable to 'get its act together' over monetary union; its economies were sluggish and sclerotic, and even its ability to defend its own continent was brought into question by the need to enlist the American military to sort out the Kosovo and Serbia crisis. Europe was a continent to visit only, a heritage theme park for vacations.

This seemed to be a view shared by Europeans themselves. For them, this whole post-1945 American narrative was simply more alluring than their own. Although the rebuilding of Europe – from the post-war rubble through the Berlin Wall to the launch of the euro – was a truly intriguing story, for young Europeans, taking their history from media journalism, the story and life of post-war Europe has simply been less compelling. It was a story of slow integration, of bureaucratic politics. It could not hold a candle to the openness of the New World, the dynamism of American business culture, the glitz of Hollywood and the smart weapons unleashed in the Gulf and Serbian conflicts. America was the most powerful nation on earth, but it was also the most attractive.

The Empire in Trouble

It all changed – swiftly and surprisingly – around the turn of the millennium, in the last years of the Clinton presidency and the first years of the presidency of George W. Bush. To Europeans, and, slowly, to Americans too, the USA became a country in trouble. There was unease that the superpower that had won the cold war was frittering away the peace in an economic bubble (fuelled by a 'hi-tech' bubble) that would soon burst. This unease was made worse by the tawdry Monica Lewinsky scandal, followed by an impeachment, and then, in 2000, by the first-ever American president to be put in office by the Supreme Court (and not the people). It was all grist for the mill of a lurking, alternative, view of America – as distorted as was the earlier, rosier, view – of an increasingly uncivil society, a nation ridden with violent crime and racial tension, with cut-throat competition, huge inequalities and without a welfare state.

These changes in European attitudes towards the USA started to reveal themselves in the opinion polls in late 2002. The fact that 71% of French people thought the 'spread of American ideas and customs is a bad thing' was high, but not surprising; what, though, was shocking was that 67% of Germans, 58% of Italians and 50% of British people thought the same thing.[26] All this prompted the leading neo-conservative Robert Kagan to argue, in his 2003 best-selling book *Paradise and Power*, that 'Americans are from Mars and Europeans are from Venus' and 'it is time to stop pretending that Americans and Europeans share a common view of the world.'[27] And, as Europeans began to change their views about the USA, their views about their own continent also changed. For the first time since 1945, many Europeans began to believe they lived in better societies than their American counterparts, that they had a higher standard of life – certainly in the cities – with less violent crime and racial tension and better welfare states. And, following the attack on the Twin Towers, the USA was just as vulnerable to terrorism as they had been. They also began to sense a power shift across the Atlantic and a geopolitical vacuum into which Europe could begin to assert itself, even become an alternative superpower.

The catalyst for these changing perceptions was the US economy. To many Europeans and Americans alike, all the perceived ills of the USA would somehow always be redeemed by its underlying economic strength which, at least, would allow them the chance to try to put things right. But by 2002, with the stock market fall-off and high-profile corporate scandals (at Enron and Arthur Anderson), it was becoming clear that the American economy possessed some serious structural weaknesses – not just troublesome accounting practices and corporate governance systems but, even more worrisome, the huge current-account deficit, the extraordinary levels of debt and the unsustainably high dollar. These economic weaknesses – which would have floored less powerful countries – could be ignored, for a time, because of the USA's status as a superpower and because any serious attempt to rectify these imbalances would have very harmful short-run consequences, affecting consumer confidence and also the broader global system where foreign businesses and economies were dependent on the American market. It was a desperate situation, in which the debt levels and the current-account deficits were getting worse and worse, and the hype and braggadocio needed for consumer confidence were getting louder and louder.

Some American policymakers, well aware of these long-term US weaknesses, were beginning to see them contributing to a geopolitical decline, especially vis-à-vis Europe and, ultimately, China. In the short run, Europe posed the most serious challenge. Former Under-Secretary of Commerce, Jeffrey E. Garten argued as early as 1998 – prophetically, and very much against the then grain in Washington and Wall Street – that the euro would pose a 'major challenge' to the USA, because 'when America's boom ends, it will still be the world's largest debtor, whereas the EMU region will be a net creditor.' And, echoing the view of a growing minority of worried Americans, he saw a future in which:

> the US will continue to run chronic trade deficits, while the
> European Union amasses large surpluses. America will not
> have reversed its super-low savings rates, while EMU members
> will have no such problems. American companies will also
> want to keep an eye on European corporate goliaths... A lot of
> experts are pointing to the need for Europe to brace for changes
> ahead. So should America.[28]

And since the 2001 Wall Street bear market (particularly in the
technology sector), the gloss had come off the much-touted American
'new economy', and also off the broader US model itself. In early
2002, even that high-priest of American capitalism, Morgan Stanley,
had issued a market commentary which made a remarkable case
that the US economy was showing so many structural weaknesses
that it was heading for a serious decline. It stated starkly that 'we
believe that the paradigm of US leadership in the global economy
and world financial markets of the last decade is coming to an end'.
And that 'we are moving from a uni-polar to a tri-polar world,
where Europe and Asia become the equals of the US in economic if
not military power.'[29]

The sputtering American economy simply made clear a hidden
reality – that during the 1990s America's power in the world may
well have been seriously overrated; conversely, Europe's and Asia's
power may have been underrated. An audit of American, European
and Asian power as it stood at the turn of the millennium is difficult
– not least because of the weight to give 'hard' and 'soft' power, and
how to measure them. In 2000, the USA had only about 300 million
people, about 5% of the world's population (whereas the EU15 had a
few million more, and China and India had over 1,000 million each).
The USA had about 31% of the world's Gross Domestic Product
(whereas the EU15 had just under 30% and China and India together
had about a sixth of the US total).

The US military, by contrast, was impressive. The Pentagon's
budget was more than the next 20 countries put together and three
eighths of total global defence spending. The American lead on
military research and development is even more impressive – four
times as much as the rest of NATO Europe put together.[30] And the US
military's potential reach is unprecedented in history, with a string
of as many as 158 bases (or 'military installations') around the world
in as many as 40 countries. American deployments stretch across

Eurasia from Western and Eastern Europe through to the Balkans (in the huge US army base at Camp Bondsteel in Kosovo picked up following the conflict with Serbia), the Middle East (including Kuwait, Oman, Saudi Arabia and now Iraq), the Indian Ocean (by courtesy of the UK in Diego Garcia) to Central Asia (with US air force bases in Tajikistan, Kyrgyzstan and Afghanistan), taking the US military right up to the Chinese border and beyond in South Korea and Japan. The only area where the Pentagon is in something of a retreat is Europe where, following the downturn in relations, US plans are to move assets out of Germany, into Poland, Bulgaria and Romania (as of 2003 the Krzesiny air base in Poznan was being prepared for the US air force).[31]

These bases were (and are) all about access, the ability at short notice for the USA's flexible forces to go anywhere in the world at any time. The architect of this new Pax Americana, Paul Wolfowitz, set out the case for them in blunt terms. 'The function of these bases,' he said, ' may be more political than actually military, they send a message to everyone.' And the message was clear: this new string of US bases girding the globe is very different from the system established during the cold war (when the bases were part of a containment policy). Now, they are no longer there for containment, but rather for pre-emption – and the implied threat has been of a US administration willing to overthrow governments believed by Washington to be dangerous. As the historian of empires Paul Kennedy ruminated in front of a transatlantic television audience in April 2003, this American system of bases was beginning to look very much like an empire in the classic old European sense.[32]

The question being increasingly posed in the USA, and around the world, before and after the 2003 Iraq war, was whether this powerful US military global reach would enable the USA, even potentially, to dominate or control, even police, the world? Could the USA in fact become the famed 'hegemon' and assume the mantle of lone super-power desired by the Bush White House and Condoleezza Rice? US forces were easily able to defeat Iraq, the world's 56th military power with no deliverable weapons of mass destruction and a country weakened by a decade of sanctions, but could they do much more than this? And were they able, as Samuel Huntingdon asked in the mid 1990s, to fight two serious wars at the same time?[33]

And was this global US military power sustainable? Would, in fact, US opinion allow future administrations to pay for its global network of bases, its hi-tech, flexible military, and the reconstruction costs of country after country whose regimes have been removed? Looked at another way, was the US an empire both overstretched and in decline, unable to sustain its power, like Rome or Britain before it? Was it destined to see other superpowers – Europe and China – rise to compete with it? And, if it continued to want to act as the world's policeman, would it need to seek to share power with Europe?

The USA at the turn of the millennium was certainly not like Rome in its latter years (Rome here meaning the empire in the west). It was not militarily weak; it had not surrendered its weapons to unassimilated bands of foreigners. It was not dependent for its supply of food on imports controlled by groups of opponents. It did not have a stagnant technology. It did not have a farm sector worked on by 90% of the population held in conditions of servitude. It did not have a hugely oppressive tax system. As yet it had not directly conquered large landmasses containing restless and resentful populations. It did not have difficult supply lines. It had lost no wars (save Vietnam). It had not yet been visited by plagues and epidemics. It did not depend on foreign mercenaries for its defence. And it did not, as yet, have a privileged, hereditary aristocracy (at least not of the type which ran Rome), nor an official and inordinately wealthy priesthood.[34]

Nor does today's USA resemble the Soviet empire before its fall. The Soviet problem was a classic case of serious overextension. Its domestic economy was simply unable to sustain the military expenditure needed to control its empire outside of its borders. Military spending was also taking far too much out of the domestic economy – to the point in the late 1980s when the Politburo came to the fateful conclusion that the USSR could no longer compete in a new arms race in space.

The US today may not resemble Rome or the Soviet Union before their falls. But it may well resemble the British empire of a century ago, in those fateful decades around 1900, before the onset of its rapid decline. Then, whilst London ruled over a global political empire on which 'the sun never set', it possessed a home base that could no longer sustain it. The British had, by global standards, a small population. So, too, do today's Americans. Britain had serious structural economic problems – not least an increasingly uncompetitive manufacturing and industrial sector that was being supplanted by other powers. Today's US structural problems – the country's massive debt owed to foreigners and its projected deficits – are no less acute.

But just as crucial was the damage inflicted by delusions of power. Imperial Britain at the zenith of empire produced an elite intoxicated with success, which slowly lost touch with reality, overestimating Britain's power and arguably leading to the blunders of the Boer War, the Great War of 1914–1918 and, at the very fag-end of empire, the 1956 Suez imbroglio. In 1921, South Africa's Anglophile Prime Minister, General Smuts, saw Britain as 'quite the greatest power in the world' and suggested that 'only unwisdom or unsound policy could rob her of her great position.'[35] And, in the view of Britain's chronicler of imperial decline, this was exactly what happened as Britain's increasingly deluded leadership allowed 'British responsibilities to vastly exceed British strength'.[36] They lost sight of the reality set out by Britain's nineteenth-century Liberal Prime Minister, William Ewart Gladstone, delivered at the height of empire: 'Rely upon it, the strength of Great Britain and Ireland is within the United Kingdom.'[37]

The American leadership in the 1990s and early 2000s was showing some of the same signs. Washington's celebration of the US 'victory' in the cold war, and Wall Street's lauding of the revolutionary 'new economy' (which some analysts predicted was even going to bring to an end the business cycle) led to a bout of excitable hubris about the USA as the world's 'only superpower', even the world's 'hegemon'. Even the measured Henry Kissinger echoed these sentiments when he said of the USA that 'at the dawn of the new millennium' it was 'enjoying a pre-eminence unrivaled by even the greatest empires of the past'.[38] It was an environment in which grandiose ideas about the superiority of American values and the need for universal conversion took root. Just as late imperial Britain talked of 'the white man's burden' and sought to bring their form of Christianity to the world by force, so the USA sought to bring its own version of 'democracy' to the world (initially the Middle East) even at the barrel of a gun.

Modern America also resembles early twentieth-century Britain in the challenge that its domestic democracy presents to its global power. As much as its faltering economy, it was Britain's developing democracy, with its visceral liberal opposition to 'colonialism' and the subjugation and domination of other peoples, which sank the empire.

Open societies are bad imperialists, as news of the harshness and moral difficulties of control and occupation abroad inevitably filter back to the homeland, creating opposition to the whole enterprise. Democracies are bad imperialists too, finding it difficult to sustain a consensus behind protracted wars abroad – as the Americans found out in Vietnam in the 1970s. Empires need elites to run them and to force through sacrifices at home. Nineteenth-century Britain possessed such an imperial elite – based upon a culture of rulership and the idea of 'noblesse oblige' – but today's American elite, based upon commerce and money, is not comfortable with such an overt political role.

Resistance to empire at home will be matched by resistance abroad. Today's Third World millions, which the USA seeks to remake in the interests of democracy and free markets, are not like the millions conquered by the Portugese, French and British over two centuries ago. Then the locals had no television, no radio, no access to what was going on about them and little ability to put it all in context. Then, too, the European imperialists did not face, as Americans do now, a highly politicized and organized religion with a gospel of resistance, and there was no international 'mullah class' of revolutionaries aiming their weapons at the heart of the homeland. Today, in America's century, foreign influence and control is both immediately known and resented and produces its inevitable reaction. The problem for the neo-conservatives in Washington who seek to 'remake' the Middle East is that they will run right up against the basic force of human dignity – few people will agree to being 'remade', even remade into democrats – from outside; sometimes even tyrants and puritan mullahs are preferable to foreigners and 'infidels'.

There is one sense in which Washington's twenty-first century form of power projection may be more sustainable than Britain's nineteenth-century type. It is more subtle and indirect. Whereas imperial London (and imperial Rome) directly ruled over the lives of millions of people around the globe, Washington does not (apart, that is, from its army of occupation in Iraq). Instead, it exercises its power on local governments through trade, aid and investment and through international institutions like the IMF and the World Bank and, increasingly, by the threat of direct military power. Modern Americans, brought up on anti-colonialist rhetoric, do not warm to the idea of empire. And, incredible though it seems to millions around the world, most Americans truly do not believe they possess one. One of the great exceptions is the novelist, biographer and essayist Gore Vidal, whose acerbic pen has chronicled and critiqued what he believes to have been the degeneration of his country from republic into empire – and a 'security state' at home to sustain it.[39] Another is the writer and academic Noam Chomsky, who sees the USA as a colonialist power like any other (following its conquests of Hawaii, the Philippines and half of Mexico).[40]

The exercise of American military power in the 1990s and early 2000s – in the first Gulf War, in Serbia and Kosovo, in Afghanistan and Iraq – has given life to Vidal's and Chomsky's themes of the American *imperium*. Even so, US power projection at the turn of the millennium was less overt and less intrusive than that used by Europe's empires. The old-style colonial power invaded, stayed and ruled – often for centuries. Today's American power projection is normally intimidatory, in order to get local rulers to 'support' US policy. Or it is of the 'hit and run' variety, which entails American military intervention (based upon air supremacy) and then leaves behind American-influenced governments to look after American interests, often with little purchase outside of the capital city, as in post-conflict Afghanistan.

Ultimately, though, American power in the coming century will not rest wholly on American military power – either through troops on the ground or through inducing local governments to do the USA's bidding. Such a strategy has its limits, never able to control all the world's peoples and constantly subject to resistance, often violently so. On the other hand, economic globalization knows far fewer limits. An inter-connected world engineered by global capitalism allied to advanced technology can, in theory, as the term itself suggests, be global in reach, and is more difficult both to identify and to resist. It is a far better carrier of 'Americanization' and has already allowed the USA to redraw parts of the world in its own image. This was the bold future predicted so confidently by Francis Fukuyama in the early 1990s in which Americanization – neo-liberal economics, liberal-democratic politics and even American moral sensibilities – would prevail the world over. It would, fantastically, be the end point of history.[41]

By the century's end, though, fewer and fewer analysts were predicting a future for Fukuyama's Americanized globe. The smart money was being placed on globalization simply fizzling out at its existing boundaries, or at redrawn, lesser boundaries. In 2002, even global bankers Morgan Stanley were reporting that globalization may well be on hold, and that it 'may now take a detour through regionalization'.[42] Such unfinished globalization was bad news for US global power. A fully Americanized world covering every corner, every nook and cranny of the globe might well be relatively stable. It would leave no space for rebellion and disobedience and, in such a homogenized world, governance would be made easier by the acceptance of common rules drawn up in the West. But, the kind of partial globalization that we have seen so far has met huge resistance – or 'blowback' as it is now called. In its starkest form, 'blowback' is seen in asymmetric terrorism against US and western targets and in the heady brew of pre-modern ideology and fundamentalist religion linked to modern terror technology. But resistance to Americanization, and modernity, will also come from traditional states as popular demagogic movements refuse to abide by IMF rules or non-proliferation agreements.

As the old century turned into the new, warnings of waning American global power were growing. But worries about overextension, about military overconfidence, about growing resistance, through terrorism, to US power and to globalization, through 'blowback' – all fell largely on deaf ears. After all, the 1990s was the decade when the USA had 'won' the cold war, and the era when America was in thrall to the great Clinton and Greenspan stock market-based boom and to the 'new economy' hype of Wall Street. To the elites in Washington and Wall Street, America was indeed the lone superpower, even the 'hegemon', and the American way was ruling the world. Talk of America losing support around the world, or of new rising superpowers (Europe and China), was against the grain, and anyway, if true, a long while off. Triumphalism was the American mood.

And then, in September 2001, the planes hit the Twin Towers of the World Trade Center in New York City. And national hubris met national tragedy, a fatal, and fateful, combination.

2

Europe Says 'No'

September 11th, Iraq and the Ruptured Alliance

At 9.38 EST on the morning of 11 September 2001, as the first plane struck the North Tower of the World Trade Center in New York, the leading lights of the American political and military establishment were going about their normal business. The newly confirmed Chairman of the Joint Chiefs, General Richard Myers, was on Capital Hill lobbying, Secretary of Defense Donald Rumsfeld was in his office at the Pentagon, Vice President Dick Cheney was in the White House complex (and about to be bundled by the secret service into the lower-floor bunker), and President Bush himself was in Florida campaigning in a school to talk about a new reading programme.

But in the days and weeks that followed the atrocity, normal politics was not resumed. A shocked Washington became a world in which 'everything changed', in which, to use the then mantra, 'nothing would ever be the same again'. And, for a short while, European leaders seemed to agree – sharing in the American grief and shock. French President Jacques Chirac, the first western leader in Washington following the attack, agreed to NATO invoking its mutual defence clause, and British Prime Minister Tony Blair talked of 'standing shoulder to shoulder' with the USA. Yet, shared grief was not to be translated into a shared view of the world; for Europeans, the atrocity of 9/11 was not ultimately to become their own 'defining moment'. In Europe, in fact, 'everything had changed' some 12 years earlier. Europe's own seminal 'defining moment' was a different 9/11 – 9 November 1989 – when the Berlin Wall came down, the cold war and the division of Europe came to an end, and suddenly the world looked very different. It was these very different defining events – and the differing views of the world they encouraged – that were to be at the heart of the Atlantic crisis that was to follow.

Europeans were never able to truly understand what the atrocity of 9/11, and the subsequent anthrax scares, meant to Americans, and the effect it had on the US political and media leadership. For many Americans it was, at bottom, a question of sudden, fearful vulnerability. Not since the war of 1812, when the British sacked the White House, had the territory of the continental USA been attacked or even threatened by outside powers. The Japanese had attacked Hawaii at Pearl Harbor in late 1941 – horrific enough to shock the country into a protracted war – but Hawaii was some three thousand miles from the homeland. September 11th, on the other hand, was subject to saturating publicity, which brought a nightmare of disaster in America's leading city to every home.

American invulnerability was central to American life. It was the platform upon which much of America's optimism, limitless possibilities and sheer geopolitical chutzpah were built. This sense of invulnerability also fuelled America's view of itself as an exceptional country – set apart and, in some sense, not essentially connected to the rest of the world.[1] The picture it had was of a huge swathe of the world outside the USA that was 'poor, nasty, brutish and short' – autocratic and tyrannical, dominated by wars, genocide and poverty. By contrast, the USA, from 'sea to shining sea', was protected by two oceans and by its sheer distance – thousands of miles – from the rest of the world. Even during the two world wars, which had involved American forces fighting and dying abroad, the continental USA remained invulnerable whilst European nations were being invaded and European cities were being bombarded and destroyed.

What the attack on the Manhattan Twin Towers achieved was hugely symbolic – showing that the citadel of capitalism in Wall Street was not invulnerable, and nor was that symbol of exuberance and superiority, the skyscraper. And almost as damaging to the sense of invulnerability was the use by the terrorists of two great pillars of domestic American commercial civilization – jet aircraft and round the clock mass media coverage (in which commercial pressures for sensationalism can increase the sense of fear).

The US population had, of course, felt fearful before – during the cold war, when Soviet missiles were capable of reaching American cities and towns in a matter of minutes. But the Soviets were seen as a traditional power whose leadership was essentially rational and could therefore be deterred and negotiated with; this took some of the sting out of the fear. Americans had also been warned about terrorism coming to the homeland. Six months ahead of the attack, the report of a commission chaired by former Senators Gary Hart and Warren Rudman had predicted such an event. They had argued prophetically that 'a direct attack against American citizens on American soil is likely over the next quarter century' and asserted that 'the combination of unconventional weapons proliferation with the persistence of international terrorism will end the relative invulnerability of the United States homeland to catastrophic attack.' But, according to Co-Chairman Gary Hart, in a sign of the sense of invulnerability of pre-9/11 America, a *New York Times* journalist walked out of the commission's press conference, saying – the exact words – 'None of this is ever going to happen'.[2]

Europeans, on the other hand, had no such sense of invulnerability. Many had, in fact, grown somewhat used to living with terrorism. The Basque separatists in Spain, the Islamic extremist bombers in Paris, the IRA in mainland Britain and political extremists in Germany and Italy had all brought terror to European cities. These terror campaigns in Europe, together with the memories of total war, particularly the aerial bombardment during the Second World War, meant that many Europeans could not share with the Americans their sudden sense of vulnerability.

Nor could they fully understand the radical American response to this 'new world' – the worldwide 'War on Terror'. European leaders agreed with Washington that al-Qaeda and other groups posed a serious threat, and the EU nations gave total backing (including military support) to the US campaign in Afghanistan to topple the Taliban. But they had many reservations about the idea of a 'War' on terror, with its black and white solutions of 'winning' and 'losing' and its proclaimed goal of 'ridding the world' of terror. Europeans who had lived with terrorism tended to believe that, ultimately, terrorism could never be fully eradicated – it could only be limited – and that the best way to limit it was by addressing the causes as well as using force. (And, as time went by, and the initial horror abated, many Europeans 'in the street' even began to share a sentiment held widely throughout the world that the Americans 'had it coming', that the Manhattan atrocity was a horrific reaction to US global power and arrogance.)

America's vulnerable mood after 9/11 had the potential not just to change the foreign policy of the country but to alter its role in the world – and Europe's role too. Isolationist instincts have never been far below the surface in contemporary America – but since George McGovern's 'Come Home America' presidential bid in 1974, they have been relegated to the margins of politics, found primarily in Pat Buchanan's 'America First' philosophy and amongst libertarians (like the influential Cato Institute in Washington, DC), who remain wary of the use and misuse of US military power. These sentiments still touch some real nerves amongst rural Americans (who see the world as a dangerous place to get involved in), labour unions (worried about exporting jobs) and women (normally somewhat more pacific than men) and can always grow quickly. Such a future 'isolationist' America – which retrenched American power around the world, closed bases, maybe even withdrew from the UN – would have big implications for Europe. For a retrenched USA would not only create a power vacuum in world politics which a uniting Europe could fill, but would also pose few objections to the emergence of the EU as a full super-state, indeed might even welcome it.

However, with US interests so heavily involved in the world beyond America's borders a new isolationism (even retrenchment) was always highly unlikely. And the immediate response of the Bush presidency in September 2001 was to renew American engagement in the world – but in a more aggressive and unilateralist manner. As George W. Bush put it to the world's governments: 'You are either with us or against us.'

It did not take the American leadership long to realize that the atrocity presented a great, even an historic, opportunity. In the great battle for the President's ear between hawks and doves, the hawks could finally make their move; and in the debate about America's role, those who believed in power (and power projection) could now win out over those who put their trust in diplomacy and economic influence. (Only a few days after the attack, the British Prime Minister, Tony Blair, as though sensing that the American leadership would indeed use the crisis to radically change their policy towards the world, made a huge claim – that when the dust from the terrorist attack on New York and Washington had settled, world politics could be reordered.)[3]

The leader of the hawks emerged very quickly. Donald Rumsfeld, a traditional conservative Republican, had been Secretary of Defense once before, in Gerald Ford's short-lived administration. With rimless spectacles and a seemingly bland demeanour, he had the deceptive look of a careful corporate bureaucrat. But in the months and years ahead Rumsfeld was to turn into a true political heavyweight, a radical who succeeded in changing American grand strategy and sold the change to the American media and public with waspish humour.

Rumsfeld saw himself as a super-realist and believed in the political power of the US military. He had once remarked, at a cocktail party in the mid 1970s, that America could 'get further with a kind word and a gun, than a kind word alone'. In the months before 9/11, Rumsfeld had been attempting to reform the US military – the so-called 'Rumsfeld Lite' reforms – to enable it to more effectively project power around the world. To this end, he wanted a military that could intervene quickly and was more mobile, technologically advanced and smaller than that advocated by traditionalists in the Pentagon, who favoured 'overwhelming force'. The public mood after 9/11 gave him the chance to put this vision into practice – first in the conflict in Afghanistan, later in the war in Iraq. He was also media savvy (if not media friendly) and was able, if not to secure the full backing of the US media, at least to ensure their neutrality.

During the 1990s, throughout their opposition years during the Clinton presidency, strategic thinking in Republican, conservative and neo-conservative circles was redefining this new role for the USA which Rumsfeld had come to represent. In Washington think tanks like the neo-conservative American Enterprise Institute, foreign policy institutes like the Centre for Strategic and International Studies, and in neo-conservative journals like *National Interest*, a new 'big idea' was taking root. In essence, it amounted – now that Soviet power had collapsed – to both defining and welcoming the USA as 'hegemon', as the sole superpower in a 'unipolar world', now able to direct and lead the globe, and, if necessary, do so on its own, unilaterally. Following the Bush victory in late 2000, this new strategic idea broke out of its laager, and began to find intellectual house room – as a serious point for debate – right across the political spectrum, from the new-right Heritage Foundation through to the prestigious journal of the liberal Carnegie Endowment, *Foreign Policy* and the journal of the establishment Council on Foreign Relations, *Foreign Affairs*. This growing consensus was simply reinforced by French Foreign Minister Hubert Vedrine's famous depiction of the USA not just as a superpower, but as a 'hyperpower'.[4]

Following the US military's performance in the Gulf War and the Serbian air campaign, a large portion of conservative and middling opinion in Washington began to believe this unipolar thesis. Washington was seized by the notion that US military predominance – particularly in smart weaponry, power projection and rapid reaction capabilities – could herald an age in which Washington could assert 'hegemony' through military power virtually anywhere in the world, as a kind of 'world policeman'. This huge American lead in military power was seen as providing Washington for a decade or two with a 'window of opportunity' for the unchallenged assertion of American interests around the world. It was a strategic vision which saw power as based primarily on military preponderance: on what the American political scientist Joseph Nye called 'hard power'. And it discounted the declining 'soft' power realities of America – its small population by global standards, its declining relative economic strength, and the growing ideological opposition to US power (often dubbed 'anti-Americanism') around the world.[5]

This developing radical vision of the USA as the world's policeman was still a minority pursuit, contained and held within Washington's think tanks, when the terrorists struck the Twin Towers in New York and the Pentagon on 11 September – and then 'everything changed'. The generalized fear engendered by the terror of the Manhattan atrocity and the anthrax scare created a new political climate in which Americans were prepared to vest authority to deal with the crisis in the President; the President himself sought to project himself as a strong and forceful leader defending a country that had been attacked on 'his watch'; and the conservatives and neo-conservatives around George W. Bush were able to convince him to adopt a radically new geo-strategic course.

It took Washington about 12 months to formulate the new strategic idea of 'hegemony' or 'dominance' into official doctrine, but by September 2002 it was ready and was published under the signature of the President in the annual *National Security Strategy of the United States* (2002). According to the evolving doctrine, 'our forces will be strong enough to dissuade potential adversaries from pursuing a military build up in hopes of surpassing, or equalling, the power of the US' and, in the Pentagon's parallel review, military doctrine became one of 'Full Spectrum Dominance'. This strategy of blocking rival powers even from 'equalling' the USA was first given an outing as early as 1991, when Zalmay Khalilzad, a member of then Defense Secretary Dick Cheney's team (and in 2002 special envoy to Afghanistan), outlined it in a book entitled *From Containment To Global Leadership*. His recommendation that US strategic doctrine should be based upon 'precluding the rise of another global rival for the indefinite future' was produced in a report of the Cheney team 'Defense Strategy for the 1990s' and reflects the thinking of Dick Cheney for some years before he became Vice President.[6]

It was a bold theme, one not normally spoken of in polite diplomatic circles, but it was to be taken up, once in the White House, by Dr Condoleezza Rice, George W. Bush's National Security Advisor. In a none-too veiled warning to Europe during the height of transatlantic tensions over Iraq she argued that other powers should not try to 'balance the United States'.[7] Then, during the Franco-German-Luxembourg-Belgium defence summit in Brussels in May 2003, President Bush himself warned the assembled powers not to create 'rivals' to the USA. By May 2003, in the immediate aftermath of the Iraq war, American diplomacy was clearly attempting to maintain its 'primacy' by a 'divide and rule' policy towards Europe. The American press was full of stories about a diplomatic strategy in which France was being punished – there was even a meeting at the White House to discuss such 'punishment' – Germany was being ignored and relations with pro-USA countries like Poland and the UK were being enhanced (Poland was given a role in occupying northern Iraq), while relations with the EU as a whole were being 'disaggregated'.

Another theme of the new doctrine unleashed by 9/11 was the idea of pre-emption. The President's new official doctrine stated boldly that in the new environment of terror 'to forestall or prevent hostile acts by our adversaries, the US will, if necessary, act pre-emptively.'[8] Since the Second World War, the USA had prided itself on never engaging in an unprovoked attack – like the 'sneak attack' on Pearl Harbor in 1941. It had, instead, relied upon containment and deterrence. But the new terrorism was so troublesome that Washington abandoned deterrence and containment because they argued that neither worked against 'rogue states'. Under this doctrine, a state opened itself to pre-emptive attack from the USA if it possessed two characteristics: if it had the capability to hurt the USA and its allies through possessing weapons of mass destruction; and if it was malign or a 'rogue'. The term 'rogue', though, was never seriously defined. Richard Haas, a moderate conservative and Director of Policy Planning at the State Department in the George W. Bush administration, has attempted to define what may be developing as a working doctrine for pursuing such 'regime change' – he suggests that a regime can rightfully be overthrown by the USA if it 'massacres its own people' or 'supports terrorism in any way'.[9] For Paul Wolfowitz, a 'rogue state' worthy of regime change would be one that was a threat to peace and/or undemocratic – and its removal would allow the USA to establish a global goal of a widening 'zone of peace and democracy' in the world. These definitions were, though, so vague that opponents of the new strategy could argue that a 'rogue state' simply amounted to any regime that 'disliked' or ideologically opposed America. Initially, three states – comprising the famous 'axis of evil' outlined by President Bush in his 2001 state of the union address – came into view as members of the club of rogue states and as candidates for pre-emption: Iraq, North Korea and Iran. By mid April 2003, two were left, and Syria, Libya, even Saudi Arabia, were being talked of as candidate members.

As Washington's new doctrine evolved in the fraught first six months of 2002, it became clear that, to the Bush administration, the threat from 'rogue states' was not so much a direct, or imminent, threat – of a Saddam Hussein lobbing a missile at the American homeland – as it was a longer-term threat. The fear was that 'rogues' could at some future date develop weapons of mass destruction and surreptitiously pass them on to terrorist groups like al-Qaeda for delivery into American cities. No amount of containment and deterrence could stop such an event, so the USA would need to act first, pre-emptively, to remove the hostile regime. Critics immediately suggested that this gave the USA huge leeway to take out any regime it simply suspected of potential terrorism at some date in the distant future – a definition which could include large numbers of nation states. President Bush's bravura declaration a few days after September 11th that, in the War on Terror, 'you are either with us or against us' was so stark that it set alarm bells ringing around the world. For it could easily be read as meaning that Washington was about to enter the business of removing regimes with weapons of mass destruction that opposed it or that it disliked – a doctrine that, following the UN imbroglio over the US-British war on Iraq, might even be cause for concern in Paris and Moscow!

The Neo-Conservative Breakthrough

By the summer of 2002, in the aftermath of the Afghanistan war, the USA and Europe were beginning to seriously diverge on strategy. Washington was warning other powers not to rival the USA, whereas leading EU nations were supporting the idea of a multi-polar world structure; the USA was embracing ideas of unilateralism (talking of Washington-led 'coalitions of the willing'), while Europe was stressing the importance of the UN; the USA talked of 'pre-empting' 'rogues', but the Europeans were worried both about 'pre-emptive' attacks on regimes (tending to fall back on traditional doctrines of containing and deterring hostile regimes) and about the problems of defining who and what amounted to a 'rogue'.

And then, in the midst of this developing transatlantic debate, President George W. Bush suddenly, and out of the blue, refocused the whole global War on Terrorism and al-Qaeda into a Middle East crisis involving Iraq and Saddam Hussein. It was this switch in policy that German Chancellor Gerhard Schroeder objected to when he argued, in the summer of 2002, that Iraq had nothing to do with the War on Terror and called the policy an 'adventure' which Germany would not support. And this new campaign against an Arab state that did not threaten the USA brought to the surface European suspicions about American motives – about whether Bush was increasingly using the War on Terror as a cover for American strategic goals in the Middle East and Eurasia – primarily for oil and in order to protect Israel. In many European eyes it came to be seen as little more than an American power play.

During 2002, Bush increasingly conflated Saddam Hussein and 'terrorism' into one terrifying image, and the question arose throughout Europe about what exactly the US administration meant by terrorism. Did it mean any sub-state group that used force to achieve its ends (a criteria that would capture within it the Nicaraguan insurgency, the father of the USA, George Washington, and his rebel army, as well as the French resistance in the Second World War)? Would it include local, national, or regional 'terror' groups that did not in any way threaten the USA (like the IRA, which had strong support amongst Irish-Americans, or the Basque guerrillas, or the Palestinian suicide bombers)?

Many Europeans saw a traumatized USA as having been drawn by September 11th (and the belief that Americans shared a similar terrorist threat to that of Israel) into an Israeli fight against Palestinians and the Arab and Muslim world. Not only Paris and Berlin, but also London, Madrid and Rome were reluctant to be drawn in as well – fearful of unnecessarily souring their relations with the Arab and Muslim worlds. Unlike many Europeans, Washington did not compare the young men and women in Palestine who used violence against their occupying power to the French and Polish resistance in the Second World War, but, rather, they saw the Palestinian suicide bombers as similar to the terrorists who attacked the World Trade Center. When the USA itself became an occupying power in Iraq, US Central Command even began to depict out-of-uniform Iraqis who attacked the invading American forces as 'terrorists'. American confusion over the definition of terrorism reached utterly bizarre heights during the Iraq war when President Bush visited Tony Blair in Belfast and sanctioned an Irish 'peace process' directly involving groups which his host had only a few years before been describing as 'terrorists'. But, in the post-9/11 atmosphere, the old adage that 'one man's terrorist is another man's freedom fighter' was, in Washington, put on hold.

In a speech to the American Enterprise Institute on 27 February 2003, President Bush deepened these suspicions. He outlined a bold post-Iraq scenario, in which a 'democratic Iraq' would become the focal point for reordering the whole Middle East. This speech was music to the ears of the neo-conservatives around Bush. Chief amongst these was Paul Wolfowitz, the No. 2 in the Pentagon. Bright, sophisticated and studious, Wolfowitz was what Washingtonians call a 'defense intellectual' (in the manner of Henry Kissinger or Zbigniew Brzezinski) and he had risen to influence in Republican circles during the Reagan years. Ever since the 1991 Gulf War, he had been a keen advocate of a tough policy towards Iraq and the main promoter in the Bush administration of regime change in Baghdad. When, some time in the early summer of 2002, Bush finally signed on to his plan, Wolfowitz, a keen supporter of Israel, was dubbed by his circle, affectionately but insensitively, as 'Wolfowitz of Arabia'.

The Wolfowitz strategy followed a radical new posture for the Middle East launched back in 1996 in a document called 'A Clean

Break: A New Strategy for Securing The Realm', the 'realm' in this case being Israel. In it, leading American neo-conservatives – Richard Perle, and strategists David Wurmser and Douglas Feith (since 2000, deputy to Paul Wolfowitz) – argued that only by a daring restructuring of the whole Middle East – by turning the then existing regimes into 'democracies' – could Arab and Iranian-backed terrorism be ended and a peace settlement secured with Israel.[10]

The American decision to attack Iraq – no matter the eventual outcome of the occupation – was a huge political boost for these neo-conservatives. They had taken a great political risk in so openly promoting the attack on Saddam. Few people in the wider world had ever heard of the genre before; and, in coming out from behind the shadowy Washington world where they mainly worked, they had become a potential political target for their opponents at home, and an actual target for those in Europe, and around the world, who opposed the war. The secret of their success was that, following September 11th, they struck when the iron was hot. In an environment willing to listen they developed a clear message with a bold vision. The American neo-conservatives in Washington and New York were few in number, and they tended to know each other (some are even related, like Bill Kristol, influential editor of *The Weekly Standard*, who is the son of the even more influential Irving Kristol, publisher of the *National Interest* and leading light in the American Enterprise Institute); and they developed an *esprit de corps* which allowed them to make a compelling case to the American, if not the European, public.

Their starting point was always the threat from 'terrorism'. In the neo-conservative world view, terrorism was enemy number one; it posed a seamless web of threat all the way from the West Bank to the heartland of America; and only the USA, by using the overwhelming might of its armed and security forces, could effectively defeat it. The neo-conservatives brought what they themselves called 'moral clarity' to the American debate. They drew a picture of the world in black and white colours, as a struggle between the terrorists (anti-American Islamists and Palestinians) and the 'good guys', solid citizens who opposed terrorism. In short, it was a struggle between good and evil – an idea well captured by the highly articulate neo-conservative, David Frum, the author of the most memorable phrase of the Bush presidency – the 'axis of evil'.

The neo-conservatives were tough on opponents and did not shirk from good old-fashioned political abuse. Europeans who questioned

American strategy in the Middle East were designated 'wimps' and 'leftists', even 'anti-Semites'. American liberals were 'anti-American'. And traditional American conservatives who did not subscribe to the invasion of Iraq, were, in an echo of the McCarthyite era, dubbed 'unpatriotic' and accused of espousing 'defeatism'.[11]

The neo-conservative plan for remaking the Middle East was grandiose enough; but, to European consternation, some strategists in Washington were going even further. Former Director of the CIA, the lean and incisive James Woolsey, was advocating a 'permanent war', or 'World War Four' (World War Three being the cold war). This extraordinary advocacy of permanent war for the USA was the brainchild of Professor Eliot Cohen, and Woolsey gave extra life to the idea by naming America's enemies in this coming conflict. They include, as of 2003: Sunni Islamists, Shiite Islamists, the Tehran mullahs, Hezbollah, Syria, Libya and Sudan – indeed anyone who opposes western-style democracy, a list which, over time, could include Saudi Arabia, Egypt, Pakistan and, maybe, even China. Woolsey, like Wolfowitz, saw the USA as creating, by force if necessary, 'a widening zone of peace and democracy' first in the Middle East and then throughout the world. And he is very hard on opponents who believe that the Arab world and other non-western societies and peoples cannot be easily democratized on the American model. He calls them 'racists'.[12]

This idea of 'permanent war' had considerable appeal in the White House, specifically to Bush's tough political guru, Karl Rove. Although no Republican would ever publicly advocate 'permanent war' (the American public would oppose the principle of a never-ending conflict), Rove saw the huge potential of a permanent state of wartime psychology for the re-election of the President. The permanent 'War on Terror' helped Bush, but was not dramatic enough. It was foreign threats, and invasions to remove them – particularly against easy targets like Saddam – that stirred patriotic sentiment and silenced or sidelined opposition. And if, in this permanent state of war, periods of high tension could be turned on and off at will, and at suitable times, so much the better.[13]

This neo-conservative-led new US strategy of bringing democracy to the Middle East region through the barrel of a gun was seen in Europe either as naïve or hypocritical. And many saw the plan – particularly if imposed by American military rule – as little more than a return to old-fashioned imperialism. An American army of occupation in the middle of Arabia, led by some kind of viceroy sent from Washington, would not, they believed, win friends, nor last for long. Sooner or later, the Americans would get bogged down and either give up and go home (leaving behind a Balkanized Iraq and radical Islamic republics) or they would have to go further, and try to remake the whole region along the lines set out by the neo-conservatives. Whatever happened afterwards, many Europeans believed that an invasion of Iraq would sour long-term relations between Europe and its neighbour – the Arab and Islamic Middle East. Washington was seen as damaging European interests.

Right up until the very last minute, there were many people in Europe who simply did not believe that the Bush administration would actually launch an unprovoked attack on a Middle Eastern state without UN approval and against the fervent opposition of key US allies and an overwhelming majority of the world's peoples. They believed Bush was bluffing. But when, at 5 a.m. Baghdad time on the morning of Friday 21 March 2003, 40 cruise missiles were fired from the Abraham Lincoln battle group in the Gulf into southern Baghdad in an attempt to 'decapitate' the Iraqi leadership and the attack began, all was clear. Bush had meant what he said; and had taken the United States of America down a new road – the raw use of power, unconstrained even by allies. Friends and opponents alike feared that this road would lead to a colonial occupation in the heart of the Arab world from which the USA could not easily extricate itself. Former US National Security Advisor, Zbigniew Brzezinski, on the eve of the Iraq war, warned his fellow Americans that the USA was more alone in the world than at any time since 1945.[14] But the President, and the new unilateralists in the US administration, hardly seemed to care.

By Monday 24 April 2003, the US Central Command in Qatar was telling the President that the USA had defeated Saddam's army in its last holdout in Tikrit. And on that day Doug Feith, a leading neo-conservative and No. 3 at the Pentagon, was convinced that he was about to see his dream of a new Middle East come true. Feith was a jovial man, whose conviviality hid a detached, razor sharp mind, honed by his legal training. But even he was hugely excited. Some weeks before, he had been asked by his bosses, Defense Secretary Donald Rumsfeld and Deputy Secretary Paul Wolfowitz, to secretly prepare the case for an immediate war with Iraq's western neighbour, Syria. And now it seemed that, buoyed by the victory over Iraq, the

President might actually order an attack on a second Arab nation and begin implementing the 'domino effect' and the neo-conservative agenda for the restructuring of the whole Middle East.

Although Feith and the neo-conservatives did not get their way that Monday – for the President decided against the attack on Syria and left Washington to campaign for his proposed tax cut – they remained convinced that the successful military overthrow of Saddam Hussein's regime had given the 'New America' – its new Middle East policy and global policy of pre-emption – a huge boost. They also felt that the Iraq war had vindicated Rumsfeld's 'light' military strategy, allowing the USA to wage war in a number of places simultaneously. To these triumphant neo-conservatives, their gamble in Iraq had paid off. America was now in the position they had worked hard for. They saw its unrivalled military power as enabling them first to remake the Middle East and then to shape a new world order.

Rupture

But, in the rarefied Washington offices of the superpower, the triumphant neo-conservatives may well have been seriously misreading the real world. The American military win in Iraq had certainly strengthened America's short-term position in the Middle East. The USA had control of the Iraqi oil fields and its ability to influence other Arab governments had been strengthened, as had its strategic partner Israel. Yet, at the same time, the Iraq war may, in the longer term, have taken a real toll on America's world position. Hatred of the USA around the world, already strong, was further strengthened. And, although oil revenues may ultimately pay for some or much of the war, the further militarization of America which the new doctrine of pre-emption involves places great new costs on the US budget – and brings into question the sustainability of the new American military empire around the world.

Above all, the war created what was not there before: an organized political opposition to US global dominance, and in the one area of the world – the European Union – which could pose a potential global challenge to the USA. In the 1990s, the EU's larger population, larger single market, equal financial power and potentially equal technological power made it an economic and civilian competitor to the USA. But Europe was politically weak, hesitant to stake out an independent role, fearful of saying 'no' to the superpower. The war in Iraq changed all that.

German Chancellor Gerhard Schroeder was the first to declare independence. But, as with many momentous decisions, it was hardly the product of a well thought-out strategy: he stumbled into it. In the summer of 2002, the German Chancellor was in the middle of a difficult election campaign, was well behind in the polls and was reaching for an issue to revive his campaign. With the economy faltering, Gerhard Schroeder's populist streak, his down to earth appeal and charismatic TV personality was not working, even against the earnest and dull but efficient Christian Democrat leader from Bavaria, Edmund Stoiber. Suddenly, in the middle of the campaign, Schroeder declared that President Bush's threatened invasion of Iraq was an 'adventure' which Germany would not support. It was a shrewd political move. Germany had supported Bush's 'War on Terrorism' and the invasion of Afghanistan, and Schroeder was genuinely surprised to see Washington suddenly switch to Iraq as a target. With Bush's case apparently so weak – with no evidence of Iraq aiding terrorism and a dubious charge that Iraq possessed weapons of mass destruction – Schroeder had the perfect opportunity to tap into both the widespread anxiety in Germany about Bush's America and the deep pacifist strain in German opinion.

The fact that Schroeder engineered a spectacular turn-around in his fortunes, and came from behind to win the election, indicated that an independent stance by a European leader was a votewinner. But more important still was the path-breaking fact that a major ally, arguably America's single most important ally, and the most Atlanticist of countries, had said 'no' to the USA and had broken with over half a century of traditionally supporting Washington. A furious Bush refused to speak to the Chancellor, and the American Defense Secretary, Donald Rumsfeld, publicly described relations between Washington and Berlin as 'poisonous'. This was not a storm in a teacup, for Schroeder stood his ground, even, some months later, lining up with President Chirac to declare a separate Franco-German Iraq policy.

This German move was momentous for, in one fell swoop, Schroeder appeared to make history. By denouncing US policy – and winning an election – he showed the rest of Europe that there was nothing to fear from an independent stance. He also realigned the West. For 50 years, Germany had placed its security relations with Washington ahead of those with France, a posture upon which NATO was built, which had ensured US leadership in Europe and had blocked all serious efforts towards a common European defence. But with Germany now aligned with France rather than Washington, a new road forward for Europe had opened up.

Schroeder's declaration of independence in the summer of 2002 may well have originated as a purely domestic political tactic; but it unleashed long-simmering feelings about Europe's subordination to America that went well beyond Germany. In fact, Germany had never been in the forefront of those Europeans who, once the cold war was over, sought greater independence from American power, unlike, say, France or Greece. But, slowly, during the 1990s, Bonn and Berlin were becoming less in thrall to American power and influence. As early as 1990, German-US relations had gone into cold storage for a month or so, in what was considered in Germany an example of American high-handedness. What happened was that in the months immediately following the collapse of the Berlin Wall and the end of the East German regime, the CIA abducted East German intelligence files, property properly belonging to the newly unified German government. At one point, so strained was the relationship that even the German government of Helmut Kohl threatened to retaliate against CIA assets in Germany.

But it was the arrival of President George W. Bush that aroused widespread public opposition to American policies amongst the public in Germany and throughout Europe. Before Bush, during the emollient presidency of Bill Clinton, growing transatlantic tensions had been smoothed over and contained. Part of this was sheer personal style: Clinton's charisma, humour and human failings played well in Europe; whereas Bush's Texan braggadocio – which he saw as straight-talking – was seen as brash and crass. More important was Clinton's decision never to push policy differences to a rupture and, thus, to avoid them and 'kick them into the long grass'. But George W. Bush's new, unabashed, go-it-alone – and, in some ways, more honest – attitude created a whole new environment. A series of unilateral decisions out of Washington – particularly the imposition of steel tariffs to protect the US steel industry, which came on the heels of Washington's exit from the Kyoto treaty and the International Criminal Court – created the impression of a new America no longer prepared to co-operate and negotiate with partners and allies.

But it was Bush's policy in the Middle East that led to rupture. Having come to office with a policy of standing aside from the Israeli-Arab conflict, President Bush soon made it clear that he was not going to follow his father's 'even-handed' policy (which put financial pressure on Israel and led to the Oslo peace process) but would instead support Israel even more fervently than had his predecessor, Bill Clinton. This American policy ran directly counter to European public opinion which was increasingly sympathetic to the occupied Palestinians, and became even more so as they witnessed the scenes of the *intifada*, the Israeli military occupation of the West Bank and tank attacks on the EU taxpayer-funded Palestinian Authority on their TV screens. When President Bush decided to attack Iraq without reinvigorating the 'peace process', European opinion hardened further against the role of the USA. Indeed, the war against Iraq became, throughout much of Europe, a symbol of unbalanced, pro-Israeli American power in the Middle East. So strong was European opinion that even Britain's Tony Blair attempted to take a stance independent of the USA and, in January 2003, took an initiative in the dispute – organizing a London conference on the future of Palestine – which had only lukewarm support from President Bush.

As well as creating real opposition in Europe to US policy, the Bush presidency and its war in Iraq may also have brought closer the elusive goal of European political unity. On the surface, the Iraq war seriously split Europe. The governments of Britain, Spain and Portugal, and to a lesser extent Italy and Denmark, supported the US action; and the 'Vilnius declaration', though not supporting the war, supported America, and was interpreted as a breaking of Europe's ranks by the newcomers. This split in Europe was seized on by US Defense Secretary Donald Rumsfeld, with one of the most effective transatlantic quips in a generation, when he described with glee what he saw as an emerging division between 'Old Europe' and 'New Europe'.

The crisis also forged a new solidarity between Europe's two leading members, France and Germany. The two countries not only joined forces in the UN to oppose a US pre-emptive military strike on Iraq, but even went as far as to openly campaign against Washington. At one point, the French Foreign Minister, Dominic de Villepaine, set off on what amounted to a campaign trip through Africa to persuade members of the Security Council to vote against

Washington's attempt to secure UN backing for the coming war. For two of America's leading allies to campaign in such a manner was unprecedented; it led the normally low-key, diplomatic Henry Kissinger to describe the French and German activity as 'outrageous'.[15]

Gerhard Schroeder had taken the first, fateful step, and France rose to the challenge. In Paris, the bleak reality of a Washington on the march gave President Chirac little choice. During this pre-war crisis, Jacques Chirac lent heavily on Dominic de Villepaine, his suave, aristocratic Foreign Minister. Like Chirac himself, de Villepaine had lived in America as a young man when his father (a senator with long experience of the Arab world) had been posted to Washington. He spoke English fluently and became a diplomatic star during the UN confrontation between the USA and France in the Security Council. He had been a close advisor to Chirac before becoming Foreign Minister (and had survived being blamed for advising Chirac to dissolve Parliament, an act which had let the socialists into government) and, with the former Prime Minister and Mayor of Bordeaux, Alain Juppé, remained part of the inner circle in the Elysée. As the crisis developed, all the advice coming into the Elysée from Chirac's inner circle, from his own UMP party and from the public, had been to stand up to Bush.

As soon as it became clear that Bush had decided to go to the UN to seek support for his war, Chirac made his decision. The USA had to be confronted. He would say 'No' to Bush and use the veto, even if it meant temporarily dividing the western world. British Prime Minister Tony Blair had been putting pressure on Chirac not to take this course. But, to the French, the Blair strategy of supporting an unprovoked American attack simply because Washington demanded it would condemn Europe to impotence. Blair may have had the President's ear, and an 'in at court' in Washington, but he was not able to influence US policy (particularly on the Israeli-Palestine issue). In any event, the French and Germans argued that when American interests differed from their own (as they did in the Middle East), Europeans should refuse to support the USA and instead pursue their own interests even if it was a strategy which ultimately would lead them to form their own power centre in the world.

What tipped the balance amongst the Elysée advisors was the historic new fact of European life – that any French initiative taken against Washington would have the support of Germany and

Russia – and mass public support throughout Europe (and also in large parts of Britain and Spain, despite their governments' pro-US stance). Chirac was well aware that Bush and Blair had given France the stage to create their long sought after rival power centre, and he was not going to miss this opportunity. And Paris played it for all it was worth. The television image – sent around the world – of a handsome and articulate French Foreign Minister lecturing America about peace and law and being clapped by the assembled world's diplomats was a true global event and a defining moment in American-European relations. It infuriated Washington, souring relations even further; but it was a rite of passage for the new Europe. Europe had finally grown up, and was joining the big league.

Seen from Paris during the calm before the storm of war, Washington's Iraq policy had played into French hands. For, as Paris saw it, no matter how Washington played it in the future, Europe would emerge with a larger role in the world. Should the Democrats win in Washington in 2004, and seek to retrench American power, then the pressures from Washington against European unity would be removed, and in the new world structure Europe would play a considerable role. On the other hand, should Bush be re-elected and the USA continue to seek to become a global policeman of an American empire, the chances were that it would spectacularly fail and Europe would be in a position not just to pick up the pieces, but also to offer an alternative western foreign policy and 'western model' – particularly to the humiliated and devastated Arab and Muslim world. But all that was in the future. By mid March 2003, President Bush was signing the orders for war against Saddam Hussein's regime. All that the French leadership, like the peoples of Europe, could do now was to sit on the sidelines and watch the Pentagon's war in the heart of the Middle East unfold on their television screens.

The strength of the American reaction to France's defiance at the UN, though, surprised Paris. The sheer vitriol of the American right, notably from the Murdoch press and television (Fox News in particular), the talk from the White House of 'punishment' for France after the war and the campaigns to boycott French wines and change 'French Fries' to 'Freedom Fries', made some French parliamentarians have second thoughts. But this American response was mainly symbolic and would likely remain so – as any official economic sanctions taken against France would meet a response from the EU as a whole, a move the faltering US economy, dependent on huge capital inflows from Europe, could do without.

Chirac and de Villepaine, as well as Schroeder and Putin, had taken a calculated gamble. They had not only opposed, but also campaigned against the will of the world's only superpower, a move which could cost them dear. Seen from Washington and London, they had split the Atlantic Alliance. And they had unleashed anti-European sentiment in the USA, particularly amongst some powerful elites in Washington. But, at the same time, they reckoned that the longer-term gains would be worth it. They believed that President Bush had made a grievous strategic error by invading an Arab state without real cause, and that this was the perfect opportunity to unfurl the European standard in the face of Bush's 'New America' and set the scene for creating a rival power by a show of European independence. They were also prepared to live with the fact that, in the short run, Europe would appear divided. Britain's Tony Blair and Spain's José Maria Aznar would stick with Washington, and the EU's Common Foreign and Security Policy (with its defence policy, the ESDP) would look dead in the water. But, in truth, the EDSP was a pretty weak vessel for as long as Britain, continuing to side with the Americans, was not part of it. So, as a spur to getting a real security policy, with real military integration and punch, Paris, with Germany and Belgium, would construct a core European military system which others, particularly the British, could join later. Real European unity had always progressed this way, from the single market to the single currency.

Above all, the Franco-German UN campaign succeeded in raising the biggest question of all: how should Europeans react to this new assertion of American power and the imminent extension, into the heart of the Middle East, of the American empire. It also highlighted the stark choice facing Europeans: whether to remain, as Paris saw Britain, as an adjunct of US power, or to create an independent superpower as a counterweight or rival. Tony Blair openly joined the debate and went public by arguing that he wanted Europe to be 'a partner not a rival'. He saw his role as being an influence on the US from the inside by being an advisor, a principal player at court.

The Franco-German campaign, and the Bush White House's reaction to it, was seen by many as representing a great historical turning point. Journalists talked of a 'shift in the tectonic plates of the West', and headlines appeared in American and European newspapers proclaiming 'a change in the map of the world' and 'the end of NATO'. Such depictions were not wholly misplaced. Never since the Suez crisis in 1956 had two major European countries agreed to oppose the USA so vehemently. And the German decision to join France and oppose America on a big security issue was indeed an historic shift. And, if France and Germany could use the aftermath of the crisis to form a core European security system excluding the USA, history would truly have been made. In the early spring of 2003, as Europeans weighed up the future in the aftermath of the American-led war in the Middle East, much of Europe was asking, could France and Germany pull it off?

'Anti-American' Europe

This 2003 Franco-German campaign against the USA at the UN did not come out of the blue. In fact, Washington and Europe had been auditioning for such a rupture in relations for some considerable time. The 1990s had witnessed a dramatic widening of the Atlantic as European and American economic interests regularly clashed, surfacing in some surprisingly bitter trade disputes. It is an unspoken rule of the transatlantic political game that tensions become acute when Europe has a single voice. For when Europe speaks 'as one' – such as on trade issues – Washington listens, and negotiates. These trade disputes can have heavy foreign and security policy undertones, such as the differing EU and US trade approaches to Cuba, Libya and Iran. Yet others represent differing European and American geopolitical interests, like the 'banana wars' dispute over EU imports from the Caribbean (where the EU sought special deals for its ex-colonial territories, deals which the USA sees as cutting across their own interests and the established trade rules), or the German business relationship with Iran, or the manoeuvrings in the 'great game' of oil. Yet others are about 'environmental' questions such as food safety – the so-called 'hormone wars' dispute over American hormone-treated beef and other genetically modified foods banned by the EU – and EU restrictions on aircraft noise, which the USA sees as a threat to US aircraft companies.

Other EU-US trade disputes were about economic advantage – such as the disputes over offshore tax havens, foreign-sales corporation tax and steel imports into the USA. These trade disputes become 'trade wars' as both the EU and US sometimes escalate from rhetoric into threats and counter-threats of sanctions. Some of the proposed sanctions have been sizeable, and serious – for instance, in the foreign-sales corporation tax dispute the EU threatened to impose $4 billion worth of sanctions against US goods imported into the EU, a threat which US trade representative Robert Zellick described as 'like dropping a nuclear bomb on the global trading system'.[16] The USA has also threatened to impose sanctions on a range of European goods traded in the USA, and issued a public list of such products in a none too veiled attempt to put pressure on individual national governments in order to split the Europeans; for instance, at one point during the dispute the British government sought to talk separately to the USA about listing Scottish cashmere products. And when the 'free-trade' Bush administration in 2002 decided to unilaterally – in a 'do what I say, not what I do' move – to impose tariffs on imported steel (in order to protect American jobs from cheap Asian steel) the EU threatened retaliation and took the USA to the WTO.

The intensity of these trade wars is a sign of the change in the fundamentals of the US-European relationship. In this newly equal relationship, Europe is like the new kid on the block, confidently feeling his new-found power and pushing up against the limits set by the older gang leader.

Many of these transatlantic trade disputes are, though, symptoms of a deeper conflict – one between the EU 'social model' of capitalism and the US 'market model'. For both sides, this conflict of 'models' was (is) more than intellectual jousting. It has become deadly serious, about preserving jobs, and even ways of life. For the Europeans, the stability of their welfare societies was at stake, for Americans the 'free market' system.

It seemed for a while in the late 1990s, however, that these trade and economic disputes, though serious, would be the worst of it; and that the growing Atlantic divide could be contained by negotiation and compromise. But, in the early months of 2001, as Bush replaced Clinton's massaging of Europe with what he saw as straight-talking in America's interests, the synthetic, patched-up unity of the Clinton years fell spectacularly apart at the seams.

And, following September 11th, once the initial sympathy had dissipated, the underlying Atlantic crisis entered a new and dangerous phase, transmuting from trade and economics to foreign and security policy – and even into fundamental questions of morality, religion and ideology. George W. Bush's personality and rhetoric became an issue with Europeans. His 'with us or against us' demand appeared childish to Europeans; his easy use of the word 'evil' (the Iraq, Iran and North Korea 'axis of evil' and the reference to the 'evildoer' and 'evil one') grated on secular European ears. And the German and French refusal to support the war on Iraq as they had supported the 'War on Terror' led to a rancorous personal bitterness amongst western politicians not seen in transatlantic relations since the highly charged personal fights of the Suez crisis in 1956. Then, the American Secretary of State, John Foster Dulles, and the British Prime Minister, Anthony Eden, had hated each other with a passion (Dulles disliking Eden's effeminate, old-fashioned manners and Eden strongly disliking Dulles's 'tactile over-familiarity' – and his halitosis).[17] In 2002, George Bush's view of Gerhard Schroeder was not reported, but his extraordinary refusal for two months to speak to the German Chancellor said it all.

Conservatives in Washington and New York were stepping their standard anti-European critiques up a gear: from normal economic jibes (at 'Eurosclerosis') to cultural wars (dubbing the French as 'cheese-eating surrender monkeys' and Europeans generally as 'anti-Semites'). And European attacks on America were going beyond normal opposition to US policy into broad condemnations, spilling over into a real and widespread anti-Americanism not seen before – entailing denunciations of American values and way of life.

In Europe, attitudes to America had undergone a series of sea changes. Pre-Second World War Europe's upper classes saw the USA as an arriviste power, and blamed it for having helped destroy European empires and undermining European interests, a charge that reared its head again as late as the Suez crisis in 1956. This European 'anti-Americanism' was, at root, the product of aristocratic and elite jealousy of America and a fear about the contagion of American democracy. The USA was considered culturally inferior to Europe, a phenomenon most openly on display in France, where jibes about the bourgeois character of the developing American republic (and about its social conformity) were standard fare: Baudelaire once compared America to Belgium. French intellectuals continued to take the lead in this disdain, summed up by the much-quoted quip attributed to their countryman, Georges Clemenceau, that 'America is the only nation in history which miraculously has gone from barbarism to degeneration without the usual interval of civilization'.[18]

For a time in the post-Second World War years, Europeans were attracted by the openness and classlessness of 'the American dream' – but by the late 1960s and early 1970s, American policy in Vietnam was causing another round of anti-Americanism, this time directed at the 'right-wing' character of the country. Not untypically for the time, Simone de Beauvoir called America 'fascist'.[19]

Anti-Vietnam protests led radicalized European youth – the breeding ground for Europe's present leaderships – to take up anti-American postures and turn against their America-supporting governments. (Intriguingly, much of this anti-Americanism was a reflection of *American* criticism of US policy which was imported into Europe from US campuses – a bizarre form of Americanization depicted by the writer Paul Hollander.)[20] And, alongside opposition to American military power, went a critique of the role of the American corporations. Although Jean-Jacques Servan Schreiber's 1967 bestseller, *Le Defi Americain*, suggested European business should emulate the best of the new global American corporations, his book became a standard-bearer for a generation of Europeans who saw the Americanization of post-war Europe as baleful.[21]

By the 1990s, the European generation who had been attracted by the 'American dream' were being replaced by those who saw no special attraction, and no special virtue, in the American way of life. For this generation of Europeans, the USA became a less positive force – no longer an exotic and successful cousin, more an old, powerful and sometimes arrogant uncle. After a century in which the USA said something decidedly new to the world, and offered something decidedly new to millions who joined the country, the special appeal of America to Europeans had run its course.

But the growing indifference and scepticism was soon to turn to widespread antipathy – particularly after the arrival of the Bush administration in the White House in 2001. This antipathy was normally not projected onto Main Street, USA or the American people, who were often seen, like the Europeans themselves, as innocent and impotent citizens of a polity and society run by the Washington and Wall Street power elites. Rather, it was largely reserved for the growth and use of American power around the world and for the leaders of what was increasingly seen as the 'American empire'. 'America' and 'empire' were words that to many European, and most American, minds used never to go together. In Europe, Emmanuel Todd's *Apres l'empire* developed the theme (although he argued that American power was waning), but it was a term being made famous by Americans themselves: by Noam Chomsky, by Gore Vidal and, to a wider audience, by the humorist and social critic, Michael Moore, whose book *Stupid White Men* was a bestseller both in the USA and in Europe.

The Bush presidency presented these opponents of American power with a focused target. So grating on European ears were Bush and those around him that many Europeans began to believe that the USA had been 'taken over' by some kind of extreme, unrepresentative gang. At the height of tensions between Berlin and Washington in the summer of 2002, a minister in the German government likened Bush to Hitler (for using war as a distraction), for which Schroeder apologized; and a British member of parliament, Bob Marshall-Andrews, echoed many in Europe when in early 2003 he attacked the Bush administration with a passion rarely displayed before in any European parliament: he argued that the Bush presidency was the worst American administration he had ever known, and that it represented 'a mixture of virulent Christian fundamentalism, ruthless Zionism and the oil lobby'.[22]

This European opposition to the policies of the Bush administration was increasingly being characterized in the USA as a manifestation of 'anti-Americanism' – the portraying of prejudice or, worse, against a whole people and culture. 'Anti-Americanism', as a term, caught on in the transatlantic debate in a way in which, intriguingly, 'anti-Europeanism' did not. And this 'anti-American' labelling of Europeans, although often used to describe a truth, was just as often used as a tactic to halt or silence opposition (as few Europeans would want to be thought of as so prejudiced). It was often used in much the same way as many prominent Europeans believed that some American Jewish organizations were using 'anti-Semitism' to depict, and traduce, Europeans who opposed Israeli and American policies in the Middle East.[23]

Some European criticism of the USA was indeed beginning to cross a line – no longer just a rejection of American strategy and policies, but amounting to a broader, and deeper, criticism of American values and the American way of life, at least as they were constantly being promoted by the Bush administration, by Hollywood and by Wall Street.[24] And this transatlantic 'values gap' was being recognized, even amongst the politicians. President George W. Bush's National Security Advisor, Condoleezza Rice, thought this 'values gap' so potentially important that she went so far as to comment publicly on it, suggesting that 'in many ways the debate over the "values gap" between the United States and Europe is the kind of self-indulgent discussion that only the very successful and well off can afford'.[25]

Increasingly, America was seen in Europe as a flawed democracy and society overly influenced by big corporate business and religious fundamentalism. It was also seen as tolerating increasing levels of inequality, with greed and materialism running rampant – the land of opportunity and the work ethic having turned into a super-rich oligarchy based increasingly on inherited wealth.[26] And the nightly diet of American TV shows on European screens portrayed the USA as violent as well as racist. In their disturbing book *Why Do People Hate America?* Ziauddin Sardar and Merryl Wyn argued that 'American history is, on many levels, a war narrative.'[27] This kind of depiction of America helps to explain why, in some European minds, the traditional 'American dream' was being replaced by something verging on 'the American nightmare'.

Yet, perversely, this new critical view of America may have huge and largely beneficial side effects for Europeans. Used to looking to America for inspiration, for the way forward (the only way forward), as well as for protection, Europeans will now be forced to look to themselves. It may well be something of a jolting experience: it will be the end of the comforting European habit of sheltering under another's umbrella – whilst at the same time criticizing the benefactor and the protector! But it can also be the beginning of the much more constructive task of building for the future.

Indeed, for Europeans, Europe itself, rather than the USA, may well now begin to represent the way forward – at least for western societies. And Europeans may well be fortified by the idea that, for a change, it is they, not the Americans, who may have the key to future success. For in the coming decades, there may be one crucial advantage for Europe over the USA – the fact is that its governing ideology does not possess an irrational hatred of the state. This could enable Europeans, rather than twenty-first century Americans, to allow state intervention in the market to limit the rampant hegemony of business and capital – thus, ironically, restoring the old entrepreneurial values of risk, work ethic and individualism that are being eroded by market capitalist inherited privilege. The lack of this irrational hatred of the state may well also allow Europe – through state and welfare programmes – to place really serious limits on the growing inequality that is now an endemic result of American-style market globalization.

But for Europe to take over from the USA as the western ideal – to replace 'the American dream' with 'the European idea' – will need more than fine ideas and well-worked values. To sustain and improve its standards it will need strategic power: the unity and punch in the world of a superpower. And, in the first years of the twenty-first century, Europe is well on the way to securing that aim.

3

The Making
of a Superpower

The Euro and Beyond?

It was the autumn of 1949, and Frenchman Jean Monnet had risen from running his father's brandy business in Cognac to become the head of France's National Economic Plan. But Monnet was more than just a powerful Paris bureaucrat. He was about to become a man of history, nothing less than an architect of today's European Union, on a par with Madison and Hamilton, the founders of the American republic.

Monnet saw himself as an heir to Aristide Briand, the inter-war French Prime Minister, whose vision of a European union based around Franco-German unity had been ruptured by depression and the bitter conflict of war. But, once the war was over, Monnet was determined to reignite the vision. In what was to become virtually an open political conspiracy, Monnet linked up with liberal Catholic Robert Schuman, a resistance fighter from Lorraine and head of the French Foreign Ministry; they also enlisted the support of prominent politicians: Frenchman Rene Pleven; Paul Henri Spaak from Belgium; and Alcide de Gasperi, an Italian from South Tyrol. They were all federalists, inspired by the idea of a united and democratic Europe rising from the ashes of the devastated continent. And in the late 1940s all things were possible. The American Dean Acheson called living in that time 'being in at the creation', and so it was. The continent's politics were in flux; Europe's nations, and nationalism, were exhausted by war; Russia had not yet fully shown her hand; America was not necessarily returning to Europe and, if she did, might even be supportive of European unity; even Churchill was talking of a United States of Europe.

The strategy of these federalists was to take up the huge and exciting opportunity for European unity presented by the Council of Europe set up in Strasbourg in August 1949. They would work through the Council, pretending to complement the new Anglo-American inspired institutions, NATO and the OECD, but all the time seeking to create their true goal of a European federal state. And in May 1950 they reckoned they had almost done it. They had gained the crucial support of the first Chancellor of the new German Federal Republic, Rhinelander Konrad Adenauer, whose main strategic aim for the newly established West Germany was to anchor it to the West through a strong link to France. With Adenauer's support, the Schumann Plan was launched in May 1950 as 'a first step in the federation of Europe'. It called for the coordination of the iron and steel industries and – incredibly to contemporary ears – for a European army. A fully fledged United States of Europe was to be built by France and Germany taking the lead as a core.

This Schumann Plan was a fast route to a new superpower. The structures needed for a European army and security policy – had they stuck – would have instantly created the supra-national architecture for a nascent global power.[1] But this daring plan for a European army (in the form of the European Defence Community) was to be scuppered by French delaying tactics and then finally by the French National Assembly in 1954. In today's Europe, this defeat is still seen as a huge, lost opportunity. Institutions, like ideas, have consequences, and once set in place can often develop a life of their own, changing history as much as great men and women or social and economic changes. As Jean Monnet himself said: 'Each man begins the world afresh. Only institutions grow wiser.'[2] Even so, this project of a European army was probably both too early and too late. It was too ambitious for a Europe which, at that time, was concentrating only on getting back on its feet. And it was too late because NATO had already been set up, in April 1949. Through NATO, the USA had fully committed itself to the defence of Western Europe a full year before the Schumann Declaration and three years before the European army proposals of the European Defence Community Treaty. So, no matter French hostility to the military project, with American money and manpower pouring into Western Europe in the early 1950s, and the cold war hotting up, Washington (and Europe's leaders) were unlikely to allow a separate power centre challenging NATO to emerge.

But Jean Monnet's grand vision of Europe did not die, or fall by the wayside, along with the European army. It simply took the slower, though surer, road – the economic route. Following the 1955 Messina conference, the Iron and Steel Community grew directly into the Common Market, and from there into the single market and then, by 1999, into the single currency.

So, by the turn of the millennium, Jean Monnet's great goal, set out 50 years earlier, had been more than realized. Europe had become a great civilian power. So much so that President Jacques Chirac of France could grandly, but not fancifully, declare that 'Europe can become the number one power in the multi-power world of tomorrow.'

Europe has, in fact, surpassed Monnet's wildest dreams. For today, the EC's successor, the EU, is on the way to acquiring all the components of a superpower. It is large, it is wealthy, it is integrating, it is enlarging, it has appeal, and it can project power around the world through its economy and, potentially at least, through military means as well. And, crucially, it is beginning to see itself, and to act, as a confident, independent player in the world.

The population of the EU two years into the new millennium – when it still comprised 15 member states – was 350 million, 40 million more than that of the USA, and 120 million more than Japan. (The new Europe of 25 has a population of 422 million.) The EU was already the world's largest single market and economy. By 2002, its GNP stood at just over $9 trillion compared to just under $9 trillion for the USA and just under $5 trillion for Japan, with a per capita income a little under that of the USA and just over half that of Japan.[3] Strikingly, its share of world trade was just about twice that of its nearest competitor – the North Atlantic Free Trade Association (NAFTA) – and about four and half times that of Japan, and four times that of the ASEAN nations.[4]

The EU single market is set to grow significantly during the first decade of the new century. During 2004, the Czech republic, Estonia, Hungary, Poland, Slovenia, Cyprus, Latvia, Lithuania, Slovakia and Malta all joined the EU as full members; a second wave, with whom negotiations began in 2000, will later likely include Bulgaria and Romania – an expansion that will take the borders of the Union right up to the shores of the Black Sea and then north to the Baltic states along the borders of Moldova, Ukraine and Belarus. The Union will then possess a population of almost 500 million, and the Euro-zone – 'Euroland' – will have 430 million inhabitants and an economy somewhat larger than that of the USA.[5] It will tower above the Japanese economy and will still dwarf those of India and China. Although all of these comparative economic statistics are highly dependent upon fluctuations in exchange rates (in the first eighteen months of its life the falling euro caused the value of the Euroland economy to fall by over 25%!), the real economy of Europe has arrived as a world power and player.

By the second decade of the new century, a successful single market will both attract and worry the scattered rest of Western Europe who by 2004 were still outside the Union – Switzerland, Norway, Iceland, Andorra, Liechtenstein, Monaco and San Marino. Also, as well as the expanded European Union, with its single market and single currency, a less formal 'House of Europe' is likely to emerge. The Balkan nations (Serbia, Croatia, Bosnia-Herzegovina, Albania, Macedonia, Kosovo and Montenegro) and the Ukraine (with 50 million people), Belarus, Azerbaijan, Georgia, Moldova and Armenia – all will become ever more enmeshed in close trade and commercial ties with the EU, and many of these countries may seek to move beyond their present partnership and cooperation agreements.

Nor is it impossible to imagine Russia in the next quarter of a century also joining this 'House of Europe' as a symbiotic economic relationship develops – as the EU opens its huge single market to Russian industry and commerce in return for special access to Russia's energy supplies. In the process, Russia may well resolve its split identity. Should its economic links with Germany and the West deepen further, then its western heritage (the Russia of Dostoevsky, Pushkin and Lenin, and of Putin) will win out over its 'Eurasian' heritage (the Russia of Trubetsko and Vernadsky, and of Stalin). General de Gaulle, in a speech to the people of Strasbourg in November 1959, had famously proclaimed that a Europe 'from the Atlantic to the Urals will decide the fate of the world'. Such a 'House of Europe' (comprising the EU and Russia in a strategic trade and even security relationship) would not dominate the world, but it would certainly become the primary force in Eurasia, and, inevitably, act to limit and contain China and India – and the USA's ambitions in Eurasia.

As early as the late 1980s, American economist Lester Thurow, in his prophetic book *Head To Head* (written before the collapse of the Soviet Union), spotted this potential for Russia to enhance Europe as a coming superpower. He suggested then that Russia's vast raw materials – and particularly the new oil flows from the Caspian Sea – as well as her scientific and educational base could be invaluable to Europe, more so than Latin America is to the USA; and that for these reasons Europe could ultimately win what he believed was the coming 'head to head' battle between the tri-lateral powers, the USA, Japan and the EU.[6] A former Member of the European Parliament, John Stevens, makes much the same point when he argues that '[the EU's] economic hinterland to the east, including Russia, is a far more attractive one than that of Central and South America.'[7]

Beyond its single market, the trade reach of the EU is growing all the time. The Lome Convention extends 'The House of Europe' through EU trading and economic influence way beyond its boundaries by linking 71 African, Caribbean and Pacific states to the EU, giving their goods preferential treatment.[8] And the 'Euro-Med Conference' links the EU's single market to 12 Mediterranean states, including the Palestinian Authority, Jordan, Syria, Turkey, Israel, Algeria and Morocco.

As for the future, as the world of the lone US superpower gives way to a world of blocs, the EU, let alone the wider and looser 'House of Europe', is already emerging as top of a crowded civilian superpower league. Some futurologists believe that by 2025 China will have the largest economy in the world, and that China and India's share of global product will equal those of the USA and the EU.[9] In the meantime, Europe could replace the USA as leader of the world economy. For, apart from the structural problems (primarily deficits) that may weaken the US economy, it is difficult to see what the USA can do from now on to dramatically improve its performance. The USA during the boom years of the 1990s was like a business that was operating at or near its full capacity; whereas Europe, by contrast, had considerable spare capacity and, particularly should it weaken the hold of economic orthodoxy in its central bank, has substantial scope to dramatically improve its performance.

In this new world, Europe, more precisely the EU, is not only a civilian giant – stable politically, attractive socially, with the world's largest economy and home market – it is also located in a pivotal global position. With its firm links to the Americas in the west, its growing strategic relationship with (and geographical proximity to) Russia in the east, its historic 'relationship' with Africa and India, and with the 'arc of Islam' stretching around its southern and south-eastern border, the EU, like no other superpower or putative superpower, is crucially placed at the centre of a web of civilizations.

Of all the attributes needed by a new superpower, one of the most important is the popular appeal of the home country – the attraction of the life, or the lifestyle, which it offers and represents. Put simply, it is a renewing asset for a superpower that those who live within its borders should want to stay, and many of those who live outside should seek to join. The collapse of the Soviet Union is testimony to this truth. In the global battle with the USA, it matched its superpower rival in population and in science and military hardware – particularly in the nuclear field. It also possessed a powerful ideology – 'socialism' – which in the propaganda battle, particularly in the Third World, was easily a match for 'freedom and democracy'. But it lost the populist battle for hearts and minds. There was no 'Soviet dream' to match 'the American dream' – the popular personal objective of achieving a middle class consumer lifestyle with large amounts of personal freedom. And in the age of modern mass communications, with knowledge about other lifestyles spreading beyond localities and national borders, it was the awareness of Soviet citizens about standards of living in the West that caused such discontent and alienation, and contributed to the ultimate downfall of the Communist Party regime. Of course, 'middle-class' lifestyles for the mass of the people can only be secured by a functioning economy – and it was the serious weaknesses in the Soviet command economy that formed the root problem.

By any test, the quality of life in the EU is one of its greatest assets. By almost any objective measure of the quality of life, 'Western Europeans are amongst the most privileged people in the world.'[10] The EU's raw economic living standards are roughly equal to those of the USA, although below those of Japan. Recent World Bank figures for per capita GNP (2001) show 12 of the EU's 15 nations in the top 30 nations in the world (out of 208 listed). Luxembourg was the highest with $39,800, and Portugal the lowest with $10,900 – with Russia at $1,750 and Turkey at $2,530 (and the USA at $34,280). Exchange-rate changes make comparisons with the USA very difficult but, by 2002, a rough calculation would place the per capita incomes of Luxembourg, Denmark, the Netherlands and Sweden slightly ahead of the USA, those of the reunited Germany, France, the UK, Belgium and Finland at roughly equal, and the rest lower.[11]

Yet, if the EU's standard of living is amongst the highest in the world, its standard of life is higher still. In all the 'quality of life indicators' used by the UN Development Programme – which measures life expectancy, infant mortality rates, population growth, calories available – all the EU countries rank extremely highly, alongside the USA and Japan. And in the UN's Human Development Index – which measures three variables: educational attainment, life expectancy and per capita income in 175 countries – the EU countries also do extremely well in the rankings: Sweden comes second in the world rankings, with Belgium fourth, the Netherlands eighth, Finland tenth, France twelfth, the UK thirteenth and Denmark fourteenth.[12]

These figures suggest that the USA's rawer, freer capitalism may have been more dynamic than Europe's social democratic variety – but not by much. And Europe's crucial advantage over the USA is that its developed and sophisticated consumer society – with excellent transport and communications systems – can also coexist with advanced welfare states which give the average European access to education and health care, and generous welfare systems.

Of course, standard of life is about more than measurable statistics about material standards; it is also about cultural variety, sophistication and depth, and about stability and security and freedom and a host of other, often intangible, attributes. By any measure in these departments Europe is 'first amongst equals', if not 'first' in the world. Take, for instance, a recent *Economist* survey of the standard of life in Germany. 'Germany,' says the survey, 'is hard to beat for the unquantifiable benefits that make a country pleasant to live in' – and it cites sleek autobahns, clean, fast railways, medical treatment second to none in the world, generous unemployment benefits, high wages, long holidays, security of employment, the best opera houses and museums and a musical and artistic infrastructure unsurpassed anywhere.[13]

But perhaps the real success of the quality of life in twenty-first-century Europe lies in its ability to combine the high growth rates and freedoms of capitalism with the civilized values of security and welfare – an elusive combination which legions of American opinion-leaders continue to argue cannot be achieved, and certainly cannot last, and is doomed to failure. Yet, as the old century turned into the new, these neo-liberal and Wall Street critics of Europe had by then been predicting such doom for well over three decades.

What, in essence, Europe may be proving is that in order to succeed, capitalism does not have to turn its back on the aspiration for equality – and certainly not on the meritocratic goal of equality of opportunity. And by placing limits on inequality, Europe ultimately secures a better democracy (with higher levels of participation) a more secure society (with less crime and violence) and a better inner-city environment, certainly than those secured in the rawer capitalist nations. Of course, today's Europe has all the critical social problems of the rest of the western world, and perhaps the most intractable one of all: the large immigrant, often Muslim, communities, in and around many of its big cities – but its attempt, through its 'social model' to limit the growth of inequality gives it, at least, a racing chance of avoiding a social explosion. During the early 1990s – a period of rapid globalization – an OECD in-depth study of inequality in the leading western nations, published in 1995, showed that the USA leads the world in inequality (with Canada coming in second, Australia third, the UK fourth, and New Zealand and France joint fifth). Intriguingly, most of the continental European nations – those shielded from the full impact of globalization by a social market or social democratic tradition – came well down the field. Norway, the Netherlands, Belgium, Finland and Sweden all needed to more than double their inequality ratios to match those of the USA. And in the USA, as in the other globalized western economies like the UK and New Zealand, the numbers of super-rich people continued to grow during the period.[14]

'Acting as One'

The size, quality, and strategic location of Europe may give the continent, and its individual nation states, great influence in the world – but a European superpower they do not make. For Europe, as for any superpower that becomes a global player, unity is all. Without unity, or 'acting and speaking as one', the two great global players of the late twentieth century, the USA and the USSR, would have had major influence, but little power. It was 'acting and speaking as one' – through its union and its single presidency – that made the several states of America into a superpower; and it was 'acting and speaking as one' – through its Communist party – that did the same for the states of the Soviet Union.

These two twentieth-century superpowers, the USA and the USSR, were forged by force of arms. And throughout history superpowers have normally been created only by force and conquest. The rise and fall of empires – though often caused by great underlying economic and social changes – are normally completed, and are often the result, of great dramatic events – of war, battles and violence. Historians tend to fix on battles – and dates of battles – as pivotal, like the birth of the Macedonian empire following the battle of Chaeronea in 338 BC, the demise of the Roman empire in the west after Odoacer overthrew Romulus Augustulus in AD 496 or, in contemporary times, when it could be argued that the rise of the Soviet empire began after the battle of Stalingrad in 1942 or the battle of Kursk in July 1943, and the American empire at Midway in June 1942 or on D-Day, 1944 (or, in the case of the death of the British Empire, the two great wars, 1914–1918 and 1939–1945). Of course, the last great fall of an empire, the collapse of the Soviet Union, came about without a major conflict or battle – but that was because general war was simply too risky in the era of weapons of mass destruction.

Superpowers are often formed by stronger neighbours simply overrunning weaker ones – as when the Parthians overran the neighbouring Seleucid kingdom to establish their empire, which lasted for over 350 years, or when the Ottomans took over the Balkans in the fourteenth century, or when the Russian empire took over large tracts of central Asia during the nineteenth. Europe has seen two (failed) attempts, by Napoleon and by Hitler, to create superpowers through the force of a dominant state. In the early nineteenth century, Napoleon's Europe was based on conquest; not, though, as a prelude to a French empire, but as an attempt to create some kind of wider, integrated European power based on French revolutionary ideas. As his armies swept across the continent, the idea of 'Europe' was always on his lips and he became an early advocate of the euro. In a letter to his brother Louis in May 1807, two years after his great victory in the battle of Austerlitz, he revealed that he wanted the whole of Europe to have one currency. 'It will make trading much easier,' he wrote.[15] Over 130 years later, Adolf Hitler's armies of conquest were also well on the way to creating a superpower in Europe; and had he succeeded he would have established a Europe based on German racial domination, a very different outcome from the Napoleonic vision of an integrated Europe based on universal ideas.

In today's Europe, no single nation, people or government has been able to so dominate the making of the Union: the prime candidate for such a domineering role, Germany, was never quite large enough (and, anyway, since the Hitler experience, modern Germans have been far too circumspect about throwing their weight around). Sometimes, seemingly marginal peoples suddenly erupt, normally violently, onto the world stage and create an empire – like the Romans, or the Arabian armies that reached all the way from Spain to northern India, or the Seljuc Turks who invaded Persia and Anatolia from central Asia, or the British as they set out from their tiny islands from the sixteenth century onwards. By contrast, today's European Union has been built not by a restless, martial people conquering others, but rather by the slow compromises of mature peoples at peace.

Often, superpowers are created by a simple power vacuum – as was the case with the USA, a serious but marginal power before 1939, catapulted to superpower status because the existing powers, the British Empire and Germany, were fighting to a finish and exhausting themselves. In his great hour of 'victory', Winston Churchill was ruefully aware that, having gone to war with Germany to save the British Empire, that same war had destroyed it – hence the startling title, 'Triumph and Tragedy', of the final volume of his history of the Second World War. The new superpowers, the USA and the Soviet Union, had moved into the power vacuum. In one sense, the emergence of the European superpower is similar: for it, too, has filled a vacuum, in this case the power vacuum created by the precipitate collapse of the Soviet Union and the end of the bi-polar world of the cold war.

But today's Europe has been built without violence or domination. And it can fairly consider itself a genuine 'first' in the world. It is truly – to use the overworked catchphrase – *sui generis*. No great world power has emerged in quite the same way as the European Union is now doing – by the peaceful coming together or merging of existing nations and states.

This remarkable story may not, though, as many Euro-enthusiasts believe, be an example of European exceptionalism, or of some kind of 'manifest destiny' of a special people engaged in a great lesson of teaching the world how to cooperate and unify peacefully under a new system of international law. Nor is it a hegemonic design, a blueprint imposed on democratic peoples by remote elites (whether French meritocrats, German industrialists or Brussels Eurocrats). Rather, the European Union may simply be the first, and so far the most integrated, of a series of new unions, from Asia to Africa and Latin America, which will be forged not by force of arms, but by economic globalization – essentially a political response to the severe litany of problems that globalization poses to all the world's peoples. Europe may simply be in the vanguard, pioneering the truly revolutionary geopolitical idea of our time: that only through political unification (not just cooperation or alliances, but actual unification) into a viable new system of larger and stronger polities – or unions – can the great questions of economics, security and environment thrown up by the modern world, begin to be dealt with.

Today's Europe may be being built by consent, but in the real world of modern Europe, whilst member states remain 'sovereign', unity will remain temporary and fragile – constantly open to challenge from both inside and outside the EU. For this reason, the real building of the EU has proceeded by 'integration' – that is, from the rich intertwining of economies, societies and polities so that unravelling it all becomes either impossible or unrealistic. This idea, understood by the founders, of 'unity through integration' is utterly fundamental to the building of a European superpower.

Today's stark reality is that only in those areas where Europe is integrated does it truly speak with one voice – and not for a day, or a year, but, as the song says, for always! And when it speaks with one voice Europe is heard, as it is heard from Washington to Peking in trade policy because on trade issues no single member state can veto a majority decision.

The results of such unity were only brought home to a wider European public in December 2003, when the EU won its high-profile battle with the USA over the steel tariffs imposed by President Bush earlier in the year. The EU had threatened to retaliate against the USA by imposing politically targeted tariffs of their own against American goods (including citrus from the electoral swing state of Florida). The steel conflict made clear, as little had before, that when the EU 'acts as one' – as it does on trade matters – it becomes an equal to the USA, negotiates from a position of strength and secures results. Quite simply, the EU's Trade Commissioner – in 2002, the tough-minded meritocratic Frenchman, Pascal Lamy – was a feared equal of his American counterpart in Washington. By comparison,

Europe's prime ministers and presidents are not equals of the American president; they are easily divided, and therefore ruled.

The Making of the Euro

As with trade, so with money. So integrated and centralized is the money of the EU that on monetary policy the Union speaks 'with one voice', and with a vengeance! The euro is the EU at its most integrated, for Europe's money is controlled exclusively by a central body, the European Central Bank in Frankfurt (the ECB). The ECB may be composed of national bankers, but not one of them can wield a national veto. So, as with trade policy, in the hugely important matter of money, Europe is unified, and it is this unity that makes the ECB, and its president, a world player on a par with the chairman of America's central bank, the Federal Reserve Board in Washington.

In a sense, the European Central Bank is the Euro-sceptics' worst nightmare, because it is living proof that Europe is on the road towards becoming a super-state. Just like the Federal Reserve in Washington, the political architecture of the ECB makes it the most highly integrated, centralized and 'supra-national' of its union's institutions. And through its interest-rate policy, its effects on jobs and living standards run all the way from Dublin to Athens (and, after 2004, up to Warsaw as well).

But the ECB is also the federalists' worst nightmare. Federalists don't mind the centralization, but do worry about the secretiveness and lack of accountability that makes Europe's central bankers so detached from public opinion. And the ECB's first president, Dr Wim Duisenberg, represented almost perfectly the technocratic detachment of the European administrator. This tall, seemingly shy, academic-looking banker from Friesland in the Netherlands is an unashamed meritocrat. As a still youngish man he took the fateful career decision to leave the hurly burly democracy of Dutch social democratic politics for the more technical and cloistered world of banking. And, having discarded his Keynesian past along with the elected politics, his financial orthodoxy grew under the influence of the rigorously independent Bundesbank and the formidable, orthodox German banker Hans Tietmeyer. Although, following the launch of the euro, and with no European president to compete with, he became the single most powerful man in Europe, he remains happy not to receive the high-profile glamour of his

American counterpart, Alan Greenspan (who, in American political life, has come to be treated as a VIP and a celebrity on a par with the President himself).

The successful completion of the euro project in 1999 was the hinge of fate for Europe – for, as French central banker Jacques Rueff once prophesied, 'Europe will be built through a currency or it will not be built at all.'[16] It was the moment of no return, for not only did it complete the single market, but it will also, inexorably, demand a single economic policy. The bankers in Frankfurt (fixing interest rates) and the politicians in Brussels (coordinating budgets) are already slowly beginning to operate a single European economic policy for a single European economy. There may, as yet, be no European Treasury Minister to match the EU Trade Commissioner or the Chairman of the ECB, but whoever ends up coordinating the budgets of Europe's nations will inevitably assume the role.

The euro project was a political project from the very beginning. The idea of a single currency emerged naturally – in the report of Luxembourg's Pierre Werner in 1970 – as an almost technical response to the crumbling of stable exchange rates in the late 1960s.[17] But it soon became clear that a single money for Europe (and a single monetary policy) was politically explosive – representing nothing less than an historic leap towards a federal Europe. German Chancellor Helmut Schmidt and French President Giscard d'Estaing were the first political leaders to put their authority behind the idea of monetary union and, at a bilateral summit to launch the next phase of the European Monetary System (EMS) in September 1978 at Aachen, the burial place of Charlemagne, the air was pregnant not with economics, but with geopolitics. The two leaders paid a visit to Charlemagne's throne, where Giscard remarked, 'Perhaps when we discussed monetary problems, the spirit of Charlemagne brooded over us.'[18] It came out later that Helmut Schmidt had overridden the mighty Bundesbank and sold the EMS plan as being required by Germany's foreign policy.

The euro project became a real plan during the genesis of serious, practical federalism in the late 1980s as the leaders of Europe fixed on a single currency as the way forward to the great goal of union and unity. And Jacques Delors became the architect. Working with Italian banker Tommaso Padoa-Schioppa on Europe's monetary life after the single market was completed in 1992, he produced the now-famous Delors Report. It had started life at a meeting held on a Sunday in Bonn, just before the Hanover summit in June 1988. Delors recalls that '[Chancellor] Kohl invited me round on a Sunday before the European Council in Hanover. I persuaded him to go for a committee of [central bank] governors and – what audacity! – to give me its chair.' So was set in motion the train to Euroland.

Jacques Delors was the epitome of the modern European federalist. Politically, he was a convinced social democrat (of the French, centre-left, kind), and entered public life as a moderate trade union official and as a supporter of Pierre Mendès-France's socialist government of 1954–1955. He was a technocrat and meritocrat who was drawn to solving problems – although someone who frequented Ronnie Scott's jazz club when in London, and adored cycling, was hardly desiccated. But he was a technocrat with a broad historical vision. As he pioneered the euro through the Byzantine structures of the EEC in the late 1980s he had a very definite sense that he was making history. He said at the time: 'history is accelerating. So must we… A qualitative jump is necessary.'[19] And he had a clear goal: 'My objective is that before the end of the millennium [Europe] should have a true federation.'[20]

Such grand claims about the historical importance of the euro (and the ECB) were not overdrawn. Napoleon had wanted one currency for Europe, and Hitler had even planned for it. It was a major world event in finance and economics, but also in geopolitics. It was clear to many at the time – and not just to the political leaders of France and Germany – that Euroland was much more than a currency union; it was to be the economic core of a new superpower created to match the USA, an underlying motivation revealed by Wim Duisenberg himself in an interview with the *New York Times* in June 2001.[21] The sheer boldness of the Euroland project was breathtaking. In the USA, the single dollar-zone (with its modern Federal Reserve) had come some hundred years after the federal structures of the USA were established. In Europe, it was coming ahead of them. Nothing on this scale – with 12 democratic nations, including Germany with its proud and independent German Bundesbank, consenting to unify their money and their monetary policy – had ever been tried before.It was not surprising that in the run-up to the Maastricht negotiations and treaty, and then in the decade before actual launch, the British and American press abounded with sceptical predictions – that the project would never get off the ground, and that if it did it wouldn't last, and would implode.

The birth of the euro at the small Dutch town of Maastricht in December 1991 was not just the result of the driving will of Jacques Delors, but also of a unique and fortuitous combination of factors converging in the late 1980s. The success of the single market programme led to a 'What Next?' culture amongst Europe's leaders; and the worldwide boom linked to the fall in oil prices gave everyone confidence in the future. Furthermore, a positive federalist political environment was engendered by Europe's top leaders, not only by Helmut Kohl and François Mitterrand, but also by Prime Ministers Lubbers of Holland, Gonzalez of Spain and Martens of Belgium – all federalists of one kind or another, all able to work together with the architect, Delors.

But Delors would not have made such startling headway without the total political support at the very highest level offered by German Chancellor Helmut Kohl. Indeed, with Delors in the Commission and Kohl in the Council they formed their very own unbeatable Franco-German axis. Intriguingly, like many Frenchmen of his generation, Delors' life and background had been marked by Germans. His father, Louis, had been badly wounded in 1916 defending the French fortress of Verdun and, in 1940, the 14-year-old Jacques and his mother and grandmother fled from Paris two days before the German army arrived; then, in early 1944, the German troops occupied his university in Clermont-Ferrand. The alliance with the German Kohl was a kind of micro example of the broader rapprochement between the two peoples that European unity represented.

If Delors was the architect, then Kohl was the founder of the euro – indeed, as the guiding force behind the Maastricht Treaty, he can reasonably be awarded the title of founder of the European Union. Brought up in provincial Rhineland-Palatinate, and rising through the regional CDU apparatus, Kohl's reputation amongst the Bonn and Berlin elites was less than sparkling. He once remarked: 'I have been underestimated for decades. I have done very well that way.'[22] Even in the early years of his long Chancellorship, Kohl was thought of as pedestrian, even a blunderer, without panache or inspiration. Yet over the years he grew into the job and he filled out both physically and politically. For many in Europe in the late 1980s and early 1990s, Kohl assumed the stature of a statesman, a man who was not only uniting Germany, but also putting his newly unified country into a wider context by building a new European home for her people. His passion for Europe was driven by the conviction, held by many of his generation, that unity would preclude future conflicts. And Kohl spelt it all out clearly in a speech at Louvain University in February 1996, when he proclaimed that 'the policy of European integration is in reality a question of war and peace in the twenty-first century.' It was this unusual sense of high purpose that set Kohl apart from other European leaders and gave him the gravity that commanded respect. And he fought hard for his federal vision. Built like a 'well-fed Sumo Wrestler' (as Bill Clinton once described him, to his face), there was a drivenness about his large presence as he bore down on lesser political mortals to get his way in the great European gatherings of the time.

Kohl was the central figure in the euro drama, not least because he used the authority of his office to overcome the serious opposition to the single currency from the orthodox bankers in the Bundesbank. It was an extraordinary political feat for a German Chancellor to abandon the independence of the Bundesbank, the most revered institution in Germany, and also to ditch the Deutschmark, the great symbol of German post-war success. Yet he did it – because of his immense authority derived from his role as the father of German unification. In fact, the fate of the euro is bound up with the great historic events swirling around Kohl and Germany in the months and years following the sudden collapse of the Berlin Wall in 1989. Not least of these was the historic meeting between Helmut Kohl and Mikhail Gorbachev in mid July 1990. Kohl was invited to Gorbachev's old political stamping ground in the Mineralnye Vody spa region near Stavropol, which only 48 years previously had been occupied by Nazi troops. In truly dramatic fashion, the Soviet leader took his guest to the foothills of the Caucasus and, during the discussion, unleashed what has been called his 'electric moment'. He agreed that a united Germany could join NATO with the Soviet Union's blessing. His price was massive financial aid, to which Kohl agreed. The two men, beaming, later met the press with Kohl declaring that 'all practical problems for German unification had been cleared up.' History was made; the highway to German unity was open; and German reunification revived all the historic French fears about German domination, and France's strategic necessity of binding this newly united Germany to the West through monetary union.

With German unity in his pocket, Kohl could now count on the crucial support of French President François Mitterrand, who, needing more than ever to tie the powerful new Germany to the West, backed the euro project with sustained aplomb. Mitterrand was acting with the grain of French thinking, and the arrival of the euro was a great victory for the whole French political class – for leading figures like Edouard Balladur, Jacques Chirac, Alain Juppé, and Jean-Claude Trichet – and for French interests. Mitterrand's crowning glory came in early February 1992 when he steered monetary union – including the tricky question of the two starting dates – through the Maastricht summit and into the treaty. At Maastricht, Franco-German leadership had been re-established, Margaret Thatcher was out of office, the rearguard action of the Bundestag was largely defeated and the great project of the euro-zone was set in train. The fact that France and Germany, although close, were not yet actually married – and that their child, the euro, 'was a bastard' – hardly mattered.[23] After all, civilian superpower Europe had just been born.

4

Towards a
Super-State

A Government for Europe

For Jacques Chirac, the year 2002 was straight out of a storybook. He had started it off with a cloud of a serious scandal hanging over him – one that might well engulf him if he were to lose his presidency in the coming election. But, after the surprising exit of Socialist candidate Lionel Jospin in the first round of voting, he had suddenly became the standard-bearer, against Jean-Marie Le Pen, of France's republican honour. And he won the election in a landslide. And, most improbably of all, by the autumn he had risen even higher – and become the 'voice of Europe' – and, as he emerged to stand up to the USA over the war in Iraq, its tribune. In a career dotted with shifts of opinion and opportunism, and with a reputation for being all things to all men, this most pliable of politicians had transformed himself into the principled statesman of a continent looking for leadership.

Jacques Chirac became this 'voice of Europe' around September of 2002, once it was clear (to almost most everyone, apart from the British Foreign Office) that the French leadership had finally decided to veto any second UN resolution which allowed the world body to sanction war against Iraq. There was a clarity, eloquent in itself, about Chirac's message to the world about American power. And he spoke for a sizeable majority of Europe's electorate (a majority to be found in every single EU country) and also for the vast majority of the world's population. Virtually overnight he assumed a role that not even de Gaulle had dared to play – that of a European leader who, in a major international crisis, not only stood up to the USA but also led a campaign against her – and was applauded through his own continent and much of the rest of the world, particularly in the Middle East and Africa. In world politics, there was a palpable sense of a new power on the scene.

There were other candidates who were also emerging as Europe's 'voice'. The German Chancellor, Gerhard Schroeder, certainly had a very good claim, for he was the first European to say 'no' to Washington in the late summer of 2002 and arguably set the anti-Bush ball rolling. But the German leader was always going to be limited by Germany's political weakness (and by the fact that she had no veto on the Security Council). Tony Blair was also trying to become a leader of Europe – through his 'reform' agenda and his surprising 1998 St Malo defence agreement with France – and, before the crisis over Iraq changed everything, rumour had it that he had secured the agreement of Chirac (and possibly Schroeder) to become the first permanent President of the European Council. Had Blair opposed America over Iraq it would have put all the other European leaders in the shade, and he might have placed himself at the head of the field – but he was handicapped by his country's Euro-scepticism and, after his role over Iraq, was beyond the pale. José Maria Aznar of Spain was also spoken of as a candidate, but was also ruled out by his pro-American role during the Iraq crisis.

But Europe's 'voice' in a crisis was no substitute for real leadership of the Union. Many began to see that 'to talk' was not the same thing as 'to act' and that a superpower could not be organized simply by words or statements or even votes at the UN by one or two of its big member states. It would need something much more if Europe's nations were going to avoid becoming a series of US satellites.

Europe's missing ingredient was a strong, central executive authority that, like Bush or Putin or the Chinese Chairman, would not only present the world with a 'single voice', but could take action swiftly and flexibly. Europe could already act in the world decisively on trade and commercial questions, and on monetary policy. Its Trade Commissioner, Pascal Lamy, had full authority to act (and negotiated from strength with his American counterpart), and its Central Bank Chairman (Wim Duisenberg and his successor Claude

Trichet) could also act decisively and spoke on equal terms with the US Federal Reserve Chairman, Alan Greenspan. But, beyond that, there was a void of leadership, particularly in the all-important new foreign and security arena. In short, federalists started arguing that Europe needed a government. In other words, it needed to be a state like any other – and because of its size it would be a super-state.

But the idea of Europe as a 'state' was highly sensitive, and Europe's leaders, even the most federalist of them, tended to steer away from this awkward issue – the words 'state' and 'Europe' rarely appearing together in any of their speeches. Even those who sought a new role for Europe in the world, and openly supported and proclaimed the arrival of Europe as a superpower, still fought shy of advocating the virtues of a super-state. In his Warsaw speech in 2000, Tony Blair perfectly represented this kind of thinking when he argued that he supported Europe as a 'superpower, not a super-state'. This formulation was a soft-focus and pleasing vision, but it was also an unlikely one. To critics, this vision of Europe was willing the ends (a superpower) but not the means (a state to organize and run it). For them, 'superpower' and 'super-state', as in the old song, went together like 'love and marriage', and 'you can't have one without the other.' And Blair's vision of a stateless superpower led leading Oxford political scientist, David Marquand, to reply that 'statehood is a precondition for power in the international arena' and that 'the question for Europe is not whether to become a superstate', but 'what kind of superstate.'[1]

But as Europeans looked around them at the way they were governed in the first years of the new century – at interest rates and budgets, at trade policies, at laws and regulations, at European Court rulings and even debates about a European army – could they be forgiven for thinking that they inhabited a state already? And that this state already had a pretty effective government in Brussels. And, if this new EU, as the saying goes, 'looks like a state, walks like a state, talks like a state' – then maybe it is a state?

Giscard d'Estaing certainly thought so. There was a palpable sense throughout political Europe that when Chairman d'Estaing opened the constitutional convention in 2002 the assembled delegates were writing the rules of a government and state that already existed. At his opening press conference, Giscard, a former French president, told journalists grandly that he compared the proceedings to 'Philadelphia' – the 1787 convention that founded the American republic and wrote the rules for what was already a new state and was to develop further into the American super-state. (Thomas Jefferson had written to John Adams at the time that this great gathering was 'really an assembly of demigods', though who exactly the contemporary equivalents of Jefferson, Madison, Washington or Pinckney might be, Giscard did not reveal.)[2]

Many, though, were still not convinced that the EU had become a 'state', at least not in the traditional sense. The EU might have the trappings of a state – a flag, an anthem, even an outline written constitution, and it may even at some point secure a single seat alongside those of China, Russia and the USA in the Security Council of the UN. It might also have increasing sway over economics and business and civil law. But, they argued, it still did not possess the key attribute of a real state – the possession of a monopoly on the legitimate use of coercion, or force. After all, they maintained, the control of the police, the security forces and the military, had not yet passed to Europe, as they were still under the control of the national governments. In this view, the EU in 2002 was more like a 'political system' or a 'polity' – something approaching, but not yet, a state.[3]

Yet, although the EU had no single police force or single army, it did possess that other great attribute of statehood – the rule and writ of law. The writ of EU law ran right throughout the Union, from Dublin to Athens, from Helsinki to Seville, with every European, and every European nation state, subject to it (as well as to the laws of their own country). And, in the clearest proof of all of its statehood, where EU and nation-state law collide, then European law takes precedence. It is this key 'legal supremacy' of the EU over its nation states that is the very heart of the case that the EU is already a state. Even sovereignty-conscious Britain consented to the legal supremacy of the EU when it adhered to the Treaty of Rome in 1973, and then again when it ratified that decision in a referendum in 1975. (Looking back on the debates of the time during Britain's referendum, this threat which Europe posed to the UK's legal supremacy was raised, loudly and clearly, and as a central issue, by the 'no' campaign – particularly by the former Conservative Cabinet Minister John Enoch Powell and the leading Labour spokesman, Michael Foot.)

This 'legal supremacy' of the EU over its the member states is the mirror image of the 'legal supremacy' clause which binds together the USA as a federal state. The historian Paul Johnson suggests that the legal supremacy of the US union over its states makes the USA an 'umbrella state' – as it brings together 'sovereign bodies to create an umbrella-state over them, to do certain things as the states should delegate to it'. For 'umbrella' here read 'federal'; and, in this sense, the EU is an 'umbrella state', or a 'federal' state, too.[4]

Yet the most powerful pointer to the fact that by the turn of the century the EU had already, in effect, become a state lies in the Union's control of Europe's money – the euro. By 2002, the Euro-zone, comprising 12 countries, had, just like the USA, one central bank and one monetary policy. And during the late twentieth century, as monetary policy became so paramount an instrument of economic policy in the West, the European Central Bank's first Chairman, Dutch banker Wim Duisenberg, and his board became every bit as influential in the European economy as was US Federal Chairman Alan Greenspan and his board in the US economy. If it is a mark of a 'state' that it issues and controls its own money then the peoples of the Euro-zone were, from 1 January 1999, citizens of a new state, and the peoples of Britain, Sweden and Denmark, still outside the Euro-zone in 2003, were not.[5]

However, the euro is not just about the management of money; for it is also the engine powering the creation of an economic government for Europe. Germany had worried for some time that following the introduction of the euro, although interest rates would be set centrally, some governments (they had in mind the Italians and the Greeks) would blast a hole in the whole enterprise and export inflation to the rest of the Union, by profligate deficit spending. And Helmut Kohl's most impressive single moment as Europe's architect may well have been the time when in 1996 he placed the first foundation stone for Europe's central government by powering through the Stability and Growth Pact, which imposed sanctions, or fines, for countries that breached the three per cent budget deficit rules. The historic achievement was not the details, but rather Kohl's securing of a European consensus behind the principle of fines.

Kohl secured the pact just ahead of the Amsterdam summit in 1997; and with him in the side room for the historic meeting was his own finance minister, Theo Waigel, together with Jacques Chirac, Wim Kok and Gerrit Zalm (Prime Minister and Finance Minister of Holland) and Jean-Claude Juncker (Prime Minister of Luxembourg). The Italians, always worried about over-harsh punishments for deficits, were absent. Chirac was attempting to water down the pact, and Theo Waigel remembers how the Dutch Prime Minister, constantly at Kohl's side, was saying, 'Helmut, be tough! Be tough!' Germany had proposed that exemptions to the fine could only be offered to countries whose economic growth had fallen by one per cent in the year. At the meeting, Chirac made the first move and offered 0.5 per cent. Kohl was silent, and then Chirac offered to go to 0.6 per cent. 'I didn't go to an elite university like you Jacques and got lower marks than you did in Maths,' said Kohl, 'but the difference between 1 per cent and 0.5 per cent is 0.75 per cent.' Kohl got his agreement, and 0.75 per cent went into the pact. And around such haggling it was resolved to set in place one of the building blocks of federal nationhood – the rules of central economic governance.[6]

So, on 1 January 1999, as the crowd gathered in Frankfurt outsider the Eurotower at Kaiserstrasse 29 to watch the giant euro light up and a new era unfold, all the existing trends and dynamics of Europe were pointing in one direction: towards and not away from more integration; towards and not away from statehood; towards Europe and the EU developing its own single government. It took only a rendition of policy areas where the EU had (and has) exclusive responsibility – monetary policy, trade policy, common commercial policy, customs union and fishery policy – or shares responsibility with the nation states – the internal market, energy, environment, agriculture, economic, social and territorial cohesion – to show the direction in which Europe was going. (And, even though a keen belief in 'subsidiarity', Euro-speak for devolved power, is now part of EU lore, it is in essence a genuflection only. For no serious powers, or competences, once secured by Brussels, have ever been repatriated back to the member states.)

What made, and still makes, this dynamic towards European super-statehood all the more unstoppable is that it is not willed by the crazed power trips of officious Brussels bureaucrats, but rather by fundamental realities. Today's big problems facing Europe – whether employment or terrorism or the environment or transport or crime and drug trafficking or geopolitical threats – are all transnational, and are simply no longer seen as soluble, even manageable, except by the Union 'acting as one'.

And this outside dynamic is complemented by an inside dynamic. Quite simply, one thing leads to another – Europe's single market leads inevitably to a single currency and thence to a single government (ultimately with a single tax and spend policy). As Wim

Duisenberg said, just after being appointed as the first Euro central banker, the EU will, in order to avoid tax competition, be bound to go down the road of more and more tax harmonization.[7] And this single government will form the central pillar of the European federal super-state. (The British government's attempt to deny this dynamic during the early years of the euro – by continuing to run a separate currency whilst staying in the single market – is Canute-like in its audacity.)

Federalists can also rely upon that great sleeper amongst Europe's institutions, the European Court of Justice, to push for 'ever closer union'. For all who wish to see, the precedent of the US Supreme Court stands out starkly. Hardly noticeable in the 1787 constitution, the US Supreme Court was to become the greatest single engine propelling the US federal state forward. In Europe's case, the judges of the European Court of Justice can be relied upon, like constitutional jurists everywhere, to make new constitutional law. And when they get their teeth into a European Charter of Rights in a European constitution, then Europeans can expect the erosion of the power not just of national courts but of national governments as well. In the Europe of 2025, the Court may well have its fingerprints on laws ranging from religion to sex, from welfare to employment.

The Federalist Push

Yet, during the 1990s, worries about the potential super-state remained widespread through Europe. And these fears developed into a growing political resistance to 'ever closer union'. Anyone with a 'national' role – national parliamentarians and national civil servants who may have jobs and careers linked to the nation-state apparatus – had at least a residual interest in resisting super-state Europe. And these elites played on broader nationalist, even xenophobic, sentiments amongst the public, while an array of anti-establishment politicians like outsiders Le Pen in France or Haider in Austria or Fortuyn in Holland, or insiders like Thatcher in Britain, gave voice to these fears.

British Prime Minister Margaret Thatcher had set the scene for a sustained campaign against federalism when she assailed the prospect of a 'European super-state' in a September 1988 speech in Bruges. It was a colourful, blunt and systematic attack on the idea of political union itself, raising, for the first time at Europe's highest level, the spectre of a future Europe as a juggernaut for unaccountable centralized power. And it was hugely successful, for the British Prime Minister articulated the hidden fears of many throughout Europe (many of these fears were, subliminally at least, about the future power of Germany, fears that turned into real anxiety after the Berlin Wall came down and Germany was reunited). And, as this war raged, most of the other governments, including the French, were grouped somewhere in between the British and German positions.

These battle lines hardened as German Chancellor Helmut Kohl, undeterred by Mrs Thatcher, stepped up his campaign for the German federalist vision. Like his fellow chancellors Helmut Schmidt before him and Gerhard Schroeder after him, he remained convinced that Europe's growing economic union needed to have a strong political union to manage it. So much so that Kohl made a fateful 'quid pro quo' agreement with French President Mitterrand whereby Germany would support the French plan for monetary union in return for French backing for increasing federalism (which, to soften the pill was to be called 'political union'). 'We [Germans] can and will not give up sovereignty over monetary policies if political union remains a "castle in the air",' declared the Chancellor in a landmark speech in Jouy-en-Josas in December 1991.[8] The French, although leaning towards the German aim of a federal European state, have never completely accepted the idea. France's great national (and nationalist) post-war leader and president, General de Gaulle, once famously remarked: 'A European Federation? Why Not? But in 50 years time.'[9] And the Gaullist legacy in French politics always put a stop to any wholehearted Gallic embrace of federalism.

Since the launch of the euro in 1999, with the obvious next step being political union, the great debate has intensified; and Europe's leaders, normally timid about the big geopolitical questions, have not been bashful in weighing in. German Foreign Minister Joschka Fischer was the very first into the arena with his May 2000 Berlin speech 'From Confederation To Federation', in which, echoing Kohl and drawing on a real domestic German consensus, he declared unabashedly for a federal future. 'I know the term "federation" irritates many Britons,' he quipped, 'but to date I have been unable to come up with another word.' He proposed a clearly defined single European government and a two-chamber Parliament.[10] A year later, this mainstream German federal vision was unfurled in the SPD document 'Responsibility for Europe'. The Germans, who had been operating a federal system for over 40 years, were now openly and systematically advancing its merits for Europe as a whole. The German blueprint envisaged nothing less than a full written constitution for a United States of Europe and a European government. It wanted power located in the European Council, amongst the leaders of the member states who would meet on a regular basis and take the big decisions; but the Council would be supplemented by a super-charged executive – in the German draft a 'strong' – European Commission. And the institution dearest to federalists, the European Parliament, would be strengthened by adding to its co-decision rights and, like all real parliaments everywhere, giving it full budgetary authority. The Parliament would also be enhanced by giving it a powerful second chamber – a Chamber of the European Nations, which would be drawn from the member states' ministers on the Council of Ministers. All this would be set down in a written constitution for the EU and, crucially, would incorporate the Charter of Basic Rights.

With the Germans quickly off the blocks, the response from Paris was eagerly awaited. And when it came it was clear that Paris was cavilling somewhat at the boldness of the German federalist vision. In late June 2000, President Jacques Chirac, whose relations with Chancellor Schroeder were then lukewarm, used the great occasion of a speech in the Bundestag to reply. On the big ideological issue of a federal future he was silent, but appeased his hosts by arguing for greater integration, and grabbed the headlines by floating the idea of a two-speed Europe, with a 'pioneer group' of nations moving ahead to further integration faster than others.

A year later, it became clear that the French political class as a whole had settled on a European vision which was less overtly federalist than the German one. In May 2001, Prime Minister Lionel Jospin spoke for many in the French political leadership when he argued that France 'could not accept' the idea of a federation on the lines of the German Länder and federal system. He described France's preference for what he called a 'federation of nation states', a subtle but real alternative to German federalism. In the future Europe, France would accept 'transferring competences' to the Union level, and, like Chirac, he proposed what amounted to the creation of an economic government for Europe. He wanted the Council of Ministers strengthened through the creation of a permanent body and Europe's leaders in the European Council to meet together every two months. Intriguingly, he also proposed that the Commission President should be elected by the European Parliament, a measure which would enhance federalism by giving the Commission greater legitimacy.[11]

The Gaullist shadow continued to fall over French politics, but as every year went by, it fell less vividly so. And German pressure remained on France to honour the informal deal made between Mitterrand and Kohl in the early 1990s to support political union in return for seeing the end of the Deutschmark. But the overriding factor that pushed Paris further and further into the federalist camp was its own interest in creating a strong central government to help manage the single market and currency, and to resist the excesses of globalization and to create a rival power to the USA. The transatlantic division over Iraq and the forging of stronger and stronger relations with Germany also softened residual resistance to federalism in France. By 2003, Paris was still refusing to use the word 'federal', but it now supported a federal Europe in all but name.

Britain, by contrast, had become more and more Euro-sceptic during the 1990s. When Blair entered office in 1997 with ambitions to join the euro and with decidedly pro-European rhetoric, it seemed a new post-Thatcher chapter had opened. By 2003, however, he was still unwilling to lead Britain into the Euro-zone, and his 2000 'confederalist' Warsaw speech continued to represent the outer limits of his constitutional thinking. (His main specific proposal was the creation of a second chamber in the European Parliament composed of representatives from national parliaments, which would act as a 'political review body' and would oversee the Common Foreign and Security Policy.)[12] As long as the British Conservatives remain the second party of UK politics – nosing out the pro-federalist Liberal Democrats – Britain will remain in Europe's nationalist camp.

And in the great game of European politics, Britain's nationalists and Euro-sceptics saw their hand strengthened during the late 1990s by the imminent arrival of Poland and the other new countries from Eastern and Central Europe who, they believed, would dilute the passion for 'ever closer union'. (And, with Britain and Spain, they could together create an 'outer Europe' that would serve to slow, if not reverse, the federalist dynamic.)

Serious federalists had been worried for most of the 1990s about this projected enlargement to the east – and the added weight it gave to the British and Spanish. And the federalist counter-attack began at Nice in December 2000 when the German Chancellor only agreed to the enlargement on condition that a written constitution be drawn up to tighten decision-making in the coming 25-member EU and make the Union workable. President Chirac was not, then, fully on board for Europe's federal destination and, under his chairmanship of the Nice summit, the coming dispensation in an enlarged Europe gave Poland and Spain almost as many votes each as allocated to the united Germany (with twice the population of each of them).

At the subsequent Laeken summit in December 2001, Berlin got its way and a convention to draw up a draft written constitution was agreed. And former French president Valéry Giscard d'Estaing was appointed its Chairman. Giscard was a natural choice for the historic job. The former French president was no fervent federalist (being a long-time adversary of the European Commission) but a supporter of 'ever closer union' nonetheless. Giscard knew his way around the European institutions and, a liberal conservative by inclination, he was not easily labelled as left or right. And his haughty, grand, detached manner was thought to suit the gravity of the portentous proceedings – he once famously kept a delegation of MEPs sent to meet him waiting whilst, under the gilt and chandeliers of the Banque de France, he played Mozart on the piano.

As things stood in the summer of 2003, the federalists, if not victorious, were in the ascendant. The Giscard draft EU constitution, bundled up and handed over to Europe's governments on 13 June 2003, had pushed the frontiers of federalism a considerable distance. The framers in the convention strengthened the role of President of the Council (by ending rotation) and the President of the Commission (by an election amongst Parliament and Council). They also streamlined the Commission (keeping 15 Commissioners in a 25-state Union). They introduced a real common policy on asylum (a more centralised visa policy and immigration law). They proposed the abolition of the veto on excise duties and corporation tax and also made provision for making the harmonization of tax rates across the EU politically easier. They aimed to create a 'European FBI' by setting up an EU public prosecutor to tackle cross-border crimes and prosecute them in the courts of nation states. And, in the controversial territory of foreign and defence policy, they proposed an EU Foreign Minister and – striking at the heart of NATO – an EU mutual defence agreement. And, in the truly controversial new territory of rights, they proposed the most federalizing of all their measures – the incorporation of the existing Charter of Fundamental Rights into the new constitution, a proposal that, through the work of the European Court of Justice, could create a rights regime for Europe as all-embracing and all-powerful as that of the USA.[13]

And France and Germany, now working hand in hand, had also secured the overthrow of the Nice formula of voting rights so that the big countries would have more say in Council decision-making (and Poland's 40 million people would no longer have virtually the same weight as Germany's 80 million population).

The Periphery Stirs

What, though, those celebrating the new draft constitution with Giscard in Brussels in late June 2003 had failed to notice was the gathering momentum against the plan which was building some 450 miles to the east in Warsaw, where Poland's leadership was girding its loins for a fight to protect itself within the Union. Over the next few months, Poland was to become the symbol of resistance to federalism. Deeply enmeshed with Washington – through the large Polish population in the USA as well as the solidarity created by US support during the cold war against the historic enemy in Moscow – Poland became a natural partner for George W. Bush, an association consummated when Poland supported the USA in the 2003 Iraq war. Spain also joined the ranks of the Euro-sceptic peripheral states. Like Poland, Spain is a medium-sized nation with a large rural, Catholic population. Post-Franco Spain had done well economically since joining the European Community in 1986, but some in the Spanish leadership felt that the country was not given the respect and power it was due, particularly by Paris. The Aznar premiership gave strong, unwavering support for George W. Bush during the Iraq war.

The Iraq war was to turn what were grumblings about the constitution in these peripheral states into a serious rift between Poland and Spain on the one hand and France and Germany on the other. Tempers aroused during the war had not really cooled by the time of the Brussels summit on 13 December 2003, when the leaders were due to meet to agree the new constitution. With neither side backing down, Brussels in December became the venue for a high-profile and high-blown European crisis. Schroeder and Chirac, in no mood to compromise with the Poles, left the weekend summit on the Saturday afternoon, after only 24 hours. Then Chairman Silvio Berlusconi announced at the post-summit press conference the complete breakdown of the talks because of 'total disagreement' about voting rights. The shambles allowed *International Herald Tribune* reporter John Vinocur, an articulate and bitter critic of European integration, to write with undisguised glee that 'the old idealistic flame of a United States of Europe lay between barest flicker and ash.'[14]

News soon started filtering out that the evening before, and anticipating the breakdown, President Chirac, Chancellor Schroeder and Belgium's federalist Prime Minister Guy Verhofstadt had met for dinner in a Japanese restaurant in the Avenue Louise where they had agreed to go ahead with radical plans for a 'Core Europe' – a pioneer grouping of countries who would integrate further and faster than the others. The German Chancellor made no bones about the idea when he stated 'there will emerge a Europe of two speeds.' This was, in all but name, a plan for a federal state within the EU, an inner super-state within the larger Union. Verhofstadt was deputed to arrange contacts with other like-minded EU countries wanting to join the Germans, French and Belgians. Initial reports suggested that those countries interested included Hungary, Austria, Greece and the Czech Republic.[15]

For some years, Paris had had a 'Plan B' for Europe. It was floated by President Jacques Chirac as early as June 2000 in his Bundestag speech when he outlined the idea for a 'pioneer group' of countries, presumably including France, Germany, Belgium, Holland and Luxembourg, to break out ahead of the rest of the EU and 'blaze the trail by making use of the new enhanced cooperation procedure... and forging, if necessary cooperation in spheres not covered by the treaty'. Chirac delivered these words in the deadening language of Euro-speak; but the content was strong stuff – with its implication of a two-tier Europe with laggard countries (presumably including Britain, Spain and Poland) being left behind, and maybe even ultimately spun-off altogether from the core.

The possibility of Core Europe had always been lurking – like Banquo's ghost – at the European feast. And it would always send alarm bells ringing throughout Europe, but particularly in the ears of successive British governments and the British Foreign Office. Yet, from London's perspective, at no point did the idea ever amount to an imminent possibility. From London's perspective, talk of Core Europe was always overblown, because Franco-German union would never get off the ground. But by December 2003, in the aftermath of the deadlock over enlargement, a Franco-German union was not looking so fanciful after all.

5

The European Core

'Charlemagna' Is Born Again

On Bastille Day, 14 July 2003, in a highly unusual turn of events, a German general, Lieutenant General Holger Kammerhoff, took the lead in the great military parade down the Champs-Elysée. And six days later, at the solemn national annual celebration of German democracy held in the grey courtyard of the old Army headquarters in the Bendlerstrasse in Berlin, there was another unprecedented event. For the first time alongside the German President, the German Chancellor and the German Defence Minister, there appeared an honoured guest from another country – the French Defence Minister.

These events were symbolic, but they signalled a new phase in the ever-tightening Franco-German alliance, and they flowed from a more substantive Franco-German get-together that had taken place in Brussels some weeks before. On Tuesday 6 May 2003, days after President Bush announced the ending of major combat in Iraq, Chancellor Gerhard Schroeder had met President Jacques Chirac in a hastily arranged special defence summit called to discuss Europe's future as a military power. This summit (as I shall argue later) may yet become an historic milestone in Europe's story. But, at the time, the US government downplayed the meeting – calling it a 'little bitty summit' – and the Anglo-American media painted it as little more than a kind of revenge meeting, an attempt to counter Bush in his hour of 'victory' and, in the process, shore up Old Europe.[1]

To take a snapshot in the aftermath of the Iraq war, Europe did indeed look like a continent divided – in US Defense Secretary Donald Rumsfeld's words – an 'old' and a 'new' Europe. There was, as Ian Buruma once suggested, a Europe divided between seafaring lands (Britain, Atlantic coastal France, Hamburg and the Hanseatic League) and a Europe of the interior (based on the old heartland of Franconia and the Holy Roman Empire, nowadays running north from Paris to Brussels, across the Rhine valley to Berlin and back down again to Munich and Rome).[2] And on top of this could be laid yet another new division, an economic/philosophical one, between heartland Europe (France and Germany) with its social market economy and welfare state, and the Latin south (Spain and Italy), where Prime Ministers Aznar and Berlusconi proclaimed and supported rawer market capitalism.

But the most serious fault-line of all was a more intangible one – between the Europe that linked itself umbilically to America, taking its inspiration from the New World, and a new Europe which was beginning to stand on its own feet, build its own new polity and move on. It was a division between American Europe and European Europe. And it was this divide that 9/11 – and the US response to it (in the war in Iraq and the Rumsfeld doctrine) – further widened.

In the long run, however, post-9/11 events may also have united contemporary Europe as never before. The Iraq crisis united (in opposition to Washington) the publics of Europe in a rare display of uniform anti-American sentiment – that is, opposition to what was seen as American power play. It also united Europe's two heartland governments (France and Germany) in opposing Washington, and, more importantly, in a new determination to create a Europe which could counterbalance American power in the world.

Before Iraq, Europe was stuck. It had the euro, and it was about to add to its single currency an historic written constitution with real supranational institutions. It had, in sum, already become Jean Monnet's 'great civilian power'. But it did not seem to possess the ability to go to the next level, to that of superpower Europe – a political union with a foreign and security policy. It was rather like a new, gleaming jumbo jet, with all the passengers on board, ready to fly, but stuck on the runway because of lack of fuel – the political will to fly.

Before Iraq, Europe had been quietly building the infrastructure of the superpower plane. The blueprint was first sketched out in the Dutch town of Maastricht in December 1991, when Europe's 'Big Two', Chancellor Helmut Kohl of Germany and the ailing President François Mitterrand of France, drew up, unnoticed amidst all the fanfare of the single currency, the first small stepping stone on the fateful pathway towards a common foreign and security policy. At Maastricht, the Union's member states agreed to a loose structure (but a structure nonetheless) called 'the Common Foreign and Security Policy' (CFSP), set it up as the 'second pillar' of the Union and also, in a truly radical step, committed themselves to 'the eventual framing of a common defence policy'. It was all about goals and aspirations, but they were goals and aspirations that were later to be built on, as Maastricht formed the foundation for the Amsterdam Treaty (1997) where Europe began to coordinate its foreign and diplomatic policy through the new office of a 'High Representative' in the person of Spaniard Javier Solana the former Secretary-General of NATO.

Solana became, if not Europe's first 'Foreign Secretary', then Europe's first 'Foreign Coordinator'. And as the Spaniard travelled the world (often with the Foreign Minister of the Council's rotating presidency), he began to be recognized as a key diplomatic player – not anything of the order of, say, US Secretary of State, Colin Powell, but taken seriously, not least because he was seen as the potential harbinger of the foreign and security policy of a nascent superpower. The great problem for Solana (and for the EU) was that, unlike his opposite number Colin Powell, he reported back not to a single European President, but to several governments (in the Council of Ministers) and shared the foreign affairs brief with the External Relations Commissioner (Chris Patten) and the Trade Commissioner (Pascal Lamy). Javier Solana represented a Europe hovering on the brink. The EU was presenting what it had long sought after – a 'face' and a 'voice' to the world – but it was unable to go beyond this, and produce a common, let alone a single, foreign policy that could challenge American domination in global geopolitics or in the coming contest for Eurasia.

This impasse, symbolized in the inadequacy of Europe's 'High Representative', was highlighting a bitter reality for federalists: that for the EU as a whole there is no swift and easy natural progression from an economic bloc to a US-style security superpower with diplomats, a foreign and security apparatus and a European army with a 'commander in chief'. The continuing absence of an EU-wide political will, the kind that created the euro, was well illuminated by the extreme caution even of the Giscard convention when it came to majority voting in foreign and defence policy.[3] For the truth of the matter is that any attempt to use the EU as a whole to balance and challenge Washington would always be blocked by Britain and maybe, too, by some of the new member states.

But if the EU as a whole could not move beyond its superpower blueprint, its two leading continental states, working closely together, could more easily do so. For, what the Iraq war did for Europe was to create that special something that was not there before – a real and lasting identity of interest and will between France and Germany about security and foreign policy. It brought into being an inner core within the EU, a core where the inexorable integration of security and defence as well as economics can proceed apace.

By 2003, France and Germany were already acting virtually as such a 'Core Europe', as a joint enterprise, a 'union within a union', 'a state within a state'; and 'Charlemagna', if not yet born, had certainly already been conceived.

And, in the summer of 2003, in the aftermath of the great transatlantic clash, this 'Charlemagna' was in the making. The two leaders, Jacques Chirac and Gerhard Schroeder, did not get on well together – there was none of the personal chemistry of Giscard and Schmidt or even of Kohl and Mitterrand – but the closeness over Iraq and the geopolitical identity of interest had more than compensated. Both knew that to build a European alternative to the USA would, first and foremost, mean changes at home. In France, it would demand the curbing of residual instinctive nationalist 'Gaullisme'; in Germany, it would mean putting its long-held Atlanticism on security issues behind it in order to secure its own growing belief in 'a European way' (within which Schroeder's 'German way' could be subsumed).

All the signs were pointing to an 'ever-closer union' of France and Germany. Some were highly symbolic – like the unprecedented gathering in 2002 of the two parliaments (the whole German Bundestag and the whole French National Assembly) at Versailles, or the German general leading the Bastille Day parade in Paris, or the French Defence Minister as the guest of honour at the Bendlerstrasse ceremony in Berlin. Some were institutional – like the deepening of cabinet and government-level contacts and integration. But the most potent sign of all of a Franco-German 'union within a union' was the increasing habit of Paris and Berlin to coordinate positions and 'act as one' within the EU on big policy questions. 2003 saw France and Germany take up common positions on policies ranging from agriculture to budgets. And, by the end of 2003, both governments had succeeded in a joint campaign to effectively remake the rules of the Growth and Stability Pact.

The idea of 'Charlemagna' has a long pedigree. As far back as the eighth century, Charlemagne, the great emperor of the Franks, the first of the German emperors of the Middle Ages, ran, from his seat in Aachen, what amounted to an earlier political union of France and Germany. The great age of nationalism, spanning four centuries, with Napoleon in the middle and Hitler at the end, then set the two countries on differing courses, and at each others' throats. But ever since the end of Hitler's war, Franco-Germany – 'Charlemagna' – has been in the air again. It was Konrad Adenauer's post-war 'western' strategy for Germany, and the politicians of the Fourth Republic who responded, that founded contemporary Franco-Germany; but when Charles de Gaulle, representing as only he could the post-war French nation, spoke in German to a Munich crowd in 1963 calling the Germans 'ein grosses Volk' ('a great people'), it was finally clear that the old enmities were truly being put aside. And the signing that same year of the Franco-German treaty confirming close cooperation between the two countries within the newly formed Common Market or 'Europe of the Six', formalized it all. Later, the duos of Helmut Schmidt and Valèry Giscard d'Estaing and then Helmut Kohl and François Mitterrand, forged an 'ever closer union' between the two countries; and Gerhard Schroeder and Jacques Chirac, have, under the impetus of the gathering clouds of Bush's America, taken Franco-Germany from an alliance into a something beginning to resemble a confederal union.

Yet, until now, Franco-Germany has always firmly worked within the context of the wider Europe that surrounds it. If St Paul was the rock on which the Christians built their church, then Franco-Germany has been the foundation stone of contemporary Europe. Franco-Germany has been rather like the ever-present host of Europe, the ever-purring engine of European unity.

Franco-Germany is, though, always potentially much more than the inner core of a Europe-wide political system. For the two countries, taken as a totality – as 'Charlemagna' – have the potential to become a superpower themselves. They certainly have everything a superpower needs. They have a population of 140 million. They have an economy which is about half that of the Euro-zone, about 40 per cent of that of the EU and of the USA, is almost equal to that of Japan and four times bigger than that of China.[4] And 'Charlemagna' would have a balanced economy with a productive manufacturing sector and large farming and service sectors. It would have immense 'soft power' – the power to attract in the world; it has a consumer society second to none with some of the world's best housing, clothing, food and drink (the combination of a society with German cars and French wine is about as good as it gets). It would have the world's richest cultural life, one of the most educated populations on the face of the globe with a vibrant intelligentsia and intellectual life. It would also be a high-tech union with the ability to keep at the forefront of technological change should it decide to. Geopolitically, Charlemagna would be the centre of a web of influence, with good contacts across the world, and in the advanced world. It would find itself (unlike the USA and Britain) with fewer real enemies in the world and the potential, at least, for decent relations with the combustible Islamic world. And it could defend itself: it would be a nuclear weapons state with the ability to deter any adversary anywhere in the world, with a large standing army. If it wanted, it could easily develop force projection to protect itself into forward areas around its borders.

In late 2003, with the crisis over the Giscard constitution unresolved, the idea of Franco-Germany reorganizing 'inner Europe' around itself into a core was beginning to swirl around Europe's capitals. On 13 November 2003, *Le Monde* reported that Paris and Berlin were actively considering a 'union of France and Germany' and the French Commissioner, Pascal Lamy, was quoted as floating the idea of a 'bund' or 'federation' which would join together the two countries.[5] The same report suggested that any such union of the two nations, any new Charlemagna, would stop far short of one leader and one electoral system. But it would need some kind of new formal structure, which most likely would be federal in character – a 'federation of nations' being a term acceptable in Paris as well as Berlin. Over time, this 'federation' could simply be extended to form the EU inner core – which, according to reports at the time, would initially comprise, as well as France and Germany, Belgium and Luxembourg. The idea was that it would be open for any other

EU state to join, and Austria, Holland, Hungary, the Czech Republic and Greece were all reported to be prime candidates to join in the first wave.[6]

This new Core Europe would take up and complete what the expanded EU 25 could not do – complete the long historic march to European integration started by the Iron and Steel Community after the war. Its *raison d'être* would be to deepen existing economic integration in 'the core' – perhaps ultimately with majority voting in the 'core' on economic policy including taxation and spending. It would begin the task of integrating the systems of justice throughout the new federation (to deal with the newly urgent issues of terrorism immigration, asylum and organized crime). And it would start to integrate the foreign and security policies of its nations (creating one diplomacy, one diplomatic corps, one arms procurement system and one military and defence system, perhaps even including a new disposition for the French nuclear deterrent). Over time, the people of this European inner federation would inhabit a single market, a single economy and single currency, a single justice system and a single foreign and security policy. The new federation will increasingly act and vote 'as one' within the European Council and the Council of Ministers (and also at the UN and in other international bodies). In short, 'Core Europe' (with, say, 200-plus million people and the world's second largest economy) would be able to act as a new state on the world stage.

This new Core Europe federated state would, though, have the great advantage of being the key player in the wider EU. It would be involved at the heart of everything the wider EU is and does. It would – rather like the USA in the global system – be the hub in a hub and spokes system. Core Europe would be the hub of the 25-member single market and trading bloc of 400 million people (the world's largest). It would also be the hub of the 22-member single currency zone (also the world's largest). It would be the hub of the passport-free 22-member Schengen group, and it would also be the hub of the EU defence system (linked, under the December 2003 agreement, with Britain, and able to develop a serious strategic military arm).

This inner core would be able to increase its political, diplomatic and military clout in the world by creating wider European 'coalitions of the willing' for specific activities or policies. However, any new core grouping would need urgently to sort out how exactly its ongoing relations with the rest of the EU would operate. For instance, in a hypothetical future, should Core Europe wish to pursue its foreign policy by imposing economic sanctions against a foreign country (because of human rights violations or aggression across borders) would it always need to go to the wider EU first before doing anything? And, what if the wider EU refused to support the projected action (as it did when Britain asked for support during its war with Argentina in 1982, and Italy threatened the veto)? Could, for instance, the sanctions policy of the Core group still be supported by a 'coalition of the willing' from outside the inner core (say, by adding Spain or Italy or Britain, or the Scandinavian countries, depending on the issue)?

Federal Endgame

This vision of a future Franco-German 'Charlemagna' flexing its muscles outside of its traditional EU context and acting alone in the world was on high-profile display well before the December constitutional crisis. It was unfurled during the Iraq war. The audacious joint posture of France and Germany in the UN, the historic anti-American UN alliance with Russia and the subsequent May 2003 'four power' defence summit (Franco-Germany plus Belgium and Luxembourg) served as a warning to the rest of Europe that Franco-Germany can, if need be, go it alone. This new strategy was couched in the diplomatic language of creating a 'pioneer' or 'vanguard' group within the EU, but the deeper implication was clear. And it is this potential to go it alone that may, more than anything else, be the catalyst that creates the European *finalité*, the security superpower. By 2003, opinion in Paris and Berlin was increasingly aware that whilst France and Germany stayed firmly and loyally within the EU context they will, inevitably, remain trapped, and Europe will remain frozen as an economic power only. They saw that as things stood, American Europe (Britain, some Eastern European countries, possibly even Italy and Spain) would simply veto European Europe's proposals for further EU security and defence integration, and France and Germany would be able to do nothing about it. For European Europe to prevail, Franco-Germany would need to continue with building 'Charlemagna' as a threat and as a magnet. Seen from Paris and Berlin, Britain would only be moved, if at all, by its traditional fear of being left behind, and alone, as a continental superpower was born on its doorstep. The other, less stubborn, supporters of American Europe (the new Eastern European member states and the governments of Spain and Italy) would be drawn automatically towards the core, as it acted like a magnet.

No matter the attraction of Core Europe, Rumsfeld's 'New Europe' – the new member states from Eastern Europe – are bound for some years to come to continue to look to the USA, for inspiration and with fond feelings. And these sentiments will provide Washington with a window of opportunity to lure Eastern Europe into its global security system. In the very year in which Poland signed the EU accession treaty it took a lead in supporting the US Iraq policy, accepted Washington's offer of a lead role as an occupying power in northern Iraq and firmed up its military and strategic links with the USA as US military personnel and bases moved out of Core Europe (Germany) into Poland. Also, the Pentagon can be expected to pursue US strategic and military links, including new basing arrangements, with a range of new and candidate members such as Bulgaria, improving US influence in the Black Sea coastal area.

Yet, in the overall geo-strategic balance, these military relationships across the Atlantic between the USA and Eastern Europe will be more than cancelled out by the increasingly dense network of economic relations between Eastern Europe and Core Europe (particularly Germany) that already exists and, after full accession and full euro membership, will become even denser.

The underlying pro-US sentiment found throughout Eastern Europe and the Baltics can also reasonably be expected to wane in the coming decades. This emotional attachment is, after all, the product of an era now passed – the cold war, and the belief amongst many Eastern Europeans that the USA was their liberator and the provider of their freedom from Russian hegemony. This fear of Russia may also weaken over time should Russia remain on a democratic path and the more general Russian-European relationship enter a very warm period. Throughout Eastern Europe, worries about Big Brother Germany (which surfaced again during the Iraq crisis) may well continue and, in the early stages of EU membership, actually intensify – but as long as Germany remains locked into the EU, or into 'Charlemagna', and does not act alone in Central Europe, such sentiments will easily be contained. In this environment, the good news for Europe is that, as time goes by, the magnet of Core Europe will remain the only real centripetal force around, and will act to pull most of the Eastern European outriders in towards her.

As well as New Europe, Italy and Spain (and Portugal) also signed up for America during the Iraq war, as the Berlusconi and Aznar governments formed a Southern European pro-American coalition. Yet, this Southern European grouping will be even easier to attract into Core Europe than will the Eastern Europeans. For what linked the three Southern European governments was not so much gut pro-American sensibility as pro-market liberalism – and a dispute between the three and Core Europe about the economic and social direction of the EU. Also, in both Italy and Spain, former fascist countries with a history of extremism, the two rightist governments of Berlusconi and Aznar were very much the products of these past internal divisions, and their strong conservatism was in part a legacy from past battles against their communist and socialist opponents.

But the hold on power of these right-wing governments in Italy and Spain was tenuous, as Prime Ministers Aznar and Berlusconi, the latter more so than the former, were mavericks; Italy could easily return to a left-of-centre administration in a future election and to a complete change in the country's approach to Core Europe – Spain already has done. Even future conservative administrations in Italy and Spain – with the economic interests of the two Euro-zone countries increasingly tied into those of France and Germany – might well see Core Europe as an irresistible magnet.

By the end of 2003, the Brussels constitutional imbroglio had plunged many Euro-federalists into deep gloom. They believed that the failure to sign the constitution and the growing rift between inner and outer states meant that their great dream of a democratic federal super-state was finally over. For them, the Giscard draft constitution, though not perfect, had been a sturdy platform on which to build. But the prize had been cruelly snatched from their grasp at the very last minute.

Such federalist pessimism was based on the belief that Europe can only make progress towards a federal future at one speed only – or not at all. Yet, for other federalists, the serious talk of building Core Europe, with its potential magnet effect, was a hugely positive turn of events. Such a Core Europe might, in fact, not just be an alternative structure to that of the enlarged EU, but might even speed up the whole process of federalizing the EU. This case was based on recent history – that Europe had always made progress through a dynamic inner core built around France and Germany, and that the European Union was itself built by a core group (the original six of the Iron and Steel Community and the Common Market) acting as a magnet to create 15 and then 25. This idea was reinforced by the history of other continents. The US federal system itself grew out of a core group of 13 states, but more relevant was the Latin American experience – when the lack of an inner core may have helped explain the failure of South America to produce a viable union on the EU model (a failure that may yet cost the continent dear). At the ill-fated Panama Congress of 1826, the two candidates, Argentina and Brazil, which could have formed an inner core (like France and Germany in today's EU), opposed the project.[7]

In reality, the idea of Core Europe amounted to a federal endrun by Germany and France round the backs of what they saw as the 'laggards'. The Franco-German game plan was clear. Core Europe would not – necessarily – become an aim in itself: for the Franco-German core, although good in itself, could also act as a magnet attracting the peripheral states (Britain, Spain, Poland and others) into closer integration. A Franco-German super-state within the EU would be up and running, and acting as one. But it would also be open to other states to join. And over time, should enough states join, then an inner-core super-state could transform itself into the cherished goal of a pan-European super-state. This 'pioneer' route, rather than breaking faith with the European ideal, was the only way to realize it.

Some supporters of the idea of Core Europe believed once the core group had expanded to, say, a majority of Europe's nations, it could adopt an updated, and more federalist, version of the Giscard draft as its written constitution. It could then invite every member of the EU to sign the new written constitution, but, crucially, unlike in 2003, 'the laggards' would not be able to block it. Those who agreed to sign and ratify the constitution would go ahead with it and those who did not would be outside.

This idea of Core Europe was changing the dynamics of European politics. By early 2004, it had so worried London that Tony Blair had, against Washington's wishes, signed up to an EU defence system with France and Germany (setting up a 'directoire' in the process). Then in early March 2004, the European Core was suddenly expanded as, following the ousting of Aznar in Spain's election, the new Spanish government adopted a pro-Core posture. Overnight, the Core had been strengthened, Britain and Poland isolated and the Giscard constitution placed back on track; in Britain, Tony Blair subsequently performed a volte-face and announced that he would (in some unspecified future) seek public approval of the constitution in a referendum. A federal future for the whole EU, not just the Core, looked more likely than not.

Giscard's draft opened the way for a key federalist aim – a single elected presidency for the Union. The 'two presidents' suggested by the Giscard draft, one for the Council and one for the Commission, was straight out of the French Fifth Republic model (with the President of the Council, together with the projected EU Foreign Minister, dealing with foreign policy, and the President of the Commission becoming a kind of Prime Minister and dealing largely with domestic policy). But these 'two presidents' could, of course, ultimately merge into one presidency. In the long run, Europe's federalists will need to decide which kind of elected executive they want – whether a 'presidential' or a 'parliamentary' model. The 'presidential' model would have an EU president elected by the people directly (or through some kind of electoral college) and the European Parliament would be elected separately. On the other hand, the parliamentary model would have the EU President elected by the European Parliament and responsible to it.

In the *finalité*, or final endgame – not unthinkable by, say, 2025 – the Council would become the upper house in the European Parliament (the present European Parliament would become the lower house) and the Commission would develop into the government and civil service of Europe – responsible to the elected presidency. A long-time ambition of federalists has been to see a strong European Parliament; but if the President (and executive) of the EU were to be elected by Parliament (as in parliamentary systems around the world) then the European Parliament would inevitably end up as a weak, whip-driven institution, rather like the parliaments of Britain and Germany.

But, whatever happens to the Council in the constitutional endgame, it will remain the EU's, and Europe's, premier institution – for as long as national governments play a role in the future of Europe. In the Giscard draft constitutional discussions, all of Europe's national leaders – not just Blair, Berlusconi and Aznar, but Chirac and Schroeder too – were determined, one way or another, to keep the Council at the heart, and as the heart, of Europe's government.

(For this reason alone it has always been a triumph of hope over experience for federalists in Brussels and Strasbourg to believe that somehow they could shoehorn the Commission or the Parliament into dominance over the Council.)

In the Brussels power game, the Council often appeared Janus-faced: all things to all men. Nationalists in Britain saw it as the great protector of states' rights where, through the veto, the ambitions of Eurocrats can be watered down. And Euro-sceptics wanted to keep it that way – an unworkable talking shop, little more than an electoral stage for any grandstanding national politician who wanted to use its forum to appeal to the folks back home. Yet, the Council can also be the cradle for decisive action, for Europe to 'act as one' – as it does on veto-less trade policy or the environment and transport and, in emergencies, even on criminal matters like arrest warrants.

For federalists, it is the veto which is the roadblock to the future – not the Council. Remove – progressively, over the years – the national veto, and the Council of Ministers becomes rather like the US Senate, where Europe's national ministers would certainly look over their shoulders at their home electorates (along with all the normal 'pork barrel' politics) but, at the same time, would take decisions for the Union as a whole *on a majority basis.*

Of course, in any future federal state the issue of 'what is a majority?' in the Council becomes crucial – it was this difficult question that sank the 2003 attempt to get a constitution! In fully functioning federal systems, like the USA and Germany, the smaller states tend to have a disproportionate say in events – in the US Senate and the German Bundesrat big populations in states like New York or North Rhine Westphalia are not fully reflected. But big states tend, ultimately, to be able to carry the day by being given their full weight through their control of some of the key institutions (in the USA through the presidency and the lower house, and in Germany through the election for the Bundestag). In the EU, power resides in the Council (with the Commission a good second and, increasingly, the Parliament a close third); so any truly federal and democratic Europe would need to create its 'majority' in the Council through a count of population rather than states. A variation on the Giscard formula of 60 per cent of the EU's population forming a 'majority' in the Council would serve both majority needs and states' rights.[8]

Federalizing Europe, though, may well be most easily secured by the European Court of Justice. And the Giscard draft constitution opened the way for such federalizing by entrenching the European Court of Justice and by its proposal for a Europe-wide public prosecutor. The Charter of Fundamental Rights may only apply to member states when they are implementing EU law, but such a Bill of Rights gives the ECJ scope to expand its writ. The history of the USA shows how a US Supreme Court, given limited powers in the original constitution, can later, through making law, expand their powers and become, in the domestic arena at least, arguably the most important of all the federal institutions.

An American Colony off the Coast: The Case of Britain

Although Eastern and Southern Europe can be expected, over time, to join Core Europe, Britain remains a different matter altogether; and it must remain an open question whether any new European core, or pioneer or vanguard group will serve to pull her into its orbit. Britain will be both the most worried about the emergence of a core and, ultimately, the most resistant to it. Its 1980s Thatcherite revolution ran very deep – making it more difficult for it than for the other peripheral states to adjust to the European economic and social model. And its political and party system, in which a pro-American tabloid media plays a pivotal role and the country's main opposition party is also pro-American, is biased against further European integration. Nor is it certain how well any new anti-Washington strategy would play in Britain; nor what the outcome would be should the British electorate ever be presented with a straight choice between an American or European destiny for the country. The real truth about Britain in the early years of the new century is that its peoples' links with the USA are deeper than those with Core Europe, although its economic interests take it in the other direction. The country could be pulled either way.

But Britain shares with Italy and Spain the real danger presented by the pull of Core Europe – that staying outside of the European core could easily destabilize these countries, all of which have powerful separatist tendencies within their borders. Should Spain stay out of Core Europe, then the core could quite quickly become a magnet attracting the Basques or the Catalonians; in Italy, northern separatists, who have long been eyeing a separate pro-European road for themselves, could well see their support grow and threaten the very unity of the republic. For these reasons, no Spanish or

Italian government can ultimately take the risk of breaking with Core Europe, even as it moves towards becoming a superpower and super-state. They will seek to protect the unity of their nation states – and the best way to ensure such unity will be to row with, not against, the European heartland.

In Britain, the political establishment of the UK is well aware that the unity of the British state could be put at risk should the country, finally, decide against a European destiny symbolized by euro membership as much as by defence integration. And a nagging fear began to stir amongst thoughtful Westminster politicians that should London take a final decision to stay out of the euro – a move that would edge the country towards leaving the EU altogether – Scotland might well seek to remain in the EU and to join the currency zone. (Also, in any referendum on the single currency England and Scotland might well vote for different outcomes: England voting 'no' and Scotland voting 'yes'.) Should Britain as a whole decide to stay out of the new Europe then there is little doubt that Scottish nationalists (which might even include a Labour breakaway to join the Scottish National Party) would begin to argue that Scotland's future prosperity demanded it join the euro, and that it could only pursue this overriding objective by securing independence. Such an independence movement, arguing that Scotland's economic future was more secure in Europe than with England, could grow rapidly, gaining Scottish independence by securing either a majority in the Scottish Parliament or a majority of Scottish MPs in the Westminster Parliament. In any event, in the aftermath of a UK decision to stay out of the euro, the Scottish Parliament would find itself in a most intriguing – and dramatic – position. If the Scots had voted to join the euro (or had pro-euro opinion poll majorities), then the Parliament in Edinburgh might even simply apply to join the Euro-zone, effectively declaring independence in the process.

Should it become clear that, following a 'no' vote in a referendum or the election of a Conservative government in Westminster, the UK, having set its face against the EU, then finds itself on the way out of the EU altogether, then the Scottish Parliament (no matter its legal relationship to Westminster) would become the focus of Scottish destiny. It could organize its own referendum and make its own deals with Brussels. There are, intriguingly, no provisions in any EU treaty for accession of a 'successor state' (that is, a part of an existing state joining or remaining in after another part has left the EU). So, the most likely outcome of this drama would be that Scotland would seek to change unions – to leave the UK union and apply to become a new member state of the EU. And, like the other new members in Eastern Europe, it would join the Euro-zone at the same time as it joined the Union.

Scotland would certainly meet the political tests of membership of the EU, and it would be in much better economic shape – that is, more 'convergent' – than many of the new member states from Eastern Europe. It could become a full member state of the EU within a year of opening negotiations. And for the English political elite who had kept Britain out of the Euro-zone, the irony of this scenario would be overwhelming: the price for staying out, of retaining British 'sovereignty', would be the break-up of the UK itself.

Outriders of the Super-State

If the core puts pressure on the peripheral states by acting as a magnet, what of those states, or parts of states, which finally decide to stay outside of the new superpower? There will not be many of them. The European Union of 25 now includes every European nation state west of Romania except Norway, Switzerland and the states of the former Yugoslavia (some of which may well apply for membership); most are there to stay. But what becomes of any future outriders? Of England? Or Norway? Or Denmark? Or, even Poland, should it find the going too tough? Each will have special circumstances, and special reasons, for staying outside the superpower. Some, like Denmark, may try to stay out of the euro, but should Sweden ultimately join the core, then Denmark may find life outside too harsh. The Poles, rather like the East German Länder after they joined the Federal Republic, may well revolt against the initial costs of joining but, over time, will find themselves increasingly dependent on the markets and economy of the core, and may find the prospect of leaving even harsher.

Only in Norway and England do some of the leadership groups contemplate a long-term outrider strategy. In Norway, the huge oil income will certainly allow the country to prosper as an outrider for some time to come. In England (with or without Scotland) many anti-euro advocates see the country as big enough to go it alone. They are inspired by Churchill's famous aphorism that if Britain ever has to 'choose between Europe and the Open Sea, then she will always choose the Open Sea'. This 'Open Sea' school would have the UK become, like the East Asians, a 'tiger economy', a 'free-market' and 'free-trading' independent player, free to make money in the global system. This vision of the English future sees the UK as 'large enough to continue to be an independent country with representation in a number of international fora and trading with the five continents of the world'.[9] This romantic, almost schoolboy, vision, plays upon well-established, nostalgic images of seafaring and empire, and it conjures up a people on the verge of an Elizabethan-like new global role. This 'offshore' strategy may, though, represent a real option for England and the English people – but not quite the one foreseen by the 'Open Sea' advocates. It would mean the full, unprotected immersion of the country and its 45 million people into the global economic system. The small size of England (or the UK) would mean that its political authorities, unlike the EU authorities, would have no option but to obey the imperatives of raw, unconstrained global capitalism. In return for attracting global capital, the country (and any other outrider country) would need to constantly renew its 'competitiveness' – that is, by lower and lower taxes and public spending (thus, lower public provision of health care, education and skills) and greater and greater 'flexibility' in its labour market (meaning more lower paid, part-time jobs) – leading inevitably, to increasing inequality and social division.[10]

Into the American Orbit?

This 'offshore' option for England will, inevitably, lead the country, and any other outrider, further and further into the American orbit. One of Britain's leading Euro-sceptics, Tory MP John Redwood, has suggested that Britain 'could try to become the 51st state of the American Union'.[11] But a British application to join the USA – either as one state or as four – if not seen in Washington as utterly facetious, is still likely to be in vain. The USA has consistently refused such overtures, even including the idea of a relatively loose English-speaking Union – between the USA, Britain and some of the dominions – which was floated in the aftermath of the Second World War. The USA is not seeking to add to its 50 states and, unlike the EU, has no constitutional provision for expansion. (Previous expansions have only added to the union existing territories, not existing nation states.) No matter the closeness of any future 'special relationship', the British would have no seats in the Senate, the House of Representatives or on the Federal Reserve Board; British voters would have no say in the election of a president; nor would British judges sit on the Supreme Court.[12]

This future for England would leave her fully exposed to all the economic forces of American-led market globalization and make her utterly dependent upon the USA for her security. Yet she would have no vote in Washington, where her destiny would be decided. Such a future would amount to the modern equivalent of 'taxation without representation'. Assuming Scotland would not accept such an indignity, England (and Wales) would, to all intents and purposes, then become a satellite within the American empire. In the greatest role reversal of all time, England would become an American colony.

There are worse fates. But, what, though, would be England's fate should the USA start reviewing its world role and retrenching? American history reveals strong isolationist impulses, a people uncomfortable with global involvement and certainly with an overt imperial role. The cold-war role of global involvement may yet be an aberration, particularly if economic globalization has run its course. A future 'Fortress America' cannot be totally discounted – for, after the first flush of reaction to the terrorist threat, the USA could still decide that it is seriously overstretched with too small a population and an insufficient economic base to take on the exacting role of world policeman.

Such a 'Fortress America' would cut back its overseas military commitments, content itself with building a National Missile Defence and only intervene in the rest of the world – selectively, powerfully, maybe pre-emptively – when 'rogue states' appear to threaten its homeland. As part of this package, the USA might well revert to a form of traditional trade protectionism.

In such an outcome, any country 'offshore' of the EU – not least still 'sovereign' England – would be in serious trouble. Outside the single currency, and marginalized in the single market, her exports to the European mainland would rapidly decline; having adopted the US economic model she would have abandoned EU-type measures of social protection. Yet, she would no longer have real access to the American market which her exports, economic growth and standard of living would be dependent upon. Caught between the two superpowers, and outside the two economic fortresses, the 'offshore' country would witness a rapid decline in living standards. This potential fate is what will, sooner or later, carry the outriders into the new superpower.

6

A Country Called 'Europe'

Identity and Democracy in an Americanized World

In November 1993, Jacques Delors was having one of his regular bouts of anxiety about the future of his great European project. He had just pulled off his greatest coup – the plan for a single currency – but he still felt that Europe was stalling. And he went onto the French radio station RTL to wonder aloud whether Europe could ever become a force on the world stage to rival America; ever, that is, become more than just a free-trade area. Would it, he asked, ever have 'a soul… a conscience… a political will?'[1]

A decade later, even after the clear success of the single currency, Europeans were still asking: are we any nearer to being 'one people', that is the 'one people' that the British, Germans, French, even Russians, Chinese and Americans believe they are?

Europe certainly had all the symbols of unity to go with its single currency and market. It had a flag, an anthem, a hugely popular football league (the Champions League) and was even negotiating a written constitution. But could it build on these to develop Jacques Delors' deeper concept of a European 'soul', or what England's leading Europeanist, Timothy Garton Ash, has called a 'sixth sense' of being European?[2] In other words, can Europe develop a common identity? Can it become a country? Will a future European Henry

Clay ever be able to say, like the US senator in 1848, 'The union, sir, is my country.'

By the turn of the century, though, Jacques Delors had little reason to worry. For, in the modern world, a European superpower may not need its people to feel 'as one' in order for it to act on the world stage. In other words, workable common European governance can, for a time at least, go hand in hand with strong national identities – as long, that is, as the still strong nations of Europe see the EU as a friend and see a united Europe as more able to further their interests and values than they, individually, can do themselves. The classic irony at work here was spotted and articulated by Professor Alan Milward in his bestselling book in the early 1990s, when he argued that, contrary to myth, European unity, rather than destroying the European nation states, would 'rescue' them.[3]

Rescue them, that is, from their growing impotence. For in the face of the globalized (and, within it, the Americanized) world that was engulfing them, some of Europe's most encrusted nationalists began to see that only Europe had the size and power to stand against these immense pressures. During the 1990s, even the most self-conscious of all the European nations, France, began to realize that French identity could only be protected by Europe. In its long-running battle with Americanized global culture – whether over films or food – many French men and women began to believe that it was only the strength of a wider, united Europe that allowed it to properly resist. The French sense of nation, and national pride, was immeasurably boosted during France's stand against the USA over Iraq; but it was bought at the price of France having to ditch residual Gaullism by working in a wider context, this time closely with Germany. And as the EU began winning some of its transatlantic trade wars (particularly the steel tariffs conflict resolved in December 2003), the British as well as French, the Dutch as well as the Germans saw the value, to them, of Europe 'acting as one' in the world.

In the long run, though, a European superpower, in order to act in the world, needs more than just cooperation from its component nationalities. It needs, no matter how weakly held, a common, integrated identity, that 'sixth sense' of being European, and of belonging. For, only such a sense of common identity can carry the superpower through bad times as well as good, can secure acquiescence in unpopular decisions as well as support for popular ones. The contrasting histories of the two global superpowers of the late twentieth century tell the tale. Whereas the USA had successfully created a common sense of being American (an American patriotism), the USSR was ultimately unable to do the same. 'Soviet man' and 'Soviet woman' could not transcend the ethnic and religious divides, and the union buckled and broke up under economic and foreign policy failure.

But how strong does this common identity need to be? In fact, who will die for Europe? And 'who will feel European in the depths of their being, and… will willingly sacrifice themselves for so abstract an ideal?'[4] That countless millions have risked their lives, and millions have died in rivers of blood, in the service of Europe's old nation states, is often seen as a measure of loyalty that modern Europe simply cannot induce. But, in today's world, the kind of sacrifices associated with the collective sentiments of nationalism in First World War trench warfare or big battles like Stalingrad and El Alamein are no longer called for. Modern superpowers, unlike old-fashioned nations, do not need to rely so much on common feelings, or a common willingness to sacrifice, and do not have to whip up intense collective sentiment (at least of the patriotic kind that during the First World War terrorized men not at the front with the infamous white feathers). Indeed, nowadays, the general willingness to sacrifice money, let alone life, has virtually disappeared altogether, and patriotic sentiment, such as it is, is essentially either superficial or contrived and phoney, based largely on a vicarious sense of valour carried forward for television entertainment.

Rather, today, a superpower needs only to be able to resource operations (and research and technology) and to pay professionals to carry out the assigned unpleasant tasks. With nuclear weapons as a deterrent and force projection as forward strategy, it is only light, or lightish, professional forces (essentially mercenaries wielding hi-tech instruments) that are needed. The American crews who carried out the air assaults on Serbia, flying directly to their targets in Europe from home bases in the Carolinas, and even the troops in real fighting situations in Iraq, saw their jobs rather like professionals everywhere – as not much to do with 'country' and 'sacrifice', and more to do with getting a job done.

2025: Europe a Nation?

Will the mere act of living within the space of a super-state help over time to forge a common European identity? Will Europe's single currency – like its flag, but much more potent – have an effect over time upon identity? Currencies have an emotional and historical content. One of Italy's leading Europeanists, Tomasso Padoa Schioppa, has said that the euro is so fundamental, that 'the single currency is only comparable to the single army.'[5] For postwar Germans, the 'mighty Deutschmark' and the Bundesbank were symbols of successful nationhood. For the British, the pound sterling was 'like the English landscape… [It] has evolved over the centuries, reflecting and sometimes leading to changes in the nation's history' and it generated 'a sense of unchanging stability of fundamental importance to the national psyche'.[6] As with the Deutschmark and sterling, so with the euro; and, as one of the EU's top former diplomats, Roy Denman, has pointed out, Europeans 'now carry with them every day a piece of Europe' and 'on the value of these notes and coins depends their prosperity'.[7]

The euro will also become a symbol of Europe's arrival on the world scene as a power to match the USA. The US dollar is one of the cornerstones of US power in the world; and as the euro goes head to head with the dollar in the world markets, and as a reserve currency, it becomes Europe's champion. Its value against the dollar has serious economic implications, for a rising euro can be a problem, particularly for Europe's exporters to the USA. But, now that the euro is a European virility symbol, a test of how superpower Europe is doing in the transatlantic contest, a high euro is good for confidence. And confidence is good for European unity.

In this contest with the dollar, the euro will provide Europeans with the all-important sense of being on the same team, or in the same boat, of being tied to the same economic future, the same destiny. And a sense of shared destiny helps Europe's diverse and disparate peoples to allow a single captain to steer the boat. Yet nothing succeeds like success, and much will depend on the strength of the boat, the accuracy of its navigation and whether, in the Atlantic race, it continues to do well.

Rights can be as important as money as a unifier – particularly if Europe is seen as protecting the rights of all Europeans, who can appeal over the heads of their national systems to a common higher court. One of Europe's foremost federalists, Euro-MP Andrew Duff, sees the creation of an EU regime of rights as a crucial building-block in the creation of what he calls a 'European federal society'.[8]

But in the creation of 'a country called Europe', more than governance is involved. Deeper questions such as history, language and security arise. In the forging of nations great myths are created around stories, not always wholly accurate, of common history, of great events and heroes, of a shared past, often of shared struggle. And Europe has a problem here, for it is not easy for Europe's builders to construct a European identity through its history. As Anthony Smith argues, Europe has few shared memories and meanings, few common meanings and myths; it is without common 'shrines and ceremonies and monuments'. (He suggests that St Pauls or Les Invalids are too national, and that Rome no longer commands the hearts and minds of Northern Europeans; that artists are either international, like Shakespeare, or national; and that there are no pan-European heroes.)[9] Although today's Europeans hold in their heads a general idea that there exists a shared history of 'European civilization', this history is replete with wars and imperial conquest, both of which, although 'shared experiences', bitterly divided Europeans rather than uniting them.

There is a sense, though, in which civil wars, although they initially fracture nations, also create nations – by resolving, usually in the manner dictated by the victors and accepted by the losers, the overall unity and direction of the total society. The divided country later looks back on its civil war as a great national event, as a crossroads, a milestone in the making of the country. France, through its revolution, defined itself as a modern, liberal society; England, following the civil war in the seventeenth century, as individualist, protestant and parliamentary; and the USA, following its own civil war between the North and South, as federal, commercial and free. As for Europe, future historians may yet point to its own great 'civil war', stretching from 1914 through to 1945, and tell the story of a bitter and bloody internal conflict that finally set Europe on the path to a united liberal democracy.

In building identity, a united Europe is essentially starting from scratch. Any future common identity simply cannot rely upon the history of its nation states, but rather will need to draw on its own short history, and future events yet unseen. Yet, one such event may have happened already, for the 2002–2003 European split with the USA over Iraq has left an indelible mark. In the creation of the political identity of nations, the struggle for 'independence' is a powerful mythic force; and a history of common political struggle against an oppressor is a great nation-builder.[10] The British state largely defined itself by its history of independence, first from Rome and then from continental Europe as a whole; the founding fathers of the American republic had, as one historian put it 'the immeasurable advantage that theirs was a project not just of invention but also of independence'.[11] Also, many ex-colonial states – including large and diverse nations like India – have created nationhood around the idea of a common achievement of independence, the throwing off of the yoke of a common foe.

Europe's future myth-makers might well start from this vantage point, as they write a story of the peaceful birth of a European super-state as it took hold of its 'independence', and threw off the yoke of the American 'empire'.

As superpower Europe emerges, and inevitably separates itself from the USA, then America could take on the new role of Europe's 'other' – the Americans would become the 'them' that defines the Europeans as the 'us', just as, for two centuries, Europe was 'the other' that defined America.[12] The USA, though, would never be the primary 'other', for Europeans may well revert to its oldest 'other' of all – Islam. A continuing 'war on terrorism', tensions between the West and Islam and the West and the Arab world, and trouble on Europe's borders with Islam, could all conspire to create in European minds a clear and present 'other' – as could future non-integrated Islamic populations in European cities, in Bradford or Berlin or Marseilles. The events of 11 September 2001 provided a transcendent cause, a common fear and a common enemy, around which most Europeans, irrespective of nationality, could unite. Within days of the atrocity the EU had its unspoken 'other' – radical, fundamentalist Islam. It quickly managed to engineer a huge leap forward in so-called second-pillar integration – by securing a common European arrest warrant, a common definition of terrorism and agreed measures to freeze assets as well as enhanced intelligence sharing – which brought the long-awaited European FBI that much closer. Suddenly, Europeans were all in the same boat, a single, powerful vessel – protecting a common civilization and common ideals from an alien force. (And such was the initial mood of European solidarity induced by the fears around 9/11 that even the British Foreign Secretary could rethink the validity of national sovereignty: 'The truth is,' he intoned, 'that 'sovereignty' has never been absolute', and that 'by sharing sovereignty a people may end up with more, not less, independence of action, more not less internal self-government and more, not less control over their lives.')[13]

In the history of nations, common identity has been created by the growing ability of people to communicate with each other. It took the revolution of the printing press to begin the creation of English national consciousness. Later, in the eighteenth century, in a quantum leap in the technology of communications, the ideas and images, the manners and codes which were to serve as the common culture of the new nation state were transmitted from one end of the islands to another. And, later still, that other huge technological leap, television, was hugely powerful in sustaining the common culture way past its sell-by date.[14] And in the twentieth century, mass communications and mass media made the US nation out of a continent. From the 1920s onwards, and particularly during the Roosevelt presidency, radio linked the country from Maine to California and Hollywood set the images and values for the new nation. Following the Second World War, television's massive penetration of society unified the culture. 200 million people across 3,000 miles were moulded by shared events, shared images and shared values.

It will take the media to make a country out of Europe too, to bind Europeans together through a common news space, common symbols and a common language – a common demos. But the organization of Europe's media is Europe's Achilles' heel. By comparison, the USA has a media fit for a superpower. Since the Second World War, more than any other US institution, its continent-wide television networks have unified its disparate and far-flung people into a common demos. To unite California and New York, Texas and Michigan, and bring them into one national political discourse would, as recently as the 1920s, have been thought a near-impossible task. And America's powerful movie industry, together with its sitcoms, relentlessly propagates the American way of life, reinforcing its values by simple, strong imagery of good (through heroes) and bad (through villains). The American media industry has a worldwide reach together with a single, simple political message (about freedom and democracy).

For highly practical reasons, the likelihood is that Europe will continue well into the next century to be divided into separate mass media markets – based primarily upon language. A Europe-wide mass media operating in a Europe-wide single market is a distant prospect. With European television and newspapers continuing to cater to their existing national markets in their national language, the media, without anyone necessarily willing it, will remain a bastion of national (and nationalist) identity. The growth of big pan-European media conglomerates (like Bertelsmann) will, over time, lessen the nationalist outlook, but profits will continue to lie (unlike in many other businesses) in exploiting national markets only.

There will, of course, be powerful countervailing forces. Businesses, through their advertisers, wanting to do business in the single market, will place pressure in a unifying direction. But all this will take time, and, in the short run, all the editorial and cultural pressures (as well as the stubbornly provincial culture of journalism) will be to appeal to existing 'national' markets.

Of course, Europe's federal authorities can try to mitigate this media bias by providing powerful unifying imagery for the media to use. The euro is a powerful media itself; but the attractive blue and yellow European flag and the powerful and evocative European anthem are underused at international sporting and entertainment events. And nothing will create a sense of European common identity more effectively than the creation of a common European sports team in competition with other continents. Europe's, and the world's, media would be fascinated by a single European Olympic team competing for Gold Medals with the Americans and Russians every four years. Already Golf's Ryder Cup – a transatlantic contest between a European team and an American – is, surprisingly for such a sedate game, one of the most exciting and patriotic occasions in all of sport.

Ultimately, but some time off, the single market itself will bring forth a Europe-wide print media which publishes the same newspaper with the same images and the same news stories, making them available to all EU citizens every day, but produced in separate languages – a kind of European *USA Today*. Europeans in Europe will then have the same service provided for Americans in Europe by the *International Herald Tribune*. A truly European CNN – with separate-language television companies drawing upon the same European and global news – would also help forward a common identity.

Yet, even if Europe's media were to become a force for European unity, Europe still has to confront the language problem. In pubs and clubs and cafés throughout the continent, wisdom still has it that Europe's separate languages remain the great, unscaleable barrier to European nationhood – and that it is a common language that, ultimately, made the USA possible but makes the USE still but a dream. But, in what amounts to the greatest unspoken reality – and the largest taboo subject – the European continent does in fact possess a common language. It is English! And English is, more powerfully even than economics and politics, pushing forward European cultural unity. English is by far the leading second language of Europe. It is the language in which Europeans conduct international business, it is the language of science and trade and air traffic. It – or its American variant – is spoken by almost all of Europe's educated elites, and by anyone seeking foreign and global contacts. English is widely spoken throughout Northern Europe, in Germany, Benelux and Scandinavia, as well as Britain and Ireland, and is even growing rapidly in France. For political reasons – and because of Brussels' politesse (to the French) – it will never be declared the official language of the EU, but within a matter of decades it could become Europe's unofficial language. The time is not far off when most Europeans with a higher education degree will speak passable English – and then language will become Europe's unifier rather than a divider, perhaps even the principal engine of European unity and nationhood. (Perversely, it may well be the much-derided Americanization of European culture – the so called 'Coca-Cola effect' – which integrationists can thank for this vast increase in the common language of spoken and written English throughout the continent.)

Europe's languages are a rich aspect of diversity, but they also present Europe with a huge democratic problem. For, whilst Europe's educated elites will be increasingly unified by their use of a single second language, Europe's less educated peoples will remain stuck in their nation-state linguistic laagers. The whole European federal level may then become an alien world to Europe's masses (much more so than Washington is to the American masses). This, potentially, is Europe's greatest democratic deficit of all; it can only be solved by the continued task of wider and wider education.

Europe's 'Big Idea'

For federalists, whilst the nature of Europe's media is a minus, Europe's message is a plus. Superpowers are built on more than power alone – they need to attract as well as impress. The two world superpowers of the twentieth century both had a big attractive idea: the Soviets had communism; the Americans had freedom. And it was these big ideas that both unified their own people and attracted millions around the world to their cause. Yet the Soviet idea collapsed amongst the Gulag camps and 1980s economic meltdown; and the American idea is today tattered and tottering, questioned around the world as never before. Not all Europeans may realize it, but their new Europe may already be filling the vacuum. For a uniting Europe is beginning to develop its own new big unifying idea that can provide the Union with a common rallying point and ideology; and which is as distinctive and powerful in its appeal as anything that has gone before. It is an idea which, as the twenty-first century unfolds, will both challenge the values of the American empire, and may even help redefine the West in the minds of the world's peoples.

This ideology of Europe is often called 'social Europe' or 'social capitalism', and it unites most of Europe's leading political players (Christian and Social Democrats, conservatives, liberals and moderate socialists alike). It amounts to a social and economic order for Europe that breaks with the American *idée fixe* about the free market. 'Social Europe' places limits on the market – particularly the market for labour – and on 'hire and fire' and 'low costs at any price' capitalism. It tolerates higher taxes – in order to secure for Europeans comprehensive welfare provision. It establishes workers rights and participation – in order to treat people with dignity (and not as chattels) in the workplace.

Above all, it believes that Europeans, whilst not abandoning the profit motive or private ownership, can provide for much more equality and social civility than does the US model. Europe's way, after the market extremism of the 1980s and 1990s, will bring the state back into a role in economic life. It will no longer believe, as did Europe's old socialists, in the moral superiority of the state – but nor in its moral inferiority! It sees a strong, unobtrusive state as the only way to create an environment (and food and drink) fit for humans and as the best way to defend its citizens. It is all about preserving – in the face of Wall Street-led global pressures – the balance between state and market, public and private. It is about placing limits on global corporations, and about using the only tool available to counter global capital – the power of government, or the state. It is about fair trade not free trade. And, most crucially of all, it is about rejecting the luxury that 'small is beautiful', and instead understanding that in today's world only a superpower and super-state can possess the power to negotiate with and regulate global capital and secure decent, humane, social conditions and wages for its people. In short, Europe's big idea is to place 'capitalism at the service of humans' not the other way round. And to show the world (and a sceptical America) that this kind of 'social capitalism' can actually work – can produce the goods.

During the 1990s, Wall Street (and Washington) watched the bedding in of Europe's 'social model' with increasing anxiety. Their critiques, sometimes surprisingly strong, even bitter, ranged from derisive (Europe's economy was 'sclerotic') to dismissive (the welfare states were 'inefficient' and hobbling to growth). The Wall Street globalist gospel proclaimed that the living standards of the peoples of the European Union were far too high to be sustainable in the early twenty-first century. Europe was, quite simply, uncompetitive in the global economy – its labour unions, welfare states, maximalist governments with high levels of public expenditure and high tax rates and social costs, could not possibly be sustained. A typical US assessment at the time was outlined by journalism's foremost and persistent American Euro-sceptic, John Vinocur of the *International Herald Tribune*. Europe, he said, creates

> more inter-governmental politics, more committees, more subsidies (for European culture), more agencies (a police force, a European prosecutor), more rules (harmonization of corporate taxes), more restrictions (on tax advantages in individual member countries and on trade competition in the world beyond), and a forced melting-pot initiative like a transnational multilingual European television network.[15]

Wall Street's fear was (and is) that Europe's social capitalism could take off. After all, a model in which global corporations and capital makes good money but at the same time does so on terms set by Europe's political communities – in which real full-time, benefited employment remains high and welfare states are protected – could become seriously alluring. And, not just to Europeans. Should the European model survive and flourish, then the rawer US style capitalism will lose its lustre – particularly amongst its own people back home in the USA, perhaps even leading to a change in American public opinion. In a huge reversal, for the very first time in American history, Europe would provide the model for Americans to follow.

Should the USA follow Europe in limiting the dominion of corporate capital then globalization would, to all intents and purposes, be dead. The system in which capital runs free around 'one world' seeking lower and lower costs will then transmute into one in which capital finds that it has to negotiate with a number of super-states (and release resources for public services and welfare). Instead of being able to dictate to local governments and local peoples, new rules of the economic game – ones that keep capitalism as an economic engine but are much more friendly to equality, and community – will come into play. And as these regional blocs – or super-states – start to emerge then the power game between global capital and the political community starts tilting back in favour of politics, and, should the super-states start cooperating, then the world will edge nearer to some form of global governance able to match global economics.

This was (is) a fearsome prospect in Wall Street. So, in order to protect themselves against such a contagion, global corporate interests in the USA, with Washington's full backing, and with considerable support from some sympathetic businesses and governments within the EU, are engaged in a real struggle to derail Europe's attempt at this new geo-economic settlement – and, ultimately, they will try to destabilize it. Europe's social-democratic model can be expected to be subjected to considerable pressure from both sides of the Atlantic.

The language of this counter-challenge is 'reform'. And, by the late 1990s, 'reformers' in Europe, led by British Prime Minister Blair and Spanish Prime Minister Aznar, began to make Wall Street's case. But they were long on rhetoric and short on success. A Thatcherite-style act of surgery which would cut into the 'social model' was simply out of the question and no serious continental European leader even began to suggest that Europe's public sector, its welfare states, its regulatory regimes and its labour and employment standards should fall to the level of those of the USA. And anyone who proposed such surgery would simply lose office.

'Core Europe' will continue to stand by the social model. From French technocrats, to Brussels civil servants, to German trade union leaders, all have an interest in preserving it. Politically, Berlin and Paris act almost as one in supporting the model. Conservative French President Jacques Chirac wanted there to be 'no question of importing the UK social model into France'.[16] Germany too

– whether a Christian Democrat or Social Democrat-led coalition rules in Berlin – is likely to continue to support all the main features of the European social democratic model: regulated labour markets, a role for trade unions, a capitalist-public mixed economy with levels of taxation (including social costs on business) set to meet the expenditure of established social provision.

By the turn of the millennium, Europe had arrived at the hard political point where concrete interests were beginning to resist the markets. No European electorate would tolerate dismantling its welfare state, just as, in the USA, the corporations would not tolerate weakening the market system, and this put the two systems on a collision course. By contrast with continental Europe, the USA (in the 1970s) and Britain (in the 1980s) had been able to let global capital fully marketize their economies without revolt. Britain's revolution was carried through by a combination of ruthlessly centralized government, Margaret Thatcher's resolve and a then still deferential people and culture. The USA had begun to dismantle its welfare social capitalism much earlier – following the defeat of LBJ's 'Great Society' in the late 1960s. And, in a later burst, it bowed to global capital when US-based corporations began downsizing their over-priced home plants and offices during the 1980s. Unlike the Europeans, the Americans could 'globalize without revolt', but for a simple reason: Americans were willing to tolerate high levels of inequality amongst their peoples. The market mentality ruled – the view that the poverty of the inner cities and the part-time, low-pay, low-welfare America are a price worth paying for a broader free and dynamic economy.

So, it now seems inevitable that in the early decades of the twenty-first century a great world drama is about to be played out in a battle between American and European capitalism – between what *Time* magazine has dubbed the 'ruthless capitalism' of the USA and Euroland's 'more caring but costly' social model. And, it is a battle royal: which can only end with one side victorious and the other needing to adapt to the other.

For Europe's social capitalism, it has become a matter of survival. Europe either takes on, and tames, the forces of globalization or it is overwhelmed by them. If its resistance fails, then Europe's road will lead directly to American-style entrenched inequality with super-rich ghettos, a squeezed, insecure, middle class and glaring inner-city poverty, violence and crime.[17] It is no exaggeration to suggest that the outcome of this historic contest will determine the course of western economic history and the way of life, not only of the European peoples, but of the West, including the USA – where those who oppose the rawer capitalist experiment are laying low and awaiting the outcome of the contest.

Who will win? Already there are very definite signs that Europe may prevail. Wall Street sages have been predicting a dire future for 'sclerotic' Europe for many years; but as every year passes Europe's living standards *do not* fall and its societies *do not* become more divided. This is a victory. For it means that in the real world, on the ground, the famed 'manic logic of global capitalism' may no longer be working its full will on everything that gets in its way – that the 'wondrous machine' may already have stalled. There may, contrary to Wall Street, be nothing inevitable about market globalization – and new rules of engagement between global markets and super-states may already have come into effect.[18]

Europe's leverage remains its huge single market, arguably the largest and most prosperous in the world, to which the global corporations seek access as a strategic priority. This strategic leverage which the single market gives to Europe was on display as early as July 1997 when, in a landmark contest, the European Union went head to head with the mighty global Boeing corporation over the social consequences of its merger with McDonnell Douglas. The EU threatened to fine the new giant ten per cent of its revenues per year, and primarily because of its need for access to the European market. Boeing, after initially refusing, finally agreed to the EU's conditions. The lesson for global corporations was clear: if you want to do business in Europe then you need to help pay for Europe's priorities – like, for instance, security in employment, adequate pensions, welfare and a decent environment – and even at the cost of marginally higher taxes, marginally higher costs and, maybe even, for a time, marginally lower growth.

Of course, European business cannot possibly compete with US businesses in low costs – in low taxes for health, pensions and the like – and in its quick 'hire and fire' labour policies. This US advantage, though, will only be at the margin; it will not lead to a stampede of capital. And the advantage will be pyrrhic: capital, if it is truly to compete globally, will press Americans into lower and lower social costs (taxes and pensions) and wages, and all at the price of an increasingly divided and policed (and imprisoned)

US society in which the number of losers grows and the number of winners declines.

Also, after the 2001–2002 stock market collapse, large questions were beginning to hang over US-style financial capitalism. The Wall Street system was looking increasingly and inherently less stable than its European capitalist sister, much more subject to hype and counter-hype, to mood and to bull and bear stampedes. And as American commentator Jim Hoagland has reported, official Washington, still living under the conventional wisdom of globalism, is having trouble taking on board the fact that the much maligned welfare states of Europe are becoming a 'zone of relative currency stability and a source of growth'.[19]

Two or so years into the crash, Main Street USA (if not Wall Street) was joining the European publics and becoming increasingly worried about job insecurity. The 2002 Enron and Arthur Anderson scandals further tarnished the image of big corporate America – as did the propensity of American corporations to shift capital, and jobs, to low-cost areas. But so strong was the hold of market ideology in the USA that, by the summer of 2003, there was still no sign of real disenchantment with the 'American model' and certainly no movement to 'reform' it. The Democratic opposition, concentrating on attacking President Bush for cutting taxes for the rich, raised few questions about the 'American model' itself. And amongst Americans who knew about, and followed, the European economy and its 'social model', the jury was still out. In Washington and New York, there was only a slight sense of an imminent economic power shift across the Atlantic from America to Europe.

Europe's challenge to the USA is about more than an alternative capitalist 'economic model'. The core idea of the coming Europe – one that will radically distinguish it from that of the USA – is to seek to promote prosperity and creativity by limiting market forces rather than unleashing them. Capitalism should be constrained, not abolished. Jacques Delors once set the compass for this 'social Europe' by suggesting that Europe should fit somewhere between the extremes of Japan and the USA; that it should seek 'balance between the individual and society' – 'more space for the individual to blossom than in Japan', but more 'civitas' and 'social' than in the USA.[20]

Its visionary aspect sees a quantum leap in civilized human development, the creation of a society that will allow the individual to flourish by lifting the oppressive anxiety and insecurity which unbridled global corporate capitalism breeds in millions, reducing them to 'wage slaves in the lands of liberty and prosperity' reliant only on small incomes, diminishing welfare and disappearing pensions.

A key element of the 'social model' are new 'human' policies in the workplace. In 2000, France introduced the 35-hour week for large companies, and, although it was greeted with much scepticism by supporters of the 'Anglo-Saxon' model, it has caught on. In Germany, long derided by Wall Street and its friends for its long holidays, companies remain attracted to the idea that a reduced working week can deliver higher productivity per labour unit. Shorter working hours, which started off in Germany as work-sharing schemes set up to avert lay-offs during the early 1990s, have become a key attribute of a humane twenty-first-century lifestyle.

This 'Slow and Easy' capitalism – not just shorter hours per week, but longer vacations, more available full-time jobs (with, where appropriate, full social security and medical cover) – could create working conditions where employees, whilst still improving their skills and remaining competitive, are not constantly looking over their shoulders at competitors, not in constant fear of losing their jobs, are not run off their feet, blighted by stress and early burnout. Should the EU continue with these social policies, it could begin a revolutionary process of putting money in its proper place. For those who had little of it, money was a great liberator; and it was also a progressive force – and, in Europe, a destroyer of old-fashioned social hierarchies. Yet the acquisition of money has taken over from quality of life as a goal and value in itself; and Europe's new direction can help restore perspective.

Europe, through its social model, can also protect civilized values and quality in leisure, entertainment and media. Market values have helped forward great advances in fast food and mass culture but, as they appeal to the lowest common denominator, they cannot help but 'dumb down' standards and, over time, the 'discerning consumer' becomes the 'bland moron'. Europe's social model – in which the state intervenes in the market where it fails – can create an environment, including niche markets, for civilized, quality living, for 'slow food' and cultivated drinking, and, crucially, for some kind of standards in media, television and cinema. It is an awkward fact, but media 'dumbing down' now seems unstoppable in market systems – as trends in British newspapers and American television amply testify. Europe's social ideal has fewer hang-ups about using the state (national, regional and local) to limit the 'dumbing down' pressures in the private sector.

Building something new – like the European Union – provides those engaged in the task with a huge advantage. They can learn from the mistakes, and build on the success, of others, and can abandon some ideas and refocus others. And their greatest opportunity lies in reanimating the tattered western ideal of democracy. During the 1980s and 1990s, the victory of market systems and market values has slowly but surely reduced the West's historic 'democratic idea' to little more than mere catering to mass tastes and opinions.

In this extreme market democracy, which is now operating freely in all walks of life in the Anglo-American economies, citizenship has been replaced by consumerism, the sovereignty of the people by a levelling down – in politics, arts, entertainment, indeed in virtually all areas of life – to a banal lowest common denominator.[21]

Because Europe puts boundaries around the role and reach of the market – particularly the global market – it has a real opportunity to develop a revived democracy in which citizenship can replace mass consumerism – in which the ideals of human merit and human rights are placed above commercially manipulated mass tastes and opinions. Such could be a real European contribution to a renewal of the powerful, but increasingly frayed, democratic reality of the West.

Europe has an advantage here because, for various reasons (not all laudatory), its political cultures have not let the market and mass democracy run free. French governance in particular has kept a meritocratic brake on mass democracy, and meritocratic instincts can also be seen in the high level of education and expertise in the European Commission in Brussels. The French and German admiration of intellectuality and intellectuals – a view not shared in the USA or Britain (where there is an innate suspicion of intellectualism) – has survived into the era of democracy, and it places another break on the tyranny of mass tastes.[22]

A Secular, Democratic Homeland

By the turn of the century, as well as 'social Europe' acting as a unifier, Europe was also beginning to see itself as a bastion of secular values

– as a secular oasis surrounded by a fundamentalist world. After 9/11, Europe's assertion of secular values – the separation of church and state – was also becoming a defining distinction between Europe and the USA. For some time, Christian fundamentalism had been informing aspects of US foreign policy. Washington had punished and rewarded less developed countries according to their abortion laws, and US support for the hardline Israeli government of Ariel Sharon was in part a product of the influence of the southern Christian right (and biblical prophecies about Israel and the second coming). And, in 2003, the US government entered the European debate when it criticized the President of France after he had announced plans to ban the wearing of 'ostentatious religious symbols' such as Islamic headscarves, Jewish skullcaps and large Christian crosses in French schools as part of a process of separation of church and state. Ambassador John Hanford, in an obvious rebuke, said 'our [US] hope is religious freedom would be non-negotiable.'[23] And even the relatively liberal *New York Times* chided Europe for what it called the continent's growing 'Secular Fundamentalism'.

Europeans were still going to church in the new century, but in fewer and fewer numbers; and, in reality, whether they were French or Italian Catholics, English Episcopals or German Lutherans, their religiosity was weak and they were increasingly embracing secular values. Large sections of European life were overtly secular and completely free from fundamentalist influence. Europe's Muslim populations were the major source of fundamentalism in Europe, but they simply did not have the same kind of purchase on political power as did the Christian fundamentalists in the USA.

Secular Europe will have real advantages in an increasingly fundamentalist world. It can become a continent where reason and science – drawing on the principles of Europe's earlier Enlightenment – can flourish, enhancing medicine, the environment and human rights. Whereas other powers – even the USA – may face religiously based objections to real advances in health care (produced by genetics) and faith-based opposition to abortion, Europe can withstand such self-defeating pressures. September 11th, widely interpreted in Europe as an act of fundamentalist-inspired religious violence, increased European awareness of its secular way of life – and the need to defend it. Professor Fred Halliday of the London School of Economics echoed a growing European sentiment when he declared that 'fundamentalism is the great problem of our age' and then, controversially and courageously, argued that non-fundamentalists should show some steel, some 'intransigence and indeed combativity, before it is too late'.[24] In late 2001, in the declared war on terrorism, the initial European consensus was that fundamentalist Islam was indeed a domestic threat to Europe – and that its practitioners within Europe will need to accept the secular principle of the division of church and state, and that the laws of the state take precedence over religious laws. It also gave a new urgency to the European debate about admitting Turkey to the Union.

Defending European values in Europe is, though, a different proposition from attempting to export values abroad as an act of policy. Europe's secular approach may well allow it to develop a geopolitics which does not look at the whole world through its own eyes, seeking to redraw the world in its own image, but tries, at least, to see, understand and respect other ways of living and thinking. It will help superpower Europe to avoid the kind of universalist, moralizing Christianity which fuelled old British colonialism and modern Republican American foreign policy.

As well as 'social Europe' and 'secular Europe', Europeans were also beginning to unite around a common value of democracy. Democracy had become a test of Union membership, as had human rights and such liberal values as opposition to the death penalty.[25] By contrast, American democracy, which had led the way for a century or more, was seen by many Europeans as degenerating into a quasi-democracy controlled by corporations and big money. The damaging reports of ballot-rigging in Florida in the 2000 presidential election, the terrifyingly low turnouts (only 50 per cent for presidential elections) and the fraying at the edges of civil rights in a new environment dominated by terror – all contributed to a European sense that their democracies were now the most advanced in the world.

The workings of the EU in Brussels, though, told a different story. As regulations poured forth, lack of scrutiny became a big issue. The fact that the Commission was unelected did not help, nor did the lack of transparency in the meetings of the Council of Ministers. A Europe-wide consensus emerged that Europe faced a 'democratic deficit', a deficit that Europe's leaders attempted to address by elevating 'subsidiarity' into an EU operating rule. But during the 1990s, Europe's critics in Wall Street and in the Anglo-American media (particularly in the Murdoch press and television empire) began demonizing the Union, tagging it not just as 'sclerotic', but also as 'undemocratic', even frighteningly so. A great fear was generated – that of a Europe of unaccountable, centralized political power, of intrusiveness into, and dictation over, the lives both of individuals and local governments. The vision – or nightmare – was of a future European government built in the image of George Orwell's Big Brother state in his powerful novel *Nineteen Eighty-Four*. The key terms used to depict this dangerous future, and repeated regularly in British 'Euro-sceptic' newspaper columns and television programmes, were 'bureaucrats' (or 'Brussels bureaucrats'), 'Eurocrats' (usually referring to the Commission) or, more generally, 'centralized power' and 'undemocratic elites'.

This Orwellian vision of a future Europe was very much in vogue in England during the 1990s, and it drew upon a long pedigree, reinforced by two world wars, of the illiberalism at the heart of continental Europe. 'Europe and the United States together invented representative democracy and human rights,' wrote liberal commentator Neal Ascherson, 'but Europe invented fascism and communism all by itself.'[26] And, in 1997, Margaret Thatcher could even compare it to the communist Soviet Union.[27] But it was while she was British Prime Minister that Margaret Thatcher – ironically presiding over the most centralized unitary state in the EU – set the seal on this undercurrent of thinking in her coruscating Bruges speech in 1988, when she raised the spectre of a 'European super-state exercising a new dominance from Brussels' and then, later, introduced the word 'federal' to describe the over-centralized monster she was fearing.

In reality, however, the EU was almost a model of democratic federalist probity. It was highly decentralized – with no federal income taxes and with the vast majority of Europe's public spending conducted at member-state level. Brussels had a small budget (1.27 per cent of the EU's GDP, compared with the national budgets which amount to 47 per cent) and a tiny bureaucracy – the Commission in Brussels employs only 13,000 staff, smaller than that of the City of Edinburgh.[28] Also, the Union, unlike many of its member states, practised the separation of powers with checks and balances (between Commission, Council, Parliament and the European Court of Justice).

By the turn of the century, it was Europe's major nation states, not the EU, which had become the democratic problem. These nation states, which had been the historic repositories of democratic expression, had now simply lost much of their democratic raison d'être. For in the new, globalized world, they were both too small and too big. They were too small to protect their citizens from the big transnational corporations, which could play one government off against another. And, as the 2003 Iraq crisis was to show, they were also too small to give their people much of a say in global politics. Individually, they were certainly no match for the US superpower, as they sat on the sidelines whilst the USA broke free from the UN and invaded Iraq.

Too small for democratic control of the global agenda, Europe's major nation states were nonetheless too big as units for local democracy. Britain, France, Spain, Italy and newcomer Poland all remain unitary states which refuse to entrench power in their localities and regions. A federal super-state will, though, be better able than Europe's nation states to protect (and express) the historic regions and nations of the continent. From the Basque country to Bavaria, from Catalonia to Scotland, the global economy threatens these historic identities and the nation-state elites continue to limit their ability to express themselves politically.

Instead of thinking about Europe as being divided into three dozen nation states, Europeans are beginning to see the continent very differently: as being divided into about 100 nationalities. These range from the Dutch and English in the coastal north, through to the Alsatians and Franconians in North-West Europe, to the Bavarians and Styrians in the Alpine area, to the Castilians and Andalusians in the Mediterranean and Finns and Karelians in the Baltic. Some of these peoples (technically known as sub-state nationalities) – like the Basques and Catalans in Spain, the Bretons in France, the Walloons in Belgium, the Scots, Welsh and Catholic Irish in the UK and, to a lesser extent, people like the Bavarians, the Lombards and the Galicians – have a highly developed sense of a separate identity which can bring them into sometimes violent conflict with their governing nation state. And already, under the impact of Europe, the old control-freak capitals of nation-state Europe have had to yield up some power to regional government. In London and Paris, used to running their countries from the centre, this has hurt.

Europeans are also beginning to see large European super-regions, often spanning parts of two or more countries, come into hard focus. The map of Europe still portrays an old-style continent of nation states but, as these borders fade, the more natural links and ties of trade and migration, some of them dating back centuries, are now emerging.

Already ten super-regions can be easily identified. They are: the 'Latin Crescent' – or the 'the Sunbelt of Europe' – stretching in an arc around the western Mediterranean from Spain, southern France and most of Italy; the 'Baltic League' – rather like the old Hanseatic League before it – uniting the Baltics with Sweden, Finland, Hamburg and the eastern half of Denmark; the 'Atlantic coastal region', incorporating Britain, Ireland, Portugal, western coasts of France, Holland and Germany up to Hamburg; 'Middle Europe', which includes the industrial and commercial heartland of the continent from Hamburg in the north to Munich in the south, Belgium in the west and Poland in the east; the 'capital district', which, rather like the Washington, Maryland and Virginia capital metropolis, forms a capital area from Brussels to Paris and Strasbourg; the small city-region of the 'financial district' of London's square mile, perhaps the financial capital of Europe (viable only with the UK as a member of the Euro-zone); the 'Alpine Arc' of Alpine regions including southern France, western Austria, Italy down to Milan and Germany up to Munich and including non-EU Switzerland; and, following future enlargements, the 'Danube Basin' (from Munich, eastern Austria, Slovakia, Hungary, Romania, Slovenia and Croatia and the Adriatic coast of Northern Italy), the 'Slavic Federation' (European Russia, Ukraine and Belarus) and 'the Balkan Peninsula' down to and including Greece.

In the coming Europe, its great cities, as well as its regions, will become the source of new modern political loyalties. European cities existed before European nations – Florence, Venice and Rome before Italy; Trier, Frankfurt and Hamburg before Germany; London, York, Winchester before the UK; Seville and Cordoba before Spain; and Paris, Orleans and Avignon before France. And today's Europe is a continent of cities as much as it is of nations. Great non-capital European cities – like Amsterdam, Antwerp, Barcelona, Birmingham, Bordeaux, Frankfurt, Glasgow, Hamburg, Lille, Lyon, Leipzig, Manchester, Marseilles, Milan, Munich, Oporto, Rotterdam, Stuttgart, Turin – as well as the great capital cities themselves – London, Paris, Rome, Berlin, Madrid, Stockholm, Helsinki, Warsaw, Prague, Budapest, Athens and the like – are, in a sense, with their hinterlands, all 'countries' in their own right with everything a civilization needs. In some cases, where they have real regional governance, like Hamburg and Berlin, they are, in effect, already city states.

Europe's Challenge to America

This 'social', 'secular' and 'democratic' Europe is not only serving to unite Europeans and provide them with a sense of common identity, it is also beginning to pose a challenge to the USA. While the USA has remained a seemingly more dynamic society, Europe has been pulling ahead as a civilized one, its democracy less beholden to corporate interests, its secular societies less divided by religion, more able to use science, its foreign policy freer from special interests and less heated about other civilizations.

Above all, Europe's 'social market' has begun to produce a higher average quality of life and higher standards and, crucially, a more sustainable brand of capitalism. By the turn of the century, American raw capitalism was beginning to resemble a pressure cooker, with the pressure rising dangerously. The system was catering well for a majority of Americans, but the 'losers' in American society were increasing in number. The crime figures, the rising prison population, the 50 per cent that do not vote, even in presidential elections, and the bitterly divided conservative versus liberal politics – all told a tale of sorts about the fragility of the consensus behind the system. And, with that bastion of America, the great American middle class, fracturing into downwardly as well as upwardly mobile groups, the number of 'losers' is growing. What's more, the constant pressures built into the American model to compete in the global economy through lower costs, lower wages and lower taxes was adding to the lists of new 'losers' by the month. By comparison, Europe's less intense but more egalitarian, inclusive and environmentally aware social capitalism, is able to keep a domestic consensus behind it; and has had far fewer pressures building up within it.

But at the end of the fateful year of 2003 – the year when the Atlantic alliance began to fracture – these growing long-term European advantages over the USA were of little interest to the politicians in Europe's capitals, in Brussels or in Washington. They were grappling with today's transatlantic problems and the geo-strategic here and now. And, from Washington's still elevated vantage point, any European superpower that might challenge the USA was still a long way off: Europe was still only half a superpower; still somewhat in thrall to US military might, only reaching towards a foreign or security policy – and still unable to fully act in its own interests.

7

Europe versus the USA

The Battle for Eurasia

Zbigniew Brzezinski was President Jimmy Carter's National Security Advisor in the White House. A Polish-American with a deep understanding of Europe, he became, alongside Henry Kissinger, one of America's leading geopolitical thinkers. No post-9/11 hawk, he had severe misgivings about the new Bush doctrine of pre-emption and regime change. Yet, like many in the Democratic foreign-policy establishment he represents, he came to support the idea of American primacy in the world and to advocate an American global policy to secure that primacy for the next century.[1] In the post-cold-war debate about global strategy, Brzezinski tended to avoid the harsh language of 'hegemony' or 'domination' used by the neo-conservatives, but only because, like his fellow Democrat former President Bill Clinton, he believed that American primacy could be secured through more subtle means. In the 1990s, Brzezinski not only supported a growing Washington consensus that American primacy could only be secured by a forward strategy for America, but he also set out the key to the forward strategy: US control of Eurasia.[2]

The father of contemporary geopolitics, Harold Mackinder, argued early in the last century that whoever 'rules the world-island [of Eurasia] commands the world'. The landmass of this 'world-island' of Eurasia stretches in the west from the Atlantic shores of Ireland and Portugal all the way across the Urals and Siberia through to China and the North Pacific Ocean and down around the shores of Southeast Asia back to India. It is, unquestionably, the key strategic area in the twenty-first century. In size it is virtually equal to the Americas (about 50,000,000 square kilometres each); but it has three quarters of the world's population, almost 70 per cent of the world's GNP and, crucially, about three quarters of the world's energy sources.[3]

During the twentieth century, Eurasia was rarely seen in this total way. Much of its mid western and eastern part was controlled by the Soviet Union and cut off from the west, as was China, following Mao's Communist revolution. 'Eurasia' appeared occasionally in the minds of thinkers – George Orwell had it as a world power bloc alongside Oceania in his *Nineteen Eighty-Four* – but it has not been a contested area since Hitler's armies reached the oil fields of Baku in 1942 and were then beaten back into Western Europe.

As things stand in the very early years of the twenty-first century, Washington, fresh from its triumph over the Soviet Union in the cold war, is still the primary power in Eurasia. Its influence is felt throughout the 'world-island' and intensely so in both west and east Eurasia. Through its bases and its economic reach, it remains hugely influential in Europe, and in the east its economic penetration of Japan and the Asian 'tiger' economies and its string of military bases girding Eurasia, from the EU to the South China Sea, make it Eurasia's unchallenged military power. In recent years, Washington has improved its military position even more through its bases in Kosovo, Iraq and the Gulf, and crucially across into the southern borders of Russia in the former Soviet Central Asian republics. By the summer of 2003, its military occupation of the oil fields of Iraq had improved its geo-strategic, if not its moral, position in the oil-rich Middle East. President George W. Bush had skilfully taken the opportunity presented by 9/11 to marshal a domestic consensus behind the massive projection of American military power into the energy-rich areas of Eurasia. And, under Bush's leadership, the USA had also become the dominant power in 'South West Asia' (comprising Iraq, the Gulf, Afghanistan and, crucially, Iran – at the junction of the Chinese, Indian, Slav and Arab worlds).

But Washington's great unspoken fear as it looks out on the coming century is that the mighty USA may well be marginalized in

Eurasia – or even ejected from the vast continent altogether. Should this indeed happen, then, by mid century, the USA – restricted to hegemony over the western hemisphere and influence around the edges of Eurasia (say, in parts of Southeast Asia and Australia) – would no longer be the 'world's only superpower'. It would be but one player amongst a number, and also considerably less wealthy.

Great challenges to America primacy in Eurasia loom on the horizon. China, and certainly any Japanese-Chinese combination, would prove formidable. But such a challenge is still some time off. More immediate, though, is the challenge now developing in Europe. Brzezinski himself worries that, as Western Europe is 'America's geo-strategic bridgehead on the Eurasian continent', then 'any ejection of America by its western partners from its perch on the western periphery [of Eurasia] would automatically spell the end of America's participation in the game on the Eurasian chessboard'.[4]

So, how secure is this perch? Much will depend on whether Europeans continue to identify themselves with the idea of a single 'West' led by America; or, instead, see the world as having two 'Wests', like the Roman Empire as it split into 'two Romes' – the empire in the west and Byzantium (which took over from the declining western empire and prospered for another seven centuries). Much will also depend on whether, even if two Wests do clearly emerge, they will see each other as part of a global joint endeavour, or partnership, or as locked in a contest.

During the cold war, both the USA and the Western European nations could rightly tell themselves that they shared a great cause – against communism. It was a cause which saw both America and Europe cooperate in a tight partnership to keep America embedded in Eurasia and to contest Soviet power throughout the 'world-island'. But ever since the collapse of the Berlin Wall in 1989, this great partnership on the western end of the 'world-island' has increasingly turned into a contest. This contest is subtle, it is usually unspoken and it is in its very early stages; but already Washington and Europe are joined in a political battle not just for influence, but for primacy in Eurasia.

Early results in the contest are mixed. The good news for Europeans is that the battle for Eurasia will take place on Europe's home turf, so to speak, thus presenting Europe with fewer problems of over-extension. The bad news for Europe may be that the USA has a huge head start. By 2003, the USA had military bases girding the 'world-island'; and, unsurprisingly (given her superpower status), her political leadership in Washington had far greater unity and strategic grasp than did the emerging European leadership. The American strategist Robert Kagan has argued that whilst Americans believe in the efficacy of power, Europeans no longer do so – and in this respect Americans and Europeans are like people from different planets (as the saying about men and women goes, from Venus and Mars). During the Iraq crisis, as Kagan himself revealed, US policymakers found it very hard to believe that leading politicians in Europe worried more about US unilateral and extra-legal action in Iraq than they worried about Saddam's regime or weapons of mass destruction.[5] Certainly, the lack of a military to match that of the USA has caused Europeans to talk and think less strategically than do Americans. The fact that the construction and expansion of the EU has involved the transcending of national law has shown Europeans the possibilities inherent in a 'world of laws and rules and transnational negotiation and cooperation'.[6] And, crucially, European leaders (particularly the French) have built their opposition to American foreign policy around a moral critique and denunciation of US unilateralism.

But, this European moralizing about process may have given Americans the wrong impression. For, in reality, it was, in part, a tactic only. The fact was that had key European interests been at stake in Iraq, and if these could no longer be pursued through the UN (blocked there by the veto), Europeans would have taken a much less moralistic and idealistic tone. (For instance, can it be envisaged that the French, faced with what they saw as an urgent threat to their interests, would refuse to take unilateral action should they face a veto in the UN?) For many of Europe's leaders (and large sections of the European public) the issue was not the unilateralism of the USA or the niceties of the process at the UN, but rather the content of what the Americans were proposing. Unlike the War on Terror, the unprovoked invasion of Iraq and its occupation was simply not seen to be in Europe's interests, and some Europeans could not understand (initially at least) why it was in America's either.

The Iraq crisis proved the point that, in the early twenty-first century, Europe simply has different interests from those held in Washington. And, crucially, Europe's own interests tend to draw her into less conflict in Eurasia (and around the rest of the world) than do the interests of the USA. The USA has a much more powerful business class than does Europe, and this class demands a 'market'-driven, globalized economy – the cause of so much anti-American 'blowback' around the world. The USA is more dependent on oil imports than Europe, and its population less willing to pay the market price for oil – and this American interest leads the country into conflict throughout oil-rich Eurasia. And, crucially, the USA, through its Christian Zionist and Israeli lobby, supports as a fundamental US national interest the expansion of the state of Israel beyond its 1967 boundaries, whereas Europe does not – a posture which brings the USA, but not Europe, into conflict with Arabia.

The intensity of this coming Atlantic contest, therefore, will ultimately depend on the extent to which Europeans see their interests as being common European interests and, then, whether they see US influence in Europe as hindering rather than protecting these interests. The USA, as I will argue later, will have a vested interest in a 'divide and rule' strategy so that no common European policy based upon these common interests can emerge. As Brzezinski himself puts it, Washington needs to 'offset, co-opt or control' any rivals, and, above all, will need to divide the European inner-core, Franco-Germany, by a 'careful management of Europe's two principal architects'.[7]

Europe's primary interest in Eurasia is in the stability of Eurasia's southern rim. This southern rim is an area stretching from Turkey and Israel across the Middle East to what is now called 'South West Asia', and then which runs from Iraq and Iran through to the former Soviet Central Asia. Without stability in this region, Europe's supplies of energy (and oil) will be at risk, terrorism will grow and migration into the EU could spiral out of control. What the Iraq crisis revealed to many Europeans was that, for all the fine words about common Atlantic interests, Washington will often march to a different drummer – its own! By contrast with Europe's needs, the USA, being 6,000 miles away from the action, can often afford to take greater risks with the stability of the 'world-island'. Also, in one part of Eurasia – the Middle East (a border area for the EU, but not for Washington) – the EU will have a greater interest in seeking stable relations by creating and sustaining existing states and by negotiating with them. By contrast, the USA, as the 2003 war in Iraq displayed, prefers a forward policy of intervention, if necessary by military conquest, to pre-empt and overthrow hostile local regimes. By the summer of 2003, this policy had led the USA into becoming an occupying power in an unstable Arab region – a strategy not geared to winning friends and influencing people. For many Europeans, occupying Arab territory was a strategic error they were loath to become associated with, let alone contribute troops towards. This new strategy of unilateral unprovoked attack, followed by occupation, fell way outside the norms of traditional peacekeeping, and represented a clear difference of policy based upon a clear difference of interest between Washington and Core Europe.

Europe and the 'War on Terror'

The transatlantic crisis over Iraq, though, served to obscure what, at least in the autumn of 2001, following 9/11, had appeared to be a growing identity of interest across the Atlantic – the so-called War on Terror. After all, like the USA, Europe's single most pressing interest was to defend itself against the potential terrorist threat to its homelands. And, for a time, Washington's War on Terror rhetoric, together with the campaign in Afghanistan, only heightened this sense of joint transatlantic endeavour, creating something akin to the atmosphere of the alliance between the western allies at the height of the cold war. For a moment, just a moment, America and Europe saw themselves as one – as a single 'civilization' under attack. Transatlantic intelligence-sharing reached a new high, and the war to remove the Taliban regime in Afghanistan and its aftermath, was a true coalition effort, involving a significant economic and military commitment from EU states (particularly Germany and Britain).

Europe had, if anything, a greater interest in a global War on Terror than the USA. For a start, Europeans saw the threat as being very close to home – smouldering on Europe's unstable borders from the Maghreb through the Balkans to the Middle East, where conflicts and religious fundamentalism could foster serious long-term terrorism. With between 12 and 15 million Muslims living in Europe's cities, all of them potentially open to fundamentalist ideas, and with considerable flows of people from Islamic countries to Europe, Europe saw itself as being in the front line should fundamentalist Islamic terrorism against the West become a real, and lasting, force.

Europe was also in the front line should instability in the EU's eastern border areas – from the Baltics down through Ukraine to Turkey – lead to population upheavals and mass migration westward.

The whole EU, but Germany and Austria in particular, had an urgent interest in stabilizing the whole Eastern European continental system – through enlargement of the EU, through economic assistance, through developing good relations with as many bordering regimes as possible and, in the Balkans, even through military intervention when border areas exploded into violence.

But, although Europe was on the front line, much European strategic thinking and literature – long before 9/11 – had become intolerant of what was seen as a Washington strategic mindset that was losing vision and breadth, becoming overly defensive, and dominated by the culture of threat-assessment and threat-reaction, and a US media determined to frighten its public to death. Amongst the European public, suspicions that 9/11 itself was manufactured by US interests were rife. And even the former Environment Minister in Tony Blair's administration, Michael Meacher, had a theory that the War on Terror was simply a political myth to 'pave the way for… the US goal of world hegemony'.[8]

By contrast, Europe's foreign-policy agenda was depicted, in Europe at least, as being altogether more rounded. Although rarely articulated by Europe's leaders or opinion-formers in the press or on television (or even by academics in learned journals), a consensus European response to the new post-cold-war threat environment was emerging. It saw threats to European societies as being as much environmental and social (for instance, food, disease, climatic changes and mass migration) as they were military and violent. Where actual violent terrorist threats could clearly be identified, Europeans tended to rely on economic, social and diplomatic solutions as well as military ones. Direct military threats to Europe from foreign governments were largely discounted. No one was going to invade or threaten to invade the EU, and certainly not Third World dictators.

Many in Europe considered that Washington had a real point about 'rogue states', but such 'rogues' were usually rational actors and could be 'kept in their box' by deterrence and containment – just as Saddam Hussein had been for a decade after the first Iraq war. (And Europeans, through the French and British, possessed a credible deterrent in their ability to deliver nuclear weapons to any place on the planet.) States needed to be enlisted on the side of the West, not destroyed and turned into failed states where terrorism would run rampant. And if, and only if, they posed an imminent threat should they be dealt with by a forward policy of pre-emption and military intervention.

This transatlantic divide over threat assessments (and responses) was suddenly widened by Washington in January 2002. The dust had hardly settled in the War on Terror in Afghanistan (and at the ghostly Ground Zero in New York) when a new imminent and urgent threat soon appeared. The nature of the threat posed to the USA was suddenly turned by President Bush from the single threat of a global terror network to a double threat – the global network plus 'rogue states' that together might use weapons of mass destruction against the West. The American President made this case in his now famous 'axis of evil' speech – naming Iraq, Iran and North Korea as these 'rogues'. This speech, and the subsequent targeting of Iraq and its dictator Saddam Hussein, was a turning point. Many Europeans simply didn't get it – and Chancellor Schroeder made clear he was genuinely perplexed, calling it 'an adventure'. The key difference between Washington and many European governments over US policy in Iraq boiled down to divergent assessments of Saddam Hussein's regime. Demonized in America, he was seen in Europe as a 'busted flush' of a dictator who posed no real threat to the West, as a secular tyrant who was hostile to al-Qaeda and other fundamentalist groups and as the only person who could keep Iraq as one nation. Europeans worried that any invasion would ultimately lead to the Balkanization of the country and to an environment ripe for creating terrorists. (And, by late 2003, with the US military mired in an occupation, and notwithstanding Saddam's capture in Tikrit in December, many European politicians were beginning to feel vindicated.)

This US targeting of Iraq only confirmed earlier European suspicions that President Bush was using the whole crisis surrounding 9/11 either for electoral purposes (to improve his position in the coming mid term elections in November) or to advance American power and interests in the world by reordering the Middle East in the interests of oil supplies and Israel. Or both. And, further, that he was picking on Iraq simply because Saddam Hussein was easily demonized and the regime was military weak, ironically possessing no useable weapons of mass destruction – a view which gained wider credence when 'rogue' state North Korea (with declared nuclear programmes) was treated differently by Washington. So deep did these suspicions run that Robert Fisk, a British journalist specializing in the Middle East, could speak for millions of Europeans – as early as two weeks after the terrorist attack on the Twin Towers – when he argued that European support for the USA's coalition against terrorism was in fact enlisting Europe 'not in a fight against terror but instead in a fight against America's enemies'.[9]

From Europe's perspective, in the War on Terror, Third World states needed to be strengthened, not weakened. But America was pushing for the exact opposite: for the overthrow of states or for their transformation into 'democracies'. Replacing dictatorships – secular or religious – with democracy was a fine aim, but could hardly be brought about at the barrel of a gun, and through American occupation of foreign lands. It would simply turn the local environment into a breeding ground for future terrorism. (Before the Iraq war, President Jacques Chirac predicted that an American invasion and occupation would lead to 'many little bin Ladens'.) To remove existing regimes unilaterally, and simply on Washington's say so, would lead to the growth of ravaged, poverty-stricken, chaotic and ungovernable twilight lands. Already, by the summer of 2003, such an arc of twilight lands – from the occupied West Bank through occupied Iraq down to parts of the Horn of Africa and up through to Afghanistan and the Afghan-Pakistan border – was emerging: a potential lethal incubus for terrorism.

Many conservative Europeans privately believed that the best way forward in the War on Terror in the Middle East was to bolster existing states – no matter how autocratic – because they would always be able to control their terrorists better than could the US military – who, even after an invasion, would be running the anti-terrorist campaign thousands of miles away in Washington. Many left-leaning Europeans tacitly agreed. They rejected the western overthrow of states – seeking instead to transform autocratic states by long-term solutions that eroded Arab poverty and indignity. Neither agreed with Washington's strategy.

Europe, Islam and Israel

These sharp differences between Washington and Europe highlighted by the war on Iraq may already amount to two distinctly separate western foreign policies operating in the Islamic world. Europe's historic relationship with Islam – from the Christian crusades through to colonialism – was, to say the least, not a happy one.

Yet, ever since the USA became the dominant power in the Middle East (following the failed Anglo-French-Israeli invasion of Egypt in 1956), Europe has been able to shelter under the American umbrella – benefiting from the secure oil flows whilst avoiding the full force of Arab and Islamic resentment and animosity.

Yet, as tensions have risen between the USA and the Islamic world – before and after 9/11 – they have inevitably spilled over into European-Islamic relations. The Maghreb (particularly Algeria), the Balkans and Turkey are all key border flashpoints between Europe and Islam. The Maghreb countries of northern Africa are amongst the most westernized in the Arab world; and the story – for over a thousand years – of Christian Europe's relations with Islam on its borders is one of peace and cooperation as well as bloody conflict.[10] Yet, in an unstable region, living under the constant threat of American military intervention, anything could happen. In Turkey, where the pro-European secular elite leadership (backed by the secular military) represents a strong bulwark, fundamentalists could easily take advantage of any instability brought about either by economic troubles, by a Kurdish uprising, or by hostility to US policy in Iraq. And in the Balkans, the prospect of a fundamentalist regime in a Greater Albania will continue to remain a constant source of anxiety.

In this tense geo-strategic environment, Europeans will be forced to make an historic choice – either to associate themselves with US policy towards the Islamic world, or to develop their own distinct approach. Europe has a real interest in developing good relations with Middle Eastern Islam. Not only does Europe share a long border with Islamic countries (many of which are susceptible to fundamentalism), but also the stability of these governments is crucial for Europe's oil supplies. There are strong European (particularly German) business interests in Iran and a host of traditional relationships – France with Algeria and Syria, Britain with Jordan and the Gulf. Looking at the geo-strategic situation in the early twenty-first century, there are no real reasons why Europe should quarrel with the governments of these Islamic lands.

An historic overture by the new European superpower to the Arab world – and, more broadly, to Islam – may also help Europe with its own Islamic populations. Islamic fundamentalism (like Christian fundamentalism) is not ultimately compatible with the life of Europe in the twenty-first century – but as long as European

Islamists draw the line at trying to establish religious supremacy over European law, no ultimate clash need occur. The French idea of encouraging Islamic integration into French society – by developing a kind of 'French Islam' – could be the way forward for calming and securing the European domestic scene.

Of course, some Europeans are less hopeful. They reckoned that even after any European break with the US policy of intervention and confrontation with Islam, it might be too late to avoid a 'clash of civilizations', which would involve Europe. In such a dire outcome a new 'cold war' between the EU and fundamentalist Islam may well serve to further unify Europe, and act as a catalyst for a fully operational European security policy.[11] It could have another dramatic effect, too, for it could create a further identity of interest between Europe and Russia – and bring into being an anti-fundamentalist 'Northern Alliance', stretching all the way across the north of the Islamic arc. Such an outcome, though, need not be necessary: if Europeans (including over time the British) can distance themselves from hostile rhetoric and policies – and specifically refuse to turn themselves into co-occupiers in the US occupation of Iraq – then the idea of stable, even good, relations between Europe and Islam need not be a fantasy.

Washington will probably continue to have a Middle East policy that causes it to remain unloved, even hated, throughout the region. And the unprovoked invasion and occupation of Iraq has only served to further increase anti-American sentiment throughout the region. Yet America has never been a formal occupying power in the Middle East before; and, even now, should Washington drop its one-sided support for Israel, it could seriously improve its standing throughout the region. As Europeans, both before and after the war, sought to understand Washington's Iraq 'adventure', a belief grew in Europe's capitals – even in London – that the beginning of an accommodation between the West and the Arab world could be secured almost overnight by pressuring Israel to yield ground in the Israeli-Palestinian dispute. The point-blank refusal of George W. Bush's Washington during 2002 to countenance any pressure on Israel – even when asked to do so by Tony Blair – took US-European relations to a new low.[12]

European frustration with this American Middle East policy is well understood in Washington – and one of America's most perceptive strategic thinkers, US State Department official and geostrategist Peter Rodman, may only be exaggerating a little when he states that 'Europeans see in US Middle East policy… the crude impulses of a domineering, arrogant Yahoo country manipulated by its Jewish lobby and masking its own self-interests in either real or feigned naïveté'.[13]

Yet, the likelihood of US policy changing simply because of European distaste is minimal. American Republican Presidents are more interested in listening to the Christian right (and its Christian Zionist lobby), and American Democratic Presidents the Israeli lobby, than they are in appeasing the Europeans. Hard though it may be for Europeans to understand, the American Christian right includes a view of Israel's future that, based upon biblical texts, believes that before the second coming of Christ, Israel will expand to its proper extent and, following the 'rapture', all Jews will be converted to Christianity. This Christian right support for Israel's expansion way beyond the 1967 borders has led to a fateful coalition between Christian Zionists (like Republican House Leader Tom DeLay), parts of the American Israeli lobby and the Likud leadership in Israel, all of which American Presidents are loath to cross. (This Christian right biblically driven geopolitics is not a feature of American political life which squares with the views of Kagan and other commentators, who see the USA as moved more by power than morality, and is usually left out of any American analysis of American-European relations.)

Of recent American Presidents, only Dwight Eisenhower, Jimmy Carter and George Bush Senior have been prepared to seriously lean on Israel – it was Bush's threat to remove the US loan guarantees to Israel that got the Oslo Peace Process started. The influence of these powerful lobbies over the US Congress will probably mean that the USA will continue to miss opportunities in the region to improve relations with the Arab and Islamic worlds – and hinder Washington's ambitions for influence more widely in Eurasia. And this will provide a real opening for EU diplomacy.

Just as Washington supplanted Europe in the Middle East in the 1950s, superpower Europe may well be able to supplant the US in the coming century. Europe has been teetering on the brink of a major Middle East initiative ever since the EEC's famous Venice Declaration, and Europe's foreign offices have seen friendly relations with the Arab and Islamic worlds as their primary interest in the region, even if it means difficult relations with Israel. But, when the chips are down, European leaders have always yielded Arab-Israeli policy to Washington, as long, that is, as the USA was promoting some initiative ('Oslo' and now the 'road map'). European leaders have understandably backed off from a direct confrontation with the USA in the region – even though the likelihood of such a confrontation is that Washington would respond by putting more pressure on Israel – pressure that could lead to a real longish-term settlement, and some kind of stability. In the short-term future, though, Washington's policymakers will only listen to Europe (more than it listens to its internal lobbies) when Europe develops its own policy in the Middle East – and is prepared to back it up with real money and perhaps even peacekeepers.

By the early years of the new century, it was becoming obvious that Europe's clear interest – fatefully distinct from that of the USA – was to calm down Arab and Islamic hatred of the West in order to secure its oil supplies and stabilize its borders – particularly in North Africa. And the EU has some cards to play. It is already the main western economic supporter of the Palestinian state; it has a special trade relationship – through the Euro-Med Conference – with Algeria, Egypt, Israel, Jordan, Lebanon, Morocco, the Palestinian authority, Syria, Tunisia and Turkey; it has good relations (through Britain) with the Gulf States and (through Germany) with Iran; and it is the nearest superpower. It could argue forcefully for the implementation of UN Security Council resolutions, and start pressuring Washington to honour them too; and it could insist on being a crucial part of any international force sent to the region. A united and consistent EU policy, backed by Russia, would challenge American control of the region and could change the whole relationship between the West and Islam.

If Europe ever seeks such a global rapprochement with the Arab and Islamic world, then the new superpower's attitude towards the state of Israel will be crucial. Ever since its Venice Declaration, Europe has seen a growing common interest in restoring the lost balance between the Palestinians and Israel and establishing alongside Israel a real Palestinian state. The obvious deal which mainstream European opinion would support is 'land for peace' – involving a retrenched Israel secure within its pre-1967 borders, the abandonment of settlements on the West Bank and in Gaza, and an acceptance of Jerusalem as the capital of a Palestinian state. (In return, the whole Arab world would be pressured to recognize Israel's 'right to exist within secure and permanent borders' and, crucially, also accept Israel as a Zionist state which would not allow exiled Palestinians a right of return to Israel proper.)

One powerful reason fuelling greater European involvement in the Middle East is Europe's history in the region. Europeans were highly influential in creating the state of Israel in 1948. The British, as the colonial power, promised a 'homeland' for the Jewish people in the Balfour Declaration, and the genocide by the leaders of the Third Reich served to created a general western sympathy for Jews and a determination to see a Jewish state secure in its boundaries. If, as millions of Arabs believe, the state of Israel is essentially a foreign colony implanted into their own lands and region, then it is a western colony and the whole western world, including Europe, is responsible.

On this reading of history, and for reasons of simple geographical proximity, the EU *should* be the major power in the region – the USA has no border with the Middle East, indeed is an ocean and a sea away. Yet, the USA's special relationship with Israel makes Washington indispensable in imposing a settlement. A future EU, though, could play an equal role with the USA should it ever decide to push its own policy on Israel-Palestine. It could press the USA to adopt a joint policy (with Russia as well) and be prepared to back up a settlement by the deployment of troops in the same way as it did in the Balkans. Superpower 'Europa' could take unilateral initiatives – from trade sanctions right through to military intervention for peacekeeping, even peacemaking.

Future EU political leaders may, though, find it very difficult to enter into the Israeli-Palestinian conflict in any really decisive way, let alone help impose a settlement. Washington will fight like a tiger to remain the key arbiter; and many Europeans – particularly Germans – will be disabled by coruscating guilt about their ancestors' role in the Nazi years. Israeli historian Fania Oz-Salzberger, has argued poignantly that 'the European Union... can only become a genuine "active mediator" if it looks Israel in the eye' and acknowledges its 'unresolved historical agony'.[14]

Modern Germans, perhaps even for another generation, may well, though, remain unable to look Israelis 'in the eye'. But such guilt does not touch many other modern Europeans, particularly those whose ancestors fought and died against Nazism. The attempt to include the whole of Europe (and the children of the wartime populations of every EU country) as somehow complicit in crimes against the Jewish people, and therefore disabled in taking positions on Middle East politics, will simply not work. Genuine civilized outrage about what happened to the Jews of Germany and Poland during the Second World War is prevalent throughout today's Europe – but it no longer provides a guide to foreign policy in the Israeli-Palestinian dispute. And even if the crimes of ancestors are to count in the balance, then the peoples of Britain, the low countries, Greece, Denmark and even France, with their wartime stand against Nazism, can without fear (with as little fear as, and in some cases less fear than, many Americans) take the lead in looking Israelis 'in the eye'.

Russia and Oil: The EU's New 'Special Relationship'

So, as superpower Europe slowly develops into a real player in the Middle East region it is unlikely to follow the USA in allowing an unbalanced support for Israel to veto its broader strategic interests – which will remain the securing of good relations with Arab governments in order to secure stability in its border areas and its oil supplies.

The EU will need stability in Eurasia's oil regions, for it is nowhere near self-sufficient in energy. In 2000, 41 per cent of the EU's energy requirements was supplied by oil (with 22 per cent supplied by natural gas, 16 per cent from coal and 15 per cent from nuclear power). A huge 76 per cent of its oil consumption was dependent on foreign supplies. The EU accounts for 20 per cent of world oil imports (compared to 26 per cent for the USA, where energy consumption per head is much higher); and the EU would be seriously hurt by any general world economic crisis caused by oil-price hikes or shortages. In the longer term, natural gas will replace oil as Europe's main energy resource, and estimates suggest gas will account for between 60 and 70 per cent of energy supply by 2020. And with 40 per cent of Europe's imported gas estimated to come from Russia by 2020, the EU will become highly dependent on Russia – but, also, should it seek to counterbalance any such dependence it will increasingly remain dependent on oil from the rest of Eurasia.

The new European superpower – with an environment friendly ideology – can be expected to try and lessen dependence upon foreign energy supplies by developing new renewable energy sources; and the EU has already set itself a target of 22 per cent renewable energy for electricity generation (12 per cent for all energy) by as early as 2010.[15] Yet, for as far into the future as anyone can see, Europe will still need barrels and barrels of oil from Eurasia; and so too – more so – will the USA. US energy supply is more dependent on oil than is the European; and by 2002 the country was importing over half, and rising, of its oil consumption; and a quarter of these imports were coming from the Middle East region of Saudi Arabia, Kuwait and the Gulf and Iraq. (These countries have half of world reserves whilst US has two per cent of reserves.)[16]

So, the EU could quite easily find itself competing, and at logger-heads, with the US in the 'great game' of oil politics. The history of the Middle East and Eurasia is littered with the twists and turns in this 'great game', in which the great powers try to outwit each other in securing the stability of price and supply of oil. And it has been deadly serious. The European powers have created and destroyed regimes and redrawn borders throughout the whole oil-rich region. And the USA has done the same: it has supported Iran, then Iraq against Iran and then, later, led a coalition against Iraq; and then, later still, overthrown the government in Iraq and introduced military bases all along the oil-rich southern rim of Russia. And there is plenty of scope for future 'games' between the USA and a European superpower in the region, and the 'games' could easily get out of hand, should the EU (and its leading states) and the USA find them-selves on opposite sides – should, say, insurgent forces threaten the governments of conservative sheiks or secular dictators; or, perhaps, find themselves with radically different policies towards Iran.

As the coming century unfolds, Europe and the USA could develop completely different strategies for securing their oil supplies from the turbulent Middle East. They could also disagree about how to keep the energy flowing from the Caspian Basin and the Western Siberian oil and gas outlets – adopting differing policies towards the nations of the Caucuses and, of course, Russia. In 1995, nearly half of EU consumption of imported gas came from Russia, and EU Commission forecasts suggest a growing demand, which could be met from Azerbaijan and the countries of Central Asia.[17]

Indeed 'avoiding the south', that is, the turbulent Middle East, could become the new goal in oil-supply strategy; particularly as large amounts of oil could reach the West from new fields in the Caspian and Kazakhstan (the huge Apsheron Trend oil field in the Caspian and the Tenghiz oil field in Kazakhstan). The new oil pipeline from Central Asia through Russia – to the increasingly important outlet at the Russian port of Novorossiysk – could become a stable supply route for European and American oil needs as it bypasses the unstable Islamic states to the south. And western reliance upon transit through Russia may come to seem much more sensible than constructing pipelines from Central Asia down through Afghanistan and Pakistan.

If both Europe and the USA build their future energy strategy on an attempt to diversify their oil and energy supplies – by building up this 'Northern Strategy' – then good relations between the West and Russia assume a new urgency. But the West may not speak as one on the question of Russia. Europe and Washington are already beginning to see Russia in rather different ways.

Since the end of the cold war the USA has had an ambiguous relationship with Russia. Washington has seen Russia as an important source of energy, but primarily as an arms-control problem (ensuring nuclear safety and plugging leakages of weapons of mass destruction to terrorists). Even as late as 2001, after 9/11, although Russia supported Washington in its War on Terror in Afghanistan, and even, British-style, sought a special strategic relationship, the George W. Bush presidency did not treat Russia well. It overrode Kremlin sensibilities as it moved its military influence into the southern borderlands of the old Soviet Union, it expanded NATO right up to the Russian border and, against Russia's pleadings, it abrogated the ABM treaty. And, in return, the initial burst of post-cold-war, pro-American sentiment in Russia turned into a degree of wariness. Wall Street's triumphalism and the imposition on the defeated Russians of a swift road to capitalism (creating the 'Wild West capitalism' of Mafiosi economics) have taken their toll on pro-American sentiment in the former superpower. And President Putin, although retaining good to cool relations with Washington, has seen those relations cooling off even more as he took the strategic decision to side with France and Germany during the Iraq crisis.

When President Putin turned up, somewhat unexpectedly, in Berlin during the diplomatic fight between Germany, France and the USA over Iraq, and was greeted on TV by a smiling German Chancellor as he announced Russia's support for the Berlin-Paris axis, the world's diplomatic tectonic plates were seen to move. But this time it was two democratic countries, not two tyrannies, that were getting together; and the meeting symbolized what had for some time, existing underneath the more glitzy Washington-Moscow relationship, been a growing unity of interest between Western Europe and Russia.

Such a European-Russian alliance had been on the cards ever since the Berlin Wall came down. And, even during the cold war, Washington was often unhappy with European overtures to Moscow. The USA was sceptical about German Chancellor Willy Brandt's *Ostpolitik* and downright hostile to French diplomacy's insistence on developing a separate relationship with the Kremlin. During the Reagan presidency, Washington and Bonn clashed publicly over the gas pipeline linking Western Siberia to Western Europe. These fissures have continued to run through into the 1990s debate over NATO enlargement – with Washington seeking to extend NATO right up to the Russia border and European leaders seeking to accommodate Russian fears.

Indeed, the dramatic agreement between Core Europe and Russia over Iraq focused minds on what was already emerging as a revolutionary geo-strategic alliance between the EU and Russia based upon joint interests. By 2002, the building blocks of such a strategic alliance were already in place. They were and are: Russian natural gas and energy supplies to Western Europe; and, in return, an increasing Russian access to Europe's markets (maybe even associate EU membership, perhaps even full membership in 25 years?). Such an 'energy for markets' deal makes eminent sense. Already, more than half of Russia's trade is with the EU, while the EU gets over a fifth of its energy needs from Russia. EU companies are the largest foreign investors in the Russian economy. The coming EU 25 will have a dense network of commercial and trade relations with Russia, which far outweighs that between Russia and the USA. But, added to energy and markets, the EU and Russia also have security interests in common – not least the need to contain the effects of any radicalization of Islam to the south.

Such a strategic security agreement would amount to a 'Northern Alliance' – and could stretch all the way from Dublin and Lisbon in the west to Vladivostok in the east. Such a 'Northern Alliance' could, for a time, work in tandem with the USA within NATO – extending the 'Northern Alliance' right across the northern part of the globe. A more likely outcome, however, is that the EU, Russia and the USA will become competitive rather than cooperative. Even before the terrorist attack on New York (and the Afghan conflict), the USA appeared to be contemplating stealing a march on the EU by creating a security presence in a vast region from the Balkans through the oil-rich Middle East to the Caspian Sea.[18]

This EU-Russia alliance could even, by the middle of the century, replace NATO as Europe's primary security system. And, in the interim, Russia could join NATO. Indeed, during 2002, both German Chancellor Gerhard Schroeder and British Prime Minister Tony Blair took the lead in developing a new, closer, institutional relationship between Russia and NATO. And, in the very long term, Russia could even join the EU.

Such a new strategic relationship between the EU and Russia – let alone a future tight security alliance – would not be welcome in Washington. And Washington can be expected to attempt to frustrate any serious get-together of this kind lest it be a prelude to Brzezinski's fearful scenario in which two Eurasian powers get together to marginalize America, or even oust her from her 'perch' on the western periphery of the continent. The fact, though, will remain that the EU is bound to Russia in a way in which the USA can never be. Both geographic proximity and the symbiotic relationship of Russian energy and EU markets make a potential EU-Russia alliance as important and lasting for Western Europe as was the NATO alliance.

By co-opting Russia into its orbit, the EU would do much more than marginalize the USA in Eurasia. It could radically redraw the map of world politics. If the USA were to lose its western 'perch' on the Eurasian continent, her position as a global superpower would be seriously weakened, as she became one superpower in a world of several. And the centre of gravity in world politics would move away from a globally dominant Washington and back towards Eurasia and its strongest power, the EU.

Superpower Politics: The EU and China

As Europe enters the global political game and develops a new freedom and independence in its foreign policy, it will make separate deals with other coming superpowers. Top of the list will be the two rising superpowers at the other end of the Eurasian landmass – China and India. Both have huge populations, the potential for spectacular economic growth and, in regional terms, considerable military power, including nuclear arsenals. Already, in the very early years of the twenty-first century, the EU, the USA, China and India are playing 'great power' politics and jockeying for position and advantage with shifting alliances and interests. The EU is already slowly establishing a separate 'western' relationship with the eastern side of Eurasia through the now annual EU-Asian summit; the euro is competing with the dollar throughout South Asia; and, as if to prove a point, even in sensitive areas where the USA normally takes a lead, the EU is now trying to establish a separate role (as when, in 2001, in the immediate aftermath of a temporary sharp downturn in US-North Korean relations, a high level EU delegation visited North Korea in order to improve relations).

Washington can hardly be expected to welcome such independent European diplomatic activity – whether with Russia, India or China. Indeed, in Bush's Washington, its own developing doctrine is based upon a future world system which is US-led, not split up between equal superpowers in a 'great power' system.[19] Washington sees China as a real long-term threat to its global dominance (more so than Europe). By 2002, China had under one tenth of the GDP of the USA and less than that of France or Germany or the UK – it was about equal to Italy.[20] But, if China's rapid growth rates continue then, at some point, she will indeed produce an economy, and a military, that will make her a superpower. Her sheer size will enable her to secure a dominant sphere of influence in her Eurasian neighbourhood to her west and south. She will then compete for the energy resources of Eurasia and will also seek to limit the Islamist agitation which is already destabilizing its Xinjiang Province. But it will be her oil needs that will likely bring her into conflict with the USA as well as with Russia.

According to one type of US strategic vision, this coming, and terrifying, Chinese challenge can only be dealt with by 'abolishing China' – that is, by subsuming her peoples within the global capitalist system so that she becomes little more than a market – a powerful market, with some limited political authority, but not one which threatens the lead position in the global system of the USA. Needless to say, the communist regime in China does not see it this way. The Chinese Communist Party seeks to make China a great power on a par with others. It seeks to harness global capitalism, not be overwhelmed by it – but will only be able to do so should the political authorities in Beijing keep ultimate control. If Beijing can combine an authoritarian political form with market growth it may well, as philosopher John Gray argues, have a real future as 'an exemplar of indigenous modernization on a par with Japan'. Such a future China would offer a real challenge to the western superpowers.[21]

The great contemporary Chinese experiment – a clever fusion of non-western political institutions and cultural heritage with western capitalism – could yet produce the greatest challenge to the West since the beginnings of its ascent in the seventeenth and eighteenth centuries. Crucially, China will challenge the western superpowers not only in the industrial sector but also in the service industries, and only the prejudiced will continue to believe that the Chinese will never be skilled enough to compete in service sectors with western populations. 'Within a generation, the burgeoning third world population will contain not only billions of unskilled workers, but hundreds of millions of scientists, engineers, architects, and other professionals willing and able to do world class work for a fraction of the payment their American counterparts expect'.[22]

The EU and the USA will continue to compete with one another in the new Chinese market. They will also engage in shifting alliances as they compete diplomatically in China and throughout the Asian part of Eurasia. There is no single 'western' policy in Asia anymore, and EU delegations, pursuing EU interests, visit and negotiate with North Korea, Beijing and the ASEAN nations, where separate European policies are pursued in order to further separate European interests.

8

Goodbye, Columbus

The End of American NATO

America's power in Europe, and therefore in Eurasia, rested on her indispensable role in resisting Soviet power during the cold war. British Foreign Secretary Ernest Bevin was no sentimental pro-American, but his fear of the Soviet Union led him during 1948 to take the European lead in setting up NATO – and to advocate deep US involvement in Western Europe as 'the last chance for saving the West'.[1] And it was this fear of Soviet power – of encroachment, even invasion across the north German plain – that led Europeans into accepting American leadership and repressing some of their interests in this wider cause.

NATO – the embodiment and instrument of American power in Europe – was a huge success. But it also induced an unhealthy relationship. Washington found itself doing most of the military heavy-lifting and resented US taxpayers having to spend more than the Europeans on defence; and the Europeans, conscious of their dependence on their superpower ally, were often reduced to carping anti-American criticism. Whilst NATO existed, Europe, particularly heartland Europe, could never fully emerge – for, as the famous maxim had it, NATO was all about 'Americans in, Russia out, Germany down'.

In 1989, though, the fall of the Berlin Wall and the Eastern bloc 'changed everything' for Europeans (just as 9/11 'changed everything' for Americans). Now that the great transatlantic anti-Soviet cause was redundant, so too was NATO. For, from then on, with the Soviet threat removed, the cold-war pattern of the European-American relationship was being constantly reassessed, and altered. Even during the cold war it had become clear that the geo-strategic situation – in which the peoples of Western Europe, with their prosperous economies and larger population than the USA – were defended by another power 3,000 miles away, one with the same GDP and a smaller population, was, in the long run, simply not tenable.

A European rebellion against American leadership of NATO, always a potential, but always suppressed, finally spilt out into the open in 2002, during the lead-up to the Iraq war. When, in late August, German Chancellor Gerhard Schroeder, said 'no' to the proposed US war on Iraq he became the first European leader to cleanly break with this thinking. Others – Charles de Gaulle, Edward Heath – had set their own courses during international crises; but Schroeder placed his rejection of Washington's war at the very centre of an election campaign. And won. Instead of an American-centred geo-strategic policy (one which advised Washington or criticized Washington) he had declared that on questions of war and peace – on, as he put it, 'existential questions' – decisions would be taken in Berlin. It was the most fundamental break with NATO-think imaginable, and it foreshadowed a new posture – that policy should be made first in Germany, and by extension, Europe, and then, and only then, coordinated with the USA.

The political and diplomatic fight at the UN between NATO members was serious enough, but the alliance was also almost torn apart on a very practical level. At the very heart of the NATO treaty was the solemn obligation on all the signatories to defend one of its members when under attack – and the US plan to attack Iraq (in part from Turkish bases) placed Turkey right in the line of potential fire from Iraq. Turkey, under the NATO treaty, asked for NATO help in air defences; but France (and Belgium) broke ranks, refused to agree to the request, and vetoed any help. (They argued, somewhat disingenuously, that Turkey was not under threat because, at the time, the US had no UN resolution to attack Iraq.) They yielded, allowing the NATO treaty to be invoked, but only at the very last minute. This Turkish crisis brought into sharp and dramatic high relief a growing European critique of Washington's approach to NATO – that the Americans now saw NATO simply as a convenient mechanism for enlisting European support for American interests around the world (almost as though Europe had no interests of her own). They saw it as a new version of the long-standing American desire to enlist Europe in the 'out of area operations' required by US global interests and more intensively required under the new US global security doctrine. But as the memory of the cold war faded, and as new transatlantic crises dominated the headlines, Europeans began to see their own, separate, interests more clearly and to understand that American interests and doctrine were not always the same. In the process, they also began to review long-held support for and deeply entrenched assumptions about NATO itself.

One such was that Europe needed the USA to defend it. But, in the post-cold-war environment, the security threats to Europe are primarily terrorist threats and, potentially too, threats from anti-western 'rogue states'. Europeans increasingly came to realize that the major difference between these new threats and the old one is that a prosperous and increasingly united Europe has the resources and the ability to handle the new ones itself. Indeed, Europeans could hardly expect the USA to defend both itself and Europe; apart from questions of dignity and self-respect, US taxpayers could hardly be expected, particularly in an era of large US deficits funding a global security mission, to add to their burdens by funding the security of equally prosperous Europe.

So the idea grew that, in this new strategic environment, Europe needed America only as much as America needed Europe. In reality, though, the new American strategic doctrine had a startling implication: that, under all the strategic rhetoric, the USA might need Europe much more than Europe needed America – for the new doctrine depended on US mobile forces operating from forward bases, and for the USA to reach anywhere in large chunks of Eurasia, Europe was crucial. By contrast, Europe had no forward strategy, no designs on Latin America or the Caribbean or Canada, and therefore hardly needed the USA for strategic purposes. From the new developing European perspective (held in France and Germany), what Europe seeks is a warm transatlantic relationship of *equal* partners ensuring good trade relations, close intelligence sharing and anti-terrorist cooperation and, when agreed, even military interventions abroad.

As well as no longer needing America for security, Europeans were no longer prepared to automatically accept American global leadership. A German Marshall Fund of the USA poll, published four months after the end of major combat in Iraq, saw a huge jump, in a year, in the proportion of Europeans who no longer thought it desirable for the USA to exert strong leadership in world affairs. As many as 49 per cent of Europeans thought US global leadership was 'undesirable' (up from 31 per cent a year previously), whereas 45 per cent thought it 'desirable'. In France, those believing US leadership to be undesirable stood at 70 per cent (up 22 per cent); in Germany it was 50 per cent (up 23 per cent); in Italy 50 per cent (up 17 per cent); and even in the Netherlands it was 41 per cent (up 18 per cent); Britain 38 per cent (up 13 per cent); and Poland 34 per cent (up 12 per cent).[2]

NATO-Think Dies Hard

Even in this new strategic environment, the assumptions of the cold war died hard. NATO-think still informed the strategic thinking of many of Europe's foreign policy elites long after the old NATO warhorse had become redundant. One reason for this lingering NATO-think was that, in the immediate aftermath of the collapse of the Berlin Wall, the necessary reassessment of the role of NATO got submerged following the eruption of the 1991 Gulf War. All the leading European governments, as part of an impressive international coalition, supported the US in expelling Iraq from Kuwait – and the war amply displayed how American military leadership was highly beneficial to Europe when European and American interests coincided. In this environment, few in Europe, outside of France, were prepared to question the underlying rationale for NATO. NATO also received another last-minute reprieve as the 1990s Yugoslav imbroglio seriously dented the claims of those who sought an independent European security policy. Germany's sudden recognition of Croatia, and the crumbling of the edifice of the Yugoslav federation, set European powers on differing sides – allowing Washington to intervene, lead a successful air war against Serbia and claim that Europe could not even resolve a crisis in its own backyard. The tragedy of the Balkans weakened the confidence of Europe just at the very time that it needed to fulfil a new role.

The divisions in Europe during the Balkans crisis led some European leaders to see a continuing relevance for Atlanticism – a strategic dependence on America – even into the new century. Rather than work together with their European neighbours to create a new security system, they continued to see themselves as important provinces of a system (or empire) led from Washington, provinces that would best make their way in the world by seeking influence in Washington, the capital of the empire.

British Prime Minister Tony Blair became the leading advocate of this rationale for post-cold-war Atlanticism – and, during the 1990s, he argued publicly that it was only his strong and unswerving support for the USA that enabled him to have a say in the councils of state in Washington. His open aim was to be recognized at court in Washington, not to link up with others to rival, and balance, the existing monarch.

During the 2002–2003 Iraq crisis, Britain became the champion of Atlanticism and Washington in Europe. So much so that Prime Minister Blair opened himself to charges of placing American interests ahead of British – and that he was becoming 'Bush's poodle', or, in a phrase used by Nelson Mandela, 'Bush's foreign minister'. Yet Downing Street stood its ground and made crystal clear its fears that should Europe alienate Washington then the Americans would simply go their own way. Blair's Foreign Secretary, Jack Straw, warned France and Germany, in a pointed outburst, to 'take care' in opposing the USA at the UN lest they 'reap the whirlwind' of American unilateralism.[3] This increasingly isolated posture was stuck to with the fervour of the true believer and was most evident amongst Britain's security establishment (its diplomats, intelligence officials and senior military). This establishment was infused with a lingering Atlanticism and 'NATO-think', but there were also vested interests at work. During the Iraq war debates, many Britons simply could not understand how a Labour Prime Minister could offer such steadfast support to a conservative Republican President's Arab war in which Britain had no interest. And, when asking who or what was behind it all, there emerged a saying in political circles: 'It's all about spooks and submariners!' The two words 'spooks' (meaning the British intelligence services) and 'submariners' (meaning the Royal Navy's nuclear Trident submarine fleet lobby) neatly captured the importance of two crucial Whitehall interest groups, both of which had become virtually operationally dependent upon the US connection. Senior figures in the UK's intelligence services felt themselves dependent because of their access to Washington's intelligence networks, and leading submariners in the Royal Navy because of the essential US help in servicing (in Norfolk, Virginia) Britain's nuclear deterrent, carried on submarines.

Britain's militant Atlanticism was not without its supporters in the outer ring of Europe. In late January 2003, eight European prime ministers signed an open letter to President Bush, which, although not technically breaching the 'Common European Position' agreed the day before of resolving the Iraq crisis through the UN Security Council, was extravagant in its pro-Washington, pro-Atlanticist language and obviously designed for the media. The letter revealed a fault line in Europe on Iraq, but more pointedly on attitudes to the USA. It was signed by the leaders of three East European nations (the Czech Republic, Poland and Hungary, all with strong cold-war attachments to Washington and some with opposition within their countries to German leadership of Europe); by Spain and Portugal (both with free-market governments at odds with the 'social model'); by Italy (under the individualistic leadership of Silvio Berlusconi); and by the UK. Intriguingly, those Western European leaders who signed were prepared to run risks with their domestic populations, as opinion polls in Italy, Spain, Portugal, the UK and Denmark were running heavily in favour of the Common European Position that the UN, not the USA, was the vehicle for resolving the crisis. Pointedly, neither President Chirac nor Chancellor Schroeder was asked to sign; and the Dutch Prime Minister, who saw it, refused to sign. The letter left a feeling of bitterness. One German Christian Democrat said, 'The race of the vassals [of Washington] has begun.'[4]

If Britain had been at one polar end of Europe's approach to NATO during the 1990s, then France was at other end. By contrast with Britain, France, even during the 40-year cold war, had taken a more independent stance – symbolized by de Gaulle's decision to remove France from the integrated military arm of NATO and NATO headquarters from Paris in 1966. Even so, during the cold war, French 'independence' was always a somewhat ambiguous concept. De Gaulle certainly built a genuinely independent nuclear system (unlike the British); but, ultimately, French security, like that of Western Europe as a whole, was still largely dependent upon the US nuclear guarantee. And, even at the height of Gaullism, France worked with the political framework of NATO. As it became increasingly clear that only a unified European security system could establish independence from US leadership, instinctive Gaullists were in a genuine bind: they willed the end (independence from the USA), but not the means (a unified European security policy in which French national interest would need to be subordinated to a greater European interest).

Over the latter years of the cold war, this hold of Gaullism on French strategic thinking weakened, opening the way for France to place security policy in a more European context. In the late 1990s and during the George W. Bush presidency, as transatlantic tensions rose (and disputes with the USA reached their zenith over Iraq policy), the French finally had their opening. Increasingly, Germany came to hold the balance and even begin to see things Paris' way. And this blossoming Franco-German strategic alliance, forged during the Iraq crisis, further Europeanized strategic thinking in Paris.

But if Europeans were eventually to consign Atlanticism and NATO to the filing cabinet of history, then even the most fervent Eurocentrics saw that Europe would need to have a new security system to put in its place. Above all, Europe would need a credible common foreign and security policy that could protect Europe in the new post-cold-war environment.

Thinking about this got underway surprisingly quickly once the Berlin Wall had come down. Not even the most ardent federalists like Helmut Kohl or the anti-Americans in Paris saw NATO as being replaced any time soon; but at the Maastricht summit in February 1992, amidst all the excitement about the launching of the plan for the euro, European leaders also launched a little-noticed outline blueprint for a European foreign and security policy, which they included in the Maastricht Treaty. Its institutions were weak – it placed foreign policy outside of the main Brussels institutions as a 'second pillar' of the EU – but its underlying long-term impact was powerful. In politics, ideas can sometimes count; and this blueprint broke an important taboo – that NATO would not be around for ever – and served notice that the European Union would one day take over from America and NATO and would form its own foreign and security policy.

So sensitive was the foreign policy question that during the 1990s, even though the EU was beginning to develop a foreign policy, it remained unannounced. But when Europe flexed its muscles in a single trade front against the USA, or when the EU announced the world's largest aid policy, or when the union supported the Kyoto Treaty and the International Criminal Court, or the ECB took major monetary decisions with global impact – these were the decisions of a superpower about the sinews of its foreign policy.

By the turn of the century, even with the euro in place, the EU was by no means a complete foreign-policy power. The veto still hobbled decision-making in too many areas of EU foreign policy (although in the USA a veto over foreign policy, exercised by institutions and powerful interest groups, was normal and accepted practice). The veto could even be exercised in an area where the EU had real clout – economic sanctions, if they were being proposed for political purposes. (Italy had blocked sanctions sought by Britain against Argentina during the Falklands war.) Yet, although progress was slow, by the end of the first year of the new century the EU possessed its first very own Foreign Minister – 'High Representative' Javier Solana who has a secretariat and a policy-planning and early warning unit reporting to him. A former NATO Secretary-General, Solana, working with the EU presidency, finally presented an EU 'face' to the world. And the Giscard draft constitution, in a clause supported by all 25 countries, went even further – creating a new Union Minister for Foreign Affairs, who would also be a Vice President of the Commission and would 'conduct the Union's common foreign and security policy'.[5]

By late 2003, Euro-optimists were sensing that Europe would, one way or another, finally emerge as a foreign-policy superpower (with foreign-policy powers and its own security institutions). It would emerge either through the new constitution or through the Franco-German core going ahead on its own. It all depended on political will. And the really big news for Europe was that, following the new US strategic doctrine unleashed by 9/11 and the subsequent Iraq crisis, that political will now existed. The foreign-policy realignment of NATO's pivotal power, Germany – away from the USA and towards France – may yet be seen as the single most important story in European security since the fall of the Berlin Wall. And, although the ten new East European member states were expected to somewhat dilute Europe's nascent common foreign policy, let alone any common actions, there has, in fact, been a surprising Europeanization of their foreign policies – attested to by their voting record in the UN which, from an EU vantage point, has been exemplary, rarely deviating from the European consensus. Also, all ten of the 'new' countries aligned themselves firmly with the EU's stance on the International Criminal Court, and have stood firm against a concerted Washington campaign to forge bilateral agreements with them that would have prevented any US national being handed over to the Court in The Hague. As of writing, on a host of issues, from Israeli-Palestine policy, to Kyoto, to transatlantic trade and the International Criminal Court, Europe's common foreign and security policy was, if not up and running, then at least beginning to stand on its own feet.

A Military Superpower?

Foreign policy, like economic policy, does not a superpower make. And in the aftermath of the Iraq crisis, an insistent question remained: can Europe back its strength with power? Few doubted that Europe had 'soft power' – the power to attract – in abundance. But could it exercise 'hard power' – the ability to make people do what they might not do otherwise?[6] It was the ability, and the will, to use the full array of 'hard power', from economic power (including sanctions) through to military force, that was becoming its first great test as a fully fledged superpower. Euro visionaries saw a coming century in which EU soldiers, in dark blue helmets with the circle of gold stars, mounted peacekeeping and peacemaking expeditions on battlefields around the world. They saw EU aircraft carriers (perhaps the existing 'Charles de Gaulle' or 'Invincible'?) and an EU defence building in Brussels as famous as the Pentagon. Some even saw EU military ranks and markings. Few, though, expected a European army (fully integrated like the US military), and the real question became whether Europe could develop a serious military apparatus of joint command which controls and coordinates armies, navies, air forces and intelligence services? And could the EU ever have the fully coordinated security system of a real superpower? Could it respond militarily to events through an accountable executive led by a president, a defence secretary and a military apparatus, all checked and balanced by a powerful parliament?

During the 1990s, EU defence became the most sensitive of issues – not just because defence was seen around Europe as the last redoubt of national power, but also because the idea of a 'separate' EU defence system cut to the vitals of the European relationship with the American superpower. Washington's reaction to any stirring of EU military independence had never been particularly friendly or helpful. The Clinton administration was emollient, saying it understood Europe's 'need to address and solve problems without always requiring US combat involvement', but warned them of the risks to alliance unity involved in the 'separate' structures.[7] But the Bush administration was much less understanding, and Secretary of Defense, Donald Rumsfeld, was at his grouchiest when thinking about it. Within months of taking over he had publicly opposed the idea, in an interview with the *Sunday Telegraph*.[8] In private, the Americans were very worried, but adopted the strategy of trying to kill European military independence with conditions – Washington said it would support the project but wanted no duplication of effort, no decoupling of Europe from America and no discrimination against non-EU members such as Turkey. Republican strategist Peter Rodman captured US thinking when he wrote, as early as 1999, that 'trying to kill [a 'separate' European defence system] would only have spurred an anti-American reaction... better to steer it in a direction compatible with NATO.'[9]

Even so, a separate EU defence system was way down the agenda of Europe's leaders for most of the 1990s. And then, intriguingly, the British Prime Minister, Tony Blair, for all his insistent Americanizing, decided to take a lead in creating a European defence identity. The political weather had changed dramatically following the 1998 NATO air war against Serbia. Quite simply, the Blair government changed its mind. Blair was shocked by the disparity between the military capabilities of the Pentagon and the EU nations that had been revealed by the air war. He had believed that Europe should be able to take the lead in a military crisis on European soil, but he watched as the European nations were, in fact, reduced – in their own backyard – to the role of bystander as Washington moved in to stabilize the region. Europe's Balkans humiliation seemingly convinced a determined Blair that the EU needed to overcome its hesitancy and become a major defence player. And, for Blair, there was another motive: soon after he came to power in 1997, he decided to delay Britain's entry into the euro; and he believed that the only way the UK could recoup a leading role in Europe was through helping forward Europe's defence. Britain's military power and prowess had become the country's only calling card in Europe.

This change of heart led Blair to cross the channel for a surprising rendezvous with President Chirac of France, where he signed an unexpected and potentially historic agreement on 4 December 1998 in the ancient French military port of St Malo. This meeting, which took the US defence establishment completely by surprise, may yet rival Maastricht, or even Rome, in the history of the making of a European superpower.

Strategic thinkers in Paris had long sought to enlist Britain in a European defence system. They acknowledged that Britain was a sizeable military power, perhaps even more formidable than the French. They saw a country spending more on defence than most of its European partners in NATO; it was a nuclear power; and, crucially, was normally able to secure public support behind military operations abroad.[10] Britain prided herself on her military history and prowess – even when it played junior partner to Washington. (When in March 2002 the Americans allocated Britain a role as peacemakers in the post-September 11th fighting in Afghanistan, 'Only The Best' beamed a *Daily Mail* headline, seemingly oblivious to the message in its subheading: 'Washington *sends* for British Marines'.)[11] By becoming a key player in a new European military force, the British were likely to make a real difference and find a real outlet for their military prowess and sensibility. The French, who were always also trying to enlist Germany into a defence agreement (primarily to help carry the financial burden), saw the possible addition of Britain as a 'troika' in the making.

Following St Malo, which the German government welcomed, Paris began to see this potential troika as able to run the defence and foreign policy of the wider Union. Not very 'communitaire', the troika would meet resistance within the wider EU, as it would be seen as an attempt at a military version of Chirac's Core Europe. But with Britain on board it need breach no EU rules, for, should London, Paris and Berlin all agree to support a policy or operation then it would be highly unlikely that, say, the Irish Taoiseach, or even the Swedish Prime Minister, would go so far as actually casting a veto. And even Poland, and other pro-American countries, shorn of the alliance with the UK, would think more than twice about doing so. As long as the big European powers agreed amongst themselves, then those who disagreed with any action would probably take the option of sitting it out rather than bringing on themselves the odium of blocking it.

At the heart of the Anglo-French initiative at St Malo was a radical vision of a future EU running its own defence policy with separate structures from NATO – including strategic planning, intelligence and military resources – to take its own defence decisions where 'the alliance as a whole is not engaged'.[12] It called for 'the progressive framing of a common defence policy' for the EU and declared that the EU 'must have the capacity for autonomous action, backed by credible military force'. To use the word 'autonomous' was, for Blair, to cross the Rubicon, to break with Washington and NATO-think by breaking the taboo that the Europeans should never act on their own. Britain's Defence Secretary, referring to the St Malo agreement, actually declared that the 'ultimate aim' of the British government was 'not so much a European Security and Defence identity but something altogether more ambitious – namely a European Defence capability'.[13] And by February 2001 at Nice, Europe's leaders had gone so far as to insist that Europe's independent defence and security policy (ESDP) should 'become operational quickly'.

St Malo was followed up by the Helsinki summit in 1999, which put some real flesh on the bones of Europe's new 'autonomy' by introducing onto the world stage Europe's great new symbol of independence, its very own Rapid Reaction Force. Blair had gone so far that France saw a choice coming – and a French official even went so far as to say that 'Britain will not be able to play a leading role in the EU unless they jettison their special relationship. Britain must choose Europe or betray it.'[14] But Blair continued to insist that no choice – between Europe and America – was needed, and he flew to Chicago where, in a speech on the 'special relationship', he attacked the idea of a choice as a 'false proposition'.[15] Blair was able to go so far down the European road only because of the emollient policy of President Bill Clinton, who was making an art form out of not upsetting the Europeans. Even so, behind the scenes, the USA was far from happy with Europe flexing its defence muscles. Clinton's No. 2 at the State Department, Strobe Talbot, responded to St Malo by stressing 'the risks and costs' of the idea, and argued that if it was mishandled it 'could create the impression – which could eventually lead to the reality – of a European-only alliance'.[16]

But Blair's great flirtation with European defence was brought to a halt by the arrival of George W. Bush in the White House and Donald Rumsfeld in the Pentagon in January 2001. Bush initially wavered on the European 'autonomous' defence issue, but Rumsfeld displayed his annoyance at Europe's defence pretensions long before 9/11. During the Iraq crisis, US policy hardened even more. The full extent of US hostility to Europe's defence initiative was on display during an extraordinary episode at the US State Department on 2

September 2003, some months after the US invasion of Iraq, but at a time when US policy was being seriously questioned at home. Hard-bitten journalists gasped with surprise when normally even-tempered US State Department spokesman Richard Boucher very undiplomatically scoffed at Franco-German plans for independent European defence and a separate European headquarters. In an unprecedented put-down, he called a Brussels meeting between France, Germany, Belgium and Luxembourg a 'little bitty summit' and then referred to the four countries – but obviously picking on Belgium – as 'the chocolate makers'.[17]

Taking his cue from US hostility, Tony Blair placed his original St Malo initiative on hold, as he waited on events. And the suspicion grew, particularly in Paris, that Blair's St Malo excursion had been nothing more than an adventure, a flirtation only; and that, when forced to choose, he would reveal that his true love lived in Washington, even in a conservative Republican White House. 9/11, and even more so the Iraq war, revived the Atlanticists throughout Europe, and for a time took the wind out of the sails of the great European defence initiative (by then renamed the ESDP).

By the early summer of 2003 – with the Americans seemingly victorious in the Iraq war – those Europeans who wanted the EU to act separately in the world from the USA saw only one way forward – to wheel out the military version of 'the Charlemagna' solution. Realizing that progress through EU institutions would always be blocked, Paris and Berlin turned, none too quietly, to the 'go it alone' strategy. On Tuesday 6 May 2003, the leaders of France, Germany, Belgium and Luxembourg met at a highly controversial defence summit in Brussels. It amounted to a direct challenge – and a public snub – to the Bush White House. It took forward the idea of the European Defence Union (EDU) that had first been floated at the crisis NATO summit in Prague in November 2002. Its key point was a major German concession to France – the setting up of a headquarters for a military command structure and an autonomous European chain of command, but the idea was also to integrate the armed forces to a higher degree than ever before, create their own rapid reaction force, their own armaments agency, improve deficiencies like air transport capacities and establish effective protection against nuclear, biological and chemical weapons. To overcome potential vetoes, this EDU is initially to be established outside the EU framework, rather like the 1985 Schengen agreement, and it remains open to others to join. These goals exactly mirror the EU's goals (in the ESDP) and are a duplication of effort, but – a crucial but – will be more effective because they bypass the veto of the Atlanticists.

Intriguingly, it was German Chancellor Schroeder who took the lead here and, in setting the tone for this 'rebel' conference, he declared that, 'In NATO, we do not have too much America, we have too little Europe.'[18] According to some German critics, this new initiative puts France in the Franco-German driving seat by giving it the military leadership of Europe. France is the EDU's one nuclear power and it spends 25 per cent more on its military than does Germany – and would thus become to Franco-Germany what the USA is to NATO. Such a short-term solution suits Paris, but is also a neat one for Schroeder and the Germans. For Germany gets the beginning of a European defence system (and one which could trigger a wider EU effort), while, at the same time, leaving the extra expenses to others. In the long run, though, the Germans will probably want the UK to join in and the full EU system to take over.

This 'rebel summit' set the alarm bells ringing in Britain. Both Downing Street and the Foreign Office feared a Franco-German military power emerging on the continent, and Blair revived the St Malo process. After interminable debates about the nuts and bolts during late November and early December 2003, Britain finally agreed to a European military planning cell being established within the EU – crucially separate from the NATO planners. It was initially to be very small (some 30 or so planners) but could rapidly be enlarged during a crisis. The agreement between London, Paris and Berlin was finally announced on 13 December 2003. For many observers this whole defence debate seemed arcane and overly bureaucratic. But, in reality, it was the birth of the 'Troika', and the final brick in the final pillar of European unity. It would not reach adulthood for a few years, but in December 2003, a superpower was born.

Germany and Superpower Europe

The Frenchwoman at the heart of France's post-9/11 military build-up, Defence Minister Michelle Alliot-Marie, pulled no punches as she came out of a meeting in Washington, DC in October 2002. 'You can't say a European foreign policy is essential,' she said brusquely to reporters, 'unless you fund Europe's defence.'[19] She was speaking for a growing consensus in France, which had come to accept that Europe would need to increase its military budgets. Although no one in France was talking about Pentagon levels of expenditure, there existed a clear understanding that the exercise of power in the modern world was, in part at least, based upon military capabilities. And for France, keen to construct the European superpower, it was becoming obvious that if Europe were not to rely upon the USA to do all the peacekeeping and peacemaking around the world, particularly in Europe's backyard border areas, it would need greater military expenditure. Also, if Europe seeks to offer an alternative to the USA's global forward strategy of intervention around the world and instead rely upon deterrence and containment, then military hardware – bombs and missiles – become an essential aid to diplomacy. Credible military forces increase power simply by their existence, not just or necessarily by their use. It was a point made by Hilaire Belloc a century earlier when he argued that, 'Whatever happens, we have got The Maxim Gun, and they have not.'[20] And the old Soviet Politburo further told the tale, for from Stalin to Brezhnev (and long before over-extension) the Soviet Union did not need to actually move their red army divisions across the north German plain, or fight anyone, to gain enormous influence in world politics; they just had to possess them.

Yet, whilst the French government was recognizing the important role of military power, other Europeans – including the German Greens and many on the wider European left – were more sceptical about exactly how much sustainable power can come out of the barrel of a gun. Even those supportive of the idea of superpower Europe – certainly when put in the context of balancing American power – remained highly dubious about the role of 'hard' military power. For them, the case of the post-1960s Soviet Union told a relevant tale – for it stood out as a lesson that military power itself, even a massive and feared military machine, does not a superpower make (at least not for long); and that Soviet-style or Pentagon-style military power certainly has no answer to terrorist 'asymmetric warfare'. Ultimately, it is economic and social strength at home that counts. According to this reading, Europe's future power and security could no longer be measured by military spending. Its advanced civilization would only endure if it rested its security policy not just on bombs and missiles, but also on 'softer security': on domestic stability, economic influence, good relations and intelligence abroad, and clever strategy.

Yet, Europe's ultimate defence problem lay not in judicious concerns about over-extension, but rather, in pacifism itself. Any visitor to modern Germany during the post-war years could sense the reluctance of Germans to become involved in military operations and adventures, even those led by the USA. Innate pacifism amongst young to middle-aged Germans, together with defensiveness amongst the older generations, produces what former French Foreign Secretary, Hubert Vedrine, has described as a contemporary German 'complex' about the use of military force. 'If something goes wrong, we will be blamed' is still a prevailing German sensibility.

The fact is that Hitler's shadow will continue to fall over the EU's largest nation for some time to come. In the USA, Britain and France the public is normally proud of their military, soldiers are seen as a 'good thing', often as heroes risking their lives for the good causes of patriotism and democracy. For Germans, however, the German role in the Second World War will continue to act as a brake upon public support for German military activity abroad – and even for any German foreign policy that even hints at a robust independent German policy. (Schroeder lost some of his domestic support during the crisis over the US Iraq policy when he talked of 'the German way'.) This continuing deep sense of guilt about the past is unlikely to be completely washed away simply because the German political leadership has signed up for a European defence system and seeks to make legitimate German ambitions into European ones. By the turn of the century, though, this very real German problem was slowly being solved, for there were real signs that Germany was not prepared, for ever, to remain an economic giant but a military worm.

For this generation of Germans, as long as Germany pursues her ambitions through Europe and her military actions through NATO, the EU or 'Charlemagna', then German public opinion will tolerate robust foreign policies, perhaps even some increases in defence expenditure. The NATO conflict with Serbia in 2001 was the key turning point, as, for the very first time since the Second World War, German forces, in this case the Luftwaffe, were used outside of Germany – ending the constitutional ban provided in the Basic Law. The US-led anti-terrorist campaign following the attack upon the World Trade Center provided a further opportunity for the Germans to play a big military role. In the immediate aftermath of 9/11, Germany even took the lead role in the NATO military presence in Macedonia and, with polls showing 65 per cent of

Germans supporting German military involvement in Afghanistan, Chancellor Schroeder offered German forces – primarily anti-chemical and anti-biological warfare forces – in support of the American military effort in that South Asian country.[21] By late 2002, Germany had more 'peacekeepers' in the field around the world than any other European power.

In a groundbreaking address to the Bundestag in October 2001, Chancellor Gerhard Schroeder declared that the era when Germany would 'avoid every direct risk [of military involvement] cannot and must not be a guideline of German foreign and security policy'.[22] And Schroeder seemed determined that Europe would become the new focus of the German military effort. He declared that the Balkans conflict had 'revealed the limited political and military power of the new Europe' and that 'it's to be regretted and must change.'[23] Some months earlier, his own party, in what in its time was a big policy switch, had dumped their Atlanticism and proclaimed that the EU must be able to act 'militarily independently' in 'cases where NATO as a whole does not become active'.[24]

Paying for the Superpower

As it constructs its global role, Europe has a great advantage over the USA. It can learn from American mistakes. Europe's defence debate may not need to be about exact percentages – whether spending should be just over two per cent of GDP (the total EU figure in 2002) or just under four per cent (the US figure). Indeed, as the European debate about security got underway after the Iraq crisis it was beginning to focus not just on money and resources, but on security needs and requirements. Europe's leaders can learn from the excesses of the US 'military-industrial complex' where strategy is increasingly driven by the Pentagon and the interests it represents. With Europe's defence industry not yet fully organized, and its relationship to a coordinated Europe-wide defence system still in its infancy, Europe's leaders can still allow security strategy to determine its military budgets, and not the other way round.

Europeans are beginning to ask what, exactly, is the right security strategy for Europe? Few disagree that Europe's advanced society needs to defend itself from serious threats both at home and abroad. No one need succumb to the kind of 'threat culture' cultivated in Bush's USA in order to believe that real threats exist. But many also believe that Europe needs to get its threats right – and therefore its responses.

On 13 December 2003, the EU, for the very first time, adopted a security strategy which, like its counterpart in the USA, set out the primary threats to Europe and how to deal with them. It had been drawn up by the EU foreign policy chief, Javier Solana, and it supported a range of 'hard power' and 'soft power' responses.[25] Unsurprisingly, at the heart of the argument of these EU strategists was the proposition that instead of old-fashioned cold-war military threats, which needed NATO, the new hierarchy of threats to Europe – the instability of Europe's borders, major environmental catastrophes and major terrorist threats – now needed Europe. For only the critical mass of military and intelligence resources drawn from the whole Union could possibly cope with them.

In capitals throughout Europe, such post-Atlanticist and post-NATO thinking was encouraging a new view of defence requirements. As no foreign state was any longer planning a land invasion of Europe, large expenditures on the large standing forces of the NATO era were no longer so necessary. A more real potential threat, in an era of developing missile technology, was of missile attack from a future hostile state. This 'rogue' problem would need a whole range of responses (from economic to military threats) amounting to 'containment and deterrence', but only in extreme contingencies – when under the threat of imminent attack (Iraq not being one of them) – pre-emptive action for regime change.

A largely unspoken difference between Washington and European strategic thinking was that many Europeans saw their security enhanced by supporting existing states, no matter how autocratic, rather than destroying them through regime change (as in Iraq) – an outcome which (as in Iraq) would only add to the number of failed states and would heighten terrorism. Western messianism (even if couched in the high-flown phraseology of 'bringing democracy') would make the West less secure – President Chirac warned on the eve of the attack on Iraq that the overthrow of Saddam would lead to hundreds of 'mini bin Ladens'.

Should Europe opt not to have a Pentagon-style global military interventionist policy, the new Euro-superpower will simply not need the huge expense of a massive mobile military to fight regular and quasi-regular armies in far-flung places throughout Eurasia. Although Europe will need some mobile units for peacekeeping operations (like UN operations in Africa), a strategy of limited power projection will place less of a burden on the European taxpayer than that placed on the American. Europe will then have more resources to allocate to the real needs of homeland defence. And a concentration on homeland defence means that counter-terrorism (and intelligence) will become Europe's spending priority – creating a financial burden that can only be borne by pooling and coordinating resources through Brussels.

Also, although rarely raised in public debate, any strategic defence of the European peoples, like those of the American or the Chinese, will, in the coming era of multiple superpowers, need to include an ability to deter other superpowers from exerting political pressure – whether they be China, India, or even close allies like Russia and the USA. In the coming world order of multiple superpowers, problems will hopefully be settled by negotiation (and, if US policy allows it, through a revived UN), but each superpower can be expected to keep a nuclear deterrent. A lesson from the cold war remains: that deterrence between superpowers works.

Yet, in the developing defence debate in Europe, some thinkers were suggesting that even a judicious superpower (with fewer ambitions than the USA) would need a bigger military. And that even should Europe get its defence house in order (with a 'separate' defence system), the continent would not be able to meet its security needs on its own – and would continue to rely upon US military support into the foreseeable future.

Raw military spending figures continue to suggest to Washington hawks that Europe greets the new century as a military weakling – as one wag put it, Europe is 'an economic giant, a political dwarf, and a military worm'. In sum, the new emperor will have no clothes. Europe certainly appears a 'weakling' when its military spending is measured against that of the Pentagon. In 2000, even before the American spending boost following September 11th, US defence spending was $294.6 billion, whereas the EU nations of NATO spent less than half of that, just $143 billion (France $34 billion, Germany $28 billion, Britain $34 billion and Italy $21 billion). According to the London-based International Institute for Strategic Studies' *Military Balance*, this represented 3 per cent of US GDP and 2.2 per cent of EU GDP[26] and this real military gap between the Pentagon and the EU lengthens when research and development expenditure, the basis of future technological capability, is compared. Since the end of the cold war, American R&D spending has been increasing year on year, whereas Europe's has been declining; and by 2001 the USA was spending a whopping $39 billion compared to the EU nations' $9 billion.[27]

Yet, the mammoth Pentagon budget – which Dwight David Eisenhower famously depicted as a 'military-industrial complex' – is not really a defence budget only. It is a social security and employment budget as well, which politicians can use to regulate the economy (as did President George W. Bush in his 2002 Keynesian pump-priming exercise) and it is one of the great vested interests in American life that cannot be seriously cut without much pain – rather like the welfare states in Europe. (Europe, though, is still in the fortunate position of being able to use its military spending simply for its security and defence needs.)

However, when comparisons with the Pentagon's 'overkill' military budget are set aside, Europe in global terms begins to appear as a military giant. In 2000, Europe had three times the power of Russia, four times the power of Japan, four times that of China and over ten times that of India. But raw figures do not tell the whole story or describe the total punch. The stark fact that two European nation states, France and the UK, can deliver weapons of mass destruction to any adversary anywhere in the world, may well make up for a lack of conventional firepower and mobility – the same being true of Pakistan in its stand-off with India (Pakistan's military budget is only a fifth of India's). Nor should it be forgotten that Europe's combined regular army size is much larger even than that of the USA. As leading American-based geo-strategic thinker Paul Kennedy once remarked – we should remember that 'four states (Germany, France, Britain and Italy) possess hundreds of major surface warships and submarines and thousands of tanks artillery and aircraft.'[28]

Critics of Europe's military unpreparedness, most of them in Washington, take a static view. They look at Europe's present, not its potential. For, the truth is that there is no single arm or facet of military power (whether it be intelligence, airlift, combat or weapons of mass destruction) that Europe does not already possess or that it could not acquire very quickly, given the political will. For the moment, Europe's great lack is not in defence, but in offence – in the mobility of its forces, in its ability to move European troops around the world at short notice. And this mobility is the expensive aspect of a modern military (as standing armies and nuclear weapons simply cost less).

Europe's good fortune is that the continent's military capabilities can be increased without increasing spending. For, unlike the Pentagon, the continent can get a 'bigger bang for the existing buck' by adopting the classic solution of economies of scale – that is, by integrating the continent's defences and pooling the total European effort. Some analysts, like Britain's retired Air Marshall Timothy Garden, are even suggesting that without such pooling Europe 'might as well get out of the military game altogether'.[29]

The simple fact is that all the main requirements of a mobile military for a modern superpower – from Pentagon-style airlift to air-to-air refuelling to combat aircraft and equipment to aircraft carriers through to a serious intelligence capacity – become possible through European defence integration and pooling. For instance, NATO's existing supranational early warning (AWACS) force – which was sent from Europe to guard the USA in the aftermath of the New York atrocity – is an example of an integrated supranational effort. Also, by pooling the large number of existing, though separately held, C130 Hercules aircraft in Europe, the EU could provide itself with a full tactical fixed-wing transport capability – of 137 such transport aircraft – before, that is, Europe's Airbus A400M transport aircraft becomes operational.[30] Again, pooling of support functions, such as air-to-air refuelling and transport ships for strategic deployment, reconnaissance and search and rescue assets, would both save costs to individual nations whilst, for a time at least, maintaining national control over the more sensitive combat capabilities.

Although it is still politically difficult to pool the all-important defensive and offensive air-power systems, such a pooling could, virtually overnight, provide the EU with a sizeable air force. For instance, a powerful EU F16 fighter force could quite quickly be assembled should Belgium, Denmark, Greece, the Netherlands and Portugal (who operate between them as many as 424 F16 aircraft) and Germany, Italy and the UK (who, even with technical differences, could contribute some of their 570 aircraft) simply merge some of these assets. And when the long-awaited Euro-fighter aircraft comes into service in five European nations, it has been suggested by analysts that 'we might perhaps imagine an operationally ready force of some 400 Euro-fighters made up of 20 multinational squadrons distributed over five airbases.'[31]

Europe could also cut costs by adopting the US system of large airbases, and also by providing one Euro HQ for the Euro-fighter. And a pooled European fleet – of aircraft or ships – would provide a common approach to the all-important European weapons and systems procurement regime, creating a single European regime to match the single regime of the Pentagon.

A pooled European defence regime would allow Europe's nations to specialize and avoid wasteful duplication. Britain, for instance, instead of sticking with its vainglorious 'full-range' military (an attempt to remain a 'mini USA'), could concentrate its talents. The UK could build the next generation of aircraft carriers – the eventual cost of which could be £10 billion – and lower its costs on other services such as the army and its regiments. A single centralized procurement programme is many years off, but an agreed common programme is possible, and military historian John Keegan has speculated that a form of informal specialization may already be underway.[32]

A big gap, though, in Europe's present defences is its lack of an independent intelligence system. For the moment, although Europe's separate civilian intelligence services are, by world standards, more than adequate, and in the new counter-terrorist environment are coordinating policies and operations, Europeans still rely heavily upon American intelligence support in a military crisis. But, as well as politics, long-standing technical differences have held up pooling and integrating the various national systems. Some experts believe that, rather than building on national intelligence systems, the EU should start from scratch, which, though costly, would allow it to establish a fully integrated, state-of-the-art system fairly quickly. It would need such big-ticket items as Unmanned Air Vehicles (the 'drones' unfurled by the USA over the skies of Afghanistan in 2002) and satellite-based strategic reconnaissance.

But with the independent European Galileo satellite navigation system due to become fully operational in 2008, the EU, after integrating it into the military, will possess an intelligence capability fit for a superpower. Galileo, which will compete with the GPS system run by the American government, will be launched by the European Space Agency, and will rely on a network of 30 satellites costing 3.2 billion euro. According to French Transport Minister Jean Claude Gaysott, 'it will allow Europe to liberate itself from dependence on the American GPS system'. Galileo faced severe opposition from factions within the US government, particularly the Pentagon, which claimed to worry about whether its signals could overlap with the GPS signals causing complications for the War on Terrorism. Paul Wolfowitz, US Deputy Defense Secretary, is reported to be have sent a letter to the EU Commission outlining fears about Galileo.[33]

Britain's special intelligence relationship with the USA remains, though, a major obstacle to pooling Europe's full intelligence potential. It also places Britain in a real intelligence bind, between a rock and a hard place. Washington simply refuses to allow the UK to pass on sensitive information gained from this 'special relationship' to its EU partners; and these 'partners' rightly argue that Britain can hardly be counted as a European power whilst it withholds information from friends. Should Britain finally decide to participate fully in the developing EU intelligence system, then it will inevitably mean a difficult break with Washington – at least for Britain's secret services.[34]

Symbols of Power

As Europe develops a strategic defence for a superpower, it will need to decide what to say about the continent's most secret and under-reported story: Europe's nuclear weapons systems. Neither at St Malo nor at Helsinki, nor in any of the EDI and EDS declarations, has the EU openly dealt with this very touchy subject. It is simply too hot to handle. The EU's two nuclear powers, Paris and London, have talked secretly about nuclear cooperation, but behind this wall of silence lies the fear is that any new Union nuclear policy, as opposed to existing national nuclear weapons, might be in breach of the non-proliferation treaty.

All that is clear is that Europe, either severally or singly – will remain a nuclear weapons state. In 2002, Europeans were opposing the Bush policy of 'pre-emption' and 'regime change' for hostile states, and advancing a defence doctrine of traditional deterrence. But deterrence – whether against 'rogue states' or against nuclear-armed superpowers which could turn anti-western (like China or India) – would need the threat of the use of nuclear weapons to back it up. Also, if Israel, South Africa and Pakistan have a nuclear capacity, opinion in Europe, even in the more pacifist countries, will inevitably ask: why not Europe?

But any European-wide nuclear security policy will call forth huge questions of control – whose finger is ultimately on the trigger? The idea that the two holders of the bomb, the French President or the British Prime Minister, would give up control of nuclear weapons to a future European Council, or even to a new President of the Council with security responsibilities, is unlikely. To see a future President of Europe followed by a colonel with nuclear codes is a long way off, and will be the very last act in the drama of a united Europe. A more likely short-term outcome – one already advocated by France – will be for France and Britain to hold these weapons in trust for Europe. France has already offered to extend its nuclear umbrella to cover Germany, but it remains less than enthusiastic about sharing the keys to its nuclear systems.

If Europe wants to remain a nuclear power it will, though, need to upgrade, as a matter of urgency, its delivery systems – better done jointly than separately. Both the British and French nuclear delivery systems are ageing. The British submarine SLBM system is dependent upon a new generation of missiles and an annual servicing – in the continental United States – of existing systems, all of which is dependent upon American goodwill. The French sea-launched and land-launched missiles are also looking somewhat weather-worn. The EU is unlikely to want the kind of massive strategic deterrent operated by the US triad system; rather, should it be in the nuclear game at all, then all it would need would be a slim-line system allowing it the ability to strike anywhere on the globe. The European Arianne rocket delivery system, which could use the smallish British and French warheads with pinpoint accuracy, could serve this function.

Europe will also have to decide whether to adopt a continental missile defence system – with or without the USA. This will depend on Europe's security doctrine: whether it is based on deterrence only, or, more likely, a mix of deterrence, pre-emption and diplomacy. Here, the outcome of the wider, American debate will be pivotal; whether the Americans will offer Europe protection under their umbrella and what the costs of this option, or an independent option, might be. Much too will depend on the technology, on whether the same protection can be afforded by close-range missile defences sited in the regions of 'rogue' states. Whatever happens, EU unity will demand a single coverage; if the EU is to mean anything then the whole of the EU will either be in or out of the system.

As well as settling the issue of 'the bomb', the other remaining question will be whether Europe really wants to join the Pentagon and get into the global force-projection business. As I have suggested, in the early years of the new century a consensus seemed to be emerging that although Europe would not want to match the USA's global power projection, the new Europe would certainly need the capability of power projection to its border areas. Instability in the Maghreb (particularly Algeria) and across the Mediterranean and Adriatic into the Balkans would need European peacekeeping and peacemaking forces and the even more combustible Middle East could see European mobile forces as part of a UN emergency. By 2002, the EU's leading military powers – Britain, France and Germany – were already providing more soldiers for peacekeeping operations around the world than were the Americans. But, outside of the Balkans, these units do not form themselves into a separate European force.

This separate force is to be provided by Europe's great new symbol of superpowerhood – the EU's Rapid Reaction Force, a European army which can be deployed anywhere in the world 'within 60 days and sustain for at least one year forces of up to 50–60,000 persons capable of the full range of Petersburg tasks' (peacekeeping and peacemaking). This force – which is backed by all of Europe's leaders, including Britain's Tony Blair – was to become a down payment by Europe, an earnest of the continent's future military unity and independence.[35] It was bold stuff, as one Eurocrat put it: 'As bold as the 1991 project to establish the euro.' And, like the euro, its ambitious start date – 2003 – was to slip.[36] Even so, some British officials believe the EU will inevitably use the force on a regular basis – at the 'upper end' of the Petersburg tasks – particularly in Africa and in the flashpoints on the European periphery.[37]

And around Europe's capitals, few were prepared to predict that it could not be done. And in Washington, Pentagon strategists were awaiting its first outing with a weird mixture of scepticism and trepidation.

But the military wing of a European superpower cannot even begin to emerge without a smooth-running centralized organization in Brussels. Ideally, future superpower Europe needs something akin to Washington's national security system, which links the President and his NSC in the White House to the Pentagon and the intelligence community. By 2004, it was on the way to getting one. The historic agreement signed in December 2003 by the troika (of Britain, France and Germany) meant that the EU Council's Political and Security Committee and Military Committee can now give directions to a couple of hundred-strong operational military planning staff officers in Brussels – a structure completely separate from NATO, and one that can quite easily grow into a fully fledged military command for the new European superpower.[38] Such operations will remain fairly limited but, as defence expert Frederick Bonnart argues, it is 'the seed corn of a full future European military planning and command headquarters'.[39] And it is hardly a big leap to see how, by say 2020, this embryonic Pentagon-style command centre could become directly responsible to a single president of Europe and the political leadership of the superpower. And French officials were pointing out that Europe could handle large operations by themselves through some of the national headquarters – and, intriguingly, they were citing the British permanent joint headquarters operation, situated in a bunker in Northwood, North-West London, which directed a 24,000 troop operation in Oman – using no NATO assets![40]

One good side effect of these Anglo-French-German debates about the way forward for European defence was that Europeans were at last beginning to think seriously about security, world politics and geo-strategy. Europe's governmental elites (in the British Foreign Office and the Quai d'Orsay) prided themselves on a sophisticated understanding of global events (though some still made the mistake of seeing Washington as a novice); but the truth was that during the cold war Europe's foreign offices and defence establishments had left serious strategic thinking to Washington and Moscow. Europeans became provincialized, riveted only on Europe (and its cold-war divisions). Paris and London had the lingering glow of a largely irrelevant imperial sensibility, and Bonn (and later Berlin) simply did not want to think about strategy at all. But, post-cold war, with increasing independence from Washington, Europeans were for the first time in a generation being forced to think strategically and globally. By 2003, even as the Union's unified defence was on the agenda, Brussels was a long way from creating a genuinely Washington-like strategic culture (that is, an ability to think about the connection between international economics, politics, history and development and the use of force). But any new superpower with military pretensions will need the kind of support that Washington has 'enjoyed' for most of the post-Second

World War period – that corpus of strategic expertise, knowledge and understanding which is brought together by a critical mass of research and opinion-forming university departments, research institutes and think-tanks, what experts have called the 'institutional confidence and processes to manage and deploy military force' as part of over-all foreign policy.[41]

Europe and America in 2020

The exact point when commentators, without hyperbole, can talk of Europe as a new superpower – of the USE in the way they talk of the USA – is difficult to divine and define. It may well be a great financial event – the euro overtaking the dollar as a world reserve currency. It might be a technological feat – a European space shot to Mars. It might be a major foreign policy clash between a united Europe and Washington. More likely, it will be something to do with armed forces. Humans are still at a stage of development when security is what governments are all about. And the moment at which Europeans come to believe that Europe, and only Europe, can guarantee their security will be the point of no return.

Yet, in security and military matters, as in life more generally, nothing succeeds like success, and when Europe's first peacekeeping or peacemaking military action 'independent of the US' takes place, much will ride on its outcome. For only with a major peacekeeping success under its belt will Europe have found its feet as a superpower. Like the euro project, it cannot afford to fail – although, unlike the euro and money, in foreign and military policy events are always much messier and their success less measurable.

If superpower Europe is truly up and running by 2020, then that in itself will have redefined the transatlantic relationship. It will then amount to an equal partnership between two superpowers – the two superpowers (in an emerging world of superpowers) that have most in common. Indeed, the old cliché will still hold – that they have more in common than divides them. The common part will be their advanced economies, democratic societies and shared ethnic background; the divided part will be their continuing differing interests in the world, and their, hopefully, relatively friendly competitive ambitions in Eurasia.

But, this redefining is bound also to impact on the more formal side of the transatlantic world, the old institutional warhorse of

NATO. And NATO will either be left to wither on the vine, a revered icon of the victory in the cold war, or if it is still taken seriously, it will be reformed. NATO could become a great overarching political alliance, linking both superpowers in a transatlantic community pledged to mutual values and to mutual defence but dropping its joint military command structure. Alternatively, it could keep its joint command system but completely overhaul it to produce equal partners in an equal structure – say, with a single EU defence command working with the single US command. Whichever way it goes, NATO will be transformed from a US-led military alliance into a real alliance between equals.

This new transatlantic world, shorn of American leadership, will take some getting used to – not just in Europe, but in the USA too. Washington will miss old NATO, probably more so than Europe will. The Pentagon will not miss European military help (for, as it found out during the Serbian air war, such help can often complicate the job at hand). But it will miss automatic access to US bases in Europe for its forward power projection and, above all, European financial assistance and political support.

But will Washington's forward global strategy survive the end of old NATO? The great Achilles heel of the Washington's power-elite's post-9/11 aggressive global strategy will be American public opinion. Most Americans remain troubled about sending US troops abroad to fight and die – and since the Vietnam conflict, all American presidents have tried to fight conflicts with air power and high-tech stand-off equipment only, and, the Gulf War included, have insisted on minimal casualties. If the US takes casualties, but is also alone and without allies, particularly European allies, public support for wars and conflicts abroad will rapidly erode.

In these circumstances, will the US begin to retrench, to withdraw from its outer empire? Or even collapse the global empire altogether, and return to a hemispheric superpower policy? Both outcomes are unlikely. What is, though, on the cards is a reorientation of Washington's global strategy. She will continue as a global power, keen, above all, to maintain a large foothold in Eurasia. But, to supplement her existing primacy in central Eurasia, the USA may well reroute itself from her 'perch' in the western landmass to a firmer bridgehead in the Pacific Rim. The USA would become an Asian power – umbilically linked to South and East Asia through its economic relationship with China.

Europe has already been slowly losing its centrality in US thinking. And, for the future, Washington's main interest may well focus on Asia – on the arc of 'rogue states' in the Middle East through to North Korea, on Islamic terrorists throughout South Asia, and principally on the economic and military destiny of China. At times, this greater interest in Asia has caused Washington to seem cavalier or even quasi-isolationist when thinking about Europe. The former NATO Supreme Allied Commander Europe, Wesley Clark, even suggested that:

> American actions and attitudes contributed significantly to pushing the Europeans towards their goal of an autonomous military capability. Let's face it, we Americans encouraged the Europeans to believe that in future security crises in Europe, we might not be there to help.[42]

Of course, the powerful business interests in North America will continue to be drawn towards Europe by the reality of the two continents economic interdependence and especially by the rich European single market. However, American Eurocentrism has always been about the links of kin, culture and heritage as much as it has been about business and economics – but it is here, in the demographic shifts in the USA, that Europe is lessening its hold. As the European-derived white population declines as a percentage of the total, and the percentage of non-whites (Blacks, Asians and, above all, the burgeoning Hispanics) increase, the writing is on the wall for the USA as a European country.

Of course, this demographic de-Europeanization of the USA may take some time because, although Europeans will cease to be a majority sometime this century, they will remain the largest single group, and they will vote in greater numbers than many non-white minorities. Yet, crucially, Europe means less and less even to the still dominant European-derived population, now third, fourth or fifth generation Europeans! Midwestern and southern whites are less and less engaged by their European background, and, in the west, most Americans, when they think of 'abroad', increasingly look to Asia. There remains a disproportionate number of Eurocentric Americans – including Anglophile 'Wasps' – in positions of power, but nowhere (not even in foreign policy circles) are they numerous enough to be decisive.

Should the USA indeed retrench around the world, concentrating upon limited global interests and its crucial economic relationship with Asia, then Europe will, of necessity, fill the vacuum as the dominant western power in Eurasia. Maintaining stable European relations with Russia, with Islam and the Middle East and, above all, China will be a tall order for the new superpower. It will amount to a heavy responsibility. But, for Europeans, the price of becoming a superpower – as Americans will readily testify – is a willingness to accept such responsibility.

Notes

Introduction

1. American neo-conservative writer Robert Kagan has called today's Europe a 'paradise of peace and relative prosperity.' See Robert Kagan, *Paradise and Power: America and Europe in the New World Order* (London, 2003), p. 3.
2. *Wall Street Journal*, 5 December 2003.
3. Phillip Bobbitt, *The Shield Of Achilles: War, Peace and the Course of History* (London, 2002).
4. Francis Fukuyama, *The End of History and The Last Man* (London, 1992).
5. See Zbigniew Brzezinski, *The Grand Chessboard: American Primacy and Its Geo-Strategic Imperatives* (New York, 1998).
6. This 'hub and spokes' model was set out by my colleague Professor Peter Gowan in: Peter Gowan, 'The New American Century', *The Spokesman*, No. 76 (London, 2002).

Chapter 1: Europe and the American Empire

1. See Paul Kennedy, *The Rise and Fall of the Great Powers: Economic Change and Military Conflict from 1500–2000* (New York, 1987), Chapter Five, for economic data on the shifting balance of world forces, 1889–1938, and for useful tables on the relative shares of world manufacturing output 1880–1938, and total industrial potential of the powers in relative perspective, 1880–1938.
2. By 'Western Europe' here, I mean Britain, Germany, France and Italy. Iron and steel figures in ibid. Table 15, p. 200.
3. Ibid. Table 27: 'Defence Expenditures of the Great Powers, 1930–1938', p. 296.
4. According to the historian Clive Ponting, Western Europe had 'low population, poor agriculture, few towns, very little trade and a very limited level of political development'. In Ponting, *World History: A New Perspective* (London, 2000), p. 490.
5. Norman Davies, *Europe: A History* (London, 1997), p. 759.

6. Italian Prime Minister Silvio Berlusconi spoke for many western progressives, more than would care to admit to it, when, at the height of tensions with the Islamic world following the terrorist attack on New York, he argued publicly that western civilization was superior to Islam specifically because of its liberal values and democratic institution. It was this view that led many Europeans (in both Europe and America) towards a 'universalism' that made liberal values the test of a society, a test applying to all peoples at all times. As Bruno Coppieters has argued, 'a universalist rhetoric is part of Europe's identity as a superior civilization, a rhetoric in which there is no significant difference between the identity of Europe and that of the US (Europe's most successful colony).' Bruno Coppieters, 'Between Europe and Asia: Security and Identity in Central Asia', in L. Aggestam and A. Hyde-Price (eds), *Security and Identity in Europe* (London, 2000), p. 210.

7. Paul Kennedy has described what he called a 'combination of economic laissez-faire, political and military pluralism, and intellectual liberty' as one of many reasons for 'Europe's miracle'. In Kennedy, *The Rise and Fall of the Great Powers*, p. 30.

8. Quoted in Davies, *Europe*, p. 597

9. It was this political, non-religious character of Europe, according to Voltaire, which set the peoples of the western Eurasian continent apart from the rest of the world. According to the great man, Europe was 'a kind of great republic divided into several states, some monarchical, the others mixed... but all corresponding with one another. They all have the same religious foundation, even if divided into several confessions. They all have the same principle of public law and politics, unknown in other parts of the world.' Quoted in Denys Hay, *Europe: The Emergence of an Idea* (Edinburgh, 1957), p. 123.

10. The erudite political theorist, the late Maurice Cranston, argued that the rule of law, and thus the authority of the state, is utterly central to ensuring the liberty of the individual. See Maurice Cranston, *Freedom: A New Analysis*, second edition (London, 1955).

11. Figures were: Total GNP in 1950: US 381 billion dollars, UK 71 billion, France 50 billion, West Germany 48 billion. Defence expenditure in 1950: US 14.5 billion dollars, UK 2.3 billion, France 1.4 billion and Italy 0.5 billion. Figures in Kennedy, *The Rise and Fall of the Great Powers*, Tables 36 and 37.

12. He said 'For the German... all of this [Hitler's political triumphs, job creation schemes etc] must have seemed like a miracle.' These remarks were presaged by 'but anyone who wishes to reduce our guilt... is trying to defend the indefensible.' Quoted in Ian Buruma, *Wages of Guilt* (London, 1994), p. 241.

13. Speech delivered in Sioux Falls, South Dakota, 8 September 1919.

14. The view of historian Allan Bullock. Bullock, *Ernest Bevin, Foreign Secretary, 1945–51* (London, 1983), p. 121; for details of the loan negotiations see Chapter Four; and see also Hugh Thomas, *Armed Truce* (New York, 1987) for a perceptive analysis of immediate post-war American foreign policy.

15. Quoted in John Charmley, *Churchill: The End of Glory* (London, 1993), p. 586.

16. For a revealing and detailed analysis of the British elite's continuing belief in the sentimental underpinning of the Anglo-American relationship, see Correlli Barnett, *The Collapse of British Power* (London, 1972).

17. For GNP figures, see Kennedy, *The Rise and Fall of the Great Powers*, Table 36, p. 369.

18. See Dean Acheson, *Present At The Creation* (New York, 1970).

19. Quoted in Bullock, *Ernest Bevin* (London, 1982), p. 414.

20. Ambassador Seitz's remarks at Pilgrim's dinner, London, 1993.

21. 'There is considerable evidence,' suggests Professor John Young, 'that, while forced to rely on the US in the short-term, in the long term Bevin hoped to build a "third force" independent of, and equal to, America, yet in the wider framework of an anti-Soviet alliance.' John W. Young, *Britain and European Unity, 1945–1992* (London, 1993). The historian John Kent even suggested that Bevin tried to organise a Euro-African bloc, bringing together Western Europe and the then African and Middle Eastern colonies. See J. Kent, 'Bevin's Imperialism and the idea of Euro-Africa', in M. Dockrill and J.W. Young (eds), *British Foreign Policy, 1945–56* (London, 1989). But Bevin was a realist. He did 'not see the creation of NATO in 1949 as a triumph... but rather as a defeat for his original vision [of a European-led third force within a broader Atlantic alliance] which proved impossible to realize', ibid. p.16.

22. Samuel Huntingdon has argued that the debate between multiculturalists and monoculturalists in the USA is important for American foreign policy. He has also suggested that the USA may, in effect, become 'de-westernised'. See Samuel Huntingdon, *The Clash of Civilizations and the Remaking of World Order* (London, 1997), p. 307.

23. Neo-conservatives used 'Finlandization' as a term of moral reproach, not as a word depicting geo-strategic realism.

24. A comment by *New York Times* columnist Flora Lewis, reported by William Wallace in 'Europe The Necessary Partner', *Foreign Affairs*, May/June 2001.

25. See, for example, Charles Krauthammer, '"The Unipolar Moment", America and The World', *Foreign Affairs* (1990/1991). And, over a decade later, also see Stephen Brooks and William Wohlforth, 'American Primacy', *Foreign Affairs*, July–August 2002.

26. Pew Research Centre national attitudes in 44 countries, published in

December 2002, reported in *The Economist*, 4 January 2003, which also reported findings revealing a widening gap in values in polls conducted in late 2002 by the German Marshall Fund, Washington, DC and Chicago Council on Foreign Relations.

27. See Kagan, *Paradise and Power*, p. 3.

28. Jeffrey Garten, 'The Euro Will Turn Europe Into a Superpower', *Business Week*, 4 May 1998.

29. Morgan Stanley, 'The Case For De-Coupling', *Market Commentary Report, Global Strategy*, 25 March 2002.

30. Figures from *The Military Balance, 2001–2* (Oxford University Press for the International Institute For Strategic Studies, October 2001). Figures for Population and GDP are from the Department of Economic and Social Affairs, UN Secretariat, 2000.

31. For information on US bases around the world, see the Centre For Defence Information, Defence Monitor series. Also see Chalmers Johnson, *The Sorrows Of Empire* (New York, 2004), Chapter Five, 'The Empire Of Bases', for an up-to-date and comprehensive account and survey of US bases.

32. Paul Wolfowitz quote to *New York Times*, reported in *The Guardian*, 21 April 2003. Paul Kennedy's interview on *Newsnight*, BBC2, April 2003.

33. Samuel Huntingdon argues that the defeat of Iraq in the first gulf war took up too large a percentage of American military capacity to allow a proper US provision for global conflict. See Huntingdon, *The Clash of Civilizations and the Remaking of World Order*, pp. 83–91.

34. This list of the characteristics of the western Roman empire in its last years was based upon an analysis in Robert Adams, *Decadent Societies* (New York, 1975).

35. Quoted in Correlli Barnett, *The Collapse of British Power*, p. 71.

36. Ibid. p. 120.

37. Ibid. p. 123.

38. Henry Kissinger, 'America at the Apex', *National Interest*, No. 64, Summer 2001.

39. Gore Vidal, *The Decline and Fall of the American Empire* (New York, 1992); *Perpetual War For Perpetual Peace* (New York, 2002); and *Dreaming War* (New York, 2003).

40. See particularly Noam Chomsky, *9-11* (New York, 2001).

41. See Francis Fukuyama, *The End of History and the Last Man*.

42. Morgan Stanley, 'The Case For De-Coupling'.

Chapter 2: Europe Says 'No'

1. In a revealing article in the prestigious American journal *Foreign Affairs*, *Newsweek* journalist Michael Hirsh shows how endemic the idea of American 'exceptionalism' might have become. Having criticized

the general idea of US exceptionalism, even he went on to argue for 'exceptional status' being granted to US forces in the International Criminal Court procedures. Hirsh, 'Bush And The World', *Foreign Affairs*, September/October 2002.

2.   Reports in *International Herald Tribune*, 9 November 2001.

3.   Speech by Tony Blair to the Labour Party Conference in Brighton, October 2001.

4.   Hubert Vedrine and Dominique Moisi, *France in An Age of Globalization* (New York, 2000).

5.   Joseph Nye, *Bound To Lead: The Changing Nature of American Power* (New York, 1990). For figures and analysis of US relative decline, see Samuel Huntingdon, *The Clash of Civilizations and The Remaking of World Order*.

6.   See later paperback edition of Zalmay M. Khalilzad, *From Containment to Global Leadership? America and the World After the Cold War* (New York, 1995).

7.   Reported in *International Herald Tribune*, 3 March 2002.

8.   The White House, 'The National Security Strategy of the United States, 2002', p. 15.

9.   Richard Haas, quoted in *New Yorker Magazine*, 1 April 2002.

10.   Douglas Feith, whilst a senior official in the Bush Defense Department, gave a revealing interview in the *New Yorker* on the eve of the Iraq war, when he named some of the states which needed to be so 'restructured'. See *New Yorker*, 17 February 2003.

11.   See David Frum, 'Unpatriotic Conservatives', *National Review*, 7 April 2003.

12.   See particularly R. James Woolsey, 'A Long War', *Wall Street Journal Europe*, 17–20 April 2003.

13.   For an analysis of Karl Rove's attitude towards the War on Terror, see James Moore and Wayne Slater, *Bush's Brain: How Karl Rove Made George Bush Presidential* (New Jersey, 2003).

14.   Interview on CNN, 2 March 2003.

15.   Interview on Fox News, 1 March 2003.

16.   *International Herald Tribune*, 12 June 2001.

17.   From an account in D.R. Thorpe, *Eden: The Life and Times of Anthony Eden, First Earl of Avon, 1897–1977* (London, 2003). See particularly p. 383.

18.   Quote attributed to Clemenceau, in *HarperCollins Concise Dictionary of Quotations* (London, 1999).

19.   Quoted in Tony Judt, 'Anti-Americans Abroad', *New York Review of Books*, 3 May 2003.

20.   See Paul Hollander, *Anti-Americanism: Critiques At Home and Abroad, 1965–1990* (New York, 1992).

21.   See Jean-Jacques Servan Schreiber, *The American Challenge*, English edition (New York, 1968).

22. Reported in *Hansard*, 22 January 2003, columns 850–2.
23. Associated Press, 9 January 2004, reported that the EU Commission President, Romano Prodi, had cancelled an EU Seminar on Anti-Semitism following criticism by leaders of the World Jewish Congress of the EU for publishing a poll reporting that Europeans had named Israel as a bigger threat to world peace than any other country. (The leading figures of the WJC argued that the EU had presented the poll in such a way as to display an 'anti-Semitic' attitude.)
24. Professor William Wallace described what he called a growing 'European disrespect for the American model', a disdain amply reciprocated by Wall Street's critique of the 'European social model'. But the term 'model' as used in the transatlantic debate tends to remain a polite way of describing judgements not just about differing economic and social policies, but values and way of life as well. See William Wallace, 'Europe, the Necessary Partner', *Foreign Affairs*, May–June 2000, p. 28.
25. Condoleezza Rice, 'America and Europe, Partners Tomorrow and The Day After', *International Herald Tribune*, 12 June 2001.
26. See Stephen Haseler, *The Super-Rich: The Unjust World Of Global Capital* (London, 2000) for a detailed analysis of hereditary wealth in the USA. The figures are stark: in 1973, 56 per cent of the total wealth held by persons aged 35–39 was given to them by their parents. Even by 1986, the figure for 35–39 baby-boomers had risen to an alarming 86 per cent. (Ibid. p. 14) And, it has been estimated that, on 1996 trends, 'the number of estates in the $1 million or more range will increase by 246 percent during the next decade; these estates will be valued (in 1990 constant dollars) at a total of more than $2 trillion ($2,000,000,000,000). But nearly the same amount will be distributed by so-called predecedent affluent parents and grandparents to their children/grandchildren.' The amounts of individual wealth transfers by inheritance are indeed staggering. Looking to the future, economist Edward Woolf has projected that should inheritance follow the lines of US wealth concentration in the 1990s then in the early years of the new century the wealth going to the top one per cent of Americans would average $3 million each, and the next richest five per cent (95–99 percentiles) would average $900,000 each. Worse still, many of today's inheritances are being used to live off. A huge private dependency culture – dependence here upon family rather than the state – is being erected. American analysts have described this derisively as 'economic outpatient care'. Such 'outpatient' welfare care is now massive: it has been estimated that a huge 46 per cent of the affluent in America give at least $15,000 worth of EOC (Economic Outpatient Care) annually to their adult children or grandchildren. If this estimate is near accurate, and 'affluent' is defined as a net worth dollar millionaire family, then there is an annual transfer from super-

rich to relatives, within the boundaries of the USA alone, of $15 billion. This super-rich welfare state involves the transfer from one generation to another of 'entire coin collections, stamp collections... payments of medical and dental expenses, plastic surgery', as well as straight cash gifts. It is estimated that 43 per cent of millionaire parents fund all or a large part of the tuition for a grandchild's private grade school and/or private high school, 32 per cent fund tuition for adult children's graduate school, 59 per cent provide financial assistance in purchasing a home, 61 per cent provide 'forgiveness loans' (those not to be repaid) to adult children, and 17 per cent give gifts of listed stock to adult children.

27.　Ziauddin Sardar and Merryl Wyn, *Why Do People Hate America?* (Cambridge, 2002).

Chapter 3: The Making of a Superpower

1.　Jean Monnet is now, though, associated with the step-by-step approach to European unity, rather than the 'big-bang' federal constitutionalist approach later favoured by Altierio Spinelli.

2.　A belief of Monnet's, adopted from the nineteenth-century diarist Henri Frederic Amiel. For an impressive account of Monnet's approach to European unity, see François Duchene, *Jean Monnet: The First Statesman of Interdependence* (Paris, 1994).

3.　Figures from the Department of Economic and Social Affairs, UN Secretariat, 2002. They always need to be adjusted to reflect exchange-rate fluctuations.

4.　World Bank figures in *World Bank Atlas* for 1999.

5.　Calculation made by Matt Marshall, *The Bank: The Birth of Europe's Central Bank And The Re-Birth of Europe's Power* (London, 1999), p. 353.

6.　See Lester Thurow, *Head To Head: The Economic Battle Among Japan, Europe and America* (New York, 1993). Thurow argues his case about Europe on pp. 252ff.

7.　John Stevens, 'Britain's European Destiny', unpublished paper, May 2001.

8.　See full list of countries in John Pinder, *The European Union: A Very Short Introduction* (Oxford, 2001), p. 147. This book is an extremely useful reference volume.

9.　Reported in H.D.S. Greenway, 'Expect the Chinese to Overtake America, and India will be Third', *International Herald Tribune*, 23 May 2001.

10.　Quotation from John McCormick, *Understanding The European Union* (Basingstoke, 1999), p. 55.

11.　Figures from World Bank, *World Bank Atlas*, 2001. Purchasing Power Parity assessments produce slightly different figures. The 1996 *World Bank Atlas* figures, taken before German reunification and the high dollar, showed per capita GNP figures had the EU average at $21,400, the USA at $26,100 and Japan at $39,400 (with non-EU semi-European countries like Russia at $2,250 and Turkey at $6,100). Individual EU countries had a higher standard of living than the US: Germany was on per capita $27,400, Sweden $23,900, Austria $26,300, and Denmark $30,000; whereas Spain at $13,000, Italy at $19,000, the UK at $18,800 and France at $24,800, were somewhat lower. From World Bank, *World Bank Atlas 1996* (Washington, DC, 1997).

12.   UN Human Development Index 2002, UN Development Programme 2002.

13.   Cited in, and also see, Giles Radice, *The New Germans* (London, 1995) p. 141.

14.   See Anthony Atkinson, Lee Rainwater and Timothy Smeeding, *Income Distribution in OECD Countries* (Paris, 1995).

15.   Quotation cited in Peter Jay, *The Oxford Dictionary of Political Quotations*, p. 264.

16.   Bernard Connolly, *The Rotten Heart Of Europe: The Dirty War For Europe's Money* (London, 1995), p. 392.

17.   The Werner Report (1970) produced a plan for economic and monetary union to be achieved by 1980, but it was never implemented.

18.   Connolly, *The Rotten Heart Of Europe*, p. 17.

19.   Speech in Bruges, 1989, cited in Charles Grant, *Delors: The House That Jacques Built* (London, 1994), p. 131.

20.   Ibid. p. 135.

21.   Quoted in Marshall, *The Bank*, p. 440.

22.   *New York Times*, 25 January 1987.

23.   Quotation from Marshall, *The Bank*, p. 94. For an informed account of the politics over the single currency at Maastricht, see pp. 349ff.

Chapter 4: Towards a Super-State

1.   David Marquand, 'Age of the Superstate', *New Statesman*, 25 June 2001.

2.   The decision of the Laeken European Council in December 2001 to establish a grand Constitutional Convention, under the chairmanship of former French President Valéry Giscard d'Estaing, to advise on the future governance of the EU has been described as 'Europe's Philadelphia' (after the convention in Philadelphia of 55 men who drew up the American constitution in 1787). Another comparison might be made with the earlier committee, set up in 1776 after the Declaration of Independence, which drew up the first American constitution, the Articles of Confederation, adopted by the fledgling USA in November 1777.

3.   The expert on European governance Simon Hix is amongst those who take the view that the EU is a 'political system' but not a 'state', because it does not have 'a monopoly of the legitimate use of coercion'. Hix, *The*

Political System of the European Union (London, 1999), p. 4. It is, though, fair to ask whether exclusive control of the police and army – although important in times of crisis – is still of any relevance to a modern European definition of statehood. It can be argued that the EU possesses the classic functions of a political system: a stable set of institutions for collective decision-making; citizens and social groups seeking to achieve ends through this political system; the collective decisions coming out of these institutions having a significant impact upon the distribution of economic resources and upon social and political values across the system; and the political process of the system being continuous and a permanent feature of political life.

4.   Although the EU treaties do not contain a formal 'supremacy clause', the supremacy of EU law over national law, should there be a conflict, was established with the European Court of Justice's landmark judgement in 1964 in the case of Costa v. ENEL and is now accepted by all national legal systems. See Hix, *The Political System of the European Union*, pp. 117–27, for an exhaustive discussion of the supremacy doctrine; see also Paul Johnson, *A History Of The American People* (London, 1997), pp. 159–66.

5.   The European Central Bank, like the US 'Fed', is composed of 'regional' bank governors, and it decides interest-rate policy (and liquidity) across the whole currency zone.

6.   For a chronicle of European Monetary Union, see Horst Ungerer, *A Concise History of European Monetary Integration* (London, 1997).

7.   Marshall, *The Bank*, p. 398.

8.   Ibid. p. 92.

9.   Quoted by Roy Denman, *International Herald Tribune*, 29 January 2003.

10.   Joschka Fischer, 'From Confederation to Federation', speech given at the Humboldt University, Berlin, 12 May 2000, published by the Federal Trust (London, 2000). Martyn Bond, a former director of London's Federal Trust, has provided by far the clearest short outline of the constitutional clash between federalists and nationalists. He argues that 'Federalists tend to favour a future structure of the Union which refers back to the Community method and assimilates the second and third pillars of the Union (Common foreign and security policy and Justice and Home affairs) to the classic Community methods of the first pillar. They want to see the Commission develop its role… as the executive of the Union… the Council of Ministers and the European Parliament develop as two arms of the legislative authority, as Chamber of the Peoples and a Chamber of the States… Intergovernmentalists, on the other hand, are reluctant to see the three pillars merged and they resist an increased role for the Commission. They wish to maintain the European Parliament in the position of junior partner vis-à-vis the

Council… They would like to enhance the role of national Parliaments, possibly by creating another Chamber at European level composed of national delegates.' In Martyn Bond, 'Introduction', in Martyn Bond and Kim Feus (eds), *The Treaty Of Nice Explained*, (London, 2001), pp. 17–18.

11.   Lionel Jospin, 'The Future Of An Enlarged Europe', 28 May 2001. Available on French government portal site: www.premier-ministre. gouv.fr/en/p.cfm?ref=24924. Also see 'Our Europe', speech by President Jacques Chirac, Bundestag, 27 June, 2000, reprinted by the Federal Trust, European essay No. 9, 2000.

12.   See Tony Blair, 'Superpower not Superstate?', speech in Warsaw, published by the Federal Trust, November 2001.

13.   Assuming Articles 20 and 21 of the Giscard draft are ultimately adopted in a constitution.

14.   See John Vinocur, *International Herald Tribune*, 15 December 2003.

15.   See *Financial Times*, 15 December 2003.

Chapter 5: The European Core

1.   Remarks, later withdrawn, by Richard Boucher at State Department Press Conference, 2 September 2003.

2.   For his analysis of European divisions, see Ian Buruma, *Anglomania: A European Love Affair* (New York, 1999).

3.   See Brendan Donnelly, 'Europe's Defense Agreement', *Wall Street Journal On-Line*, November 2003.

4.   Figures from: UN Statistics, UN Secretariat, 2002.

5.   *Le Monde*, reported in *The Independent*, 13 November 2003.

6.   Reported in the *Financial Times*, 14 December 2003.

7.   For an interesting analysis of the Panama Congress, see Stefano Spoltore, 'The Panama Congress: A Failed Attempt at Latin American Union', *The Federalist: A political review*, No. 1, Pavia, Italy, 2003.

8.   The Giscard proposal included this 60 per cent rule but, to get a 'majority' in the Council, a majority of the states was needed as well. Also, I use the term 'Council'. There are though two Councils. One is the European Council of heads of government; the other is a legislative body, the Council of Ministers (for ministers). They both represent national governments, and I use the terms interchangeably throughout this book.

9.   John Redwood, *Stars and Strife: The Coming Conflicts Between the USA and the EU* (London, 2001), p. 27.

10.   This thesis about the social effects of globalized economies on domestic inequalities is set forth in, amongst other works, Hans-Peter Martin and Harald Schumann, *The Global Trap: Globalisation and the Assault on Prosperity and Democracy* (London and New York, 1997). Also see

William Greider, *One World, Ready Or Not: The Manic Logic Of Global Capitalism* (London, 1997); Edward Luttwak, *Turbo Capitalism* (New York, 1999); and Stephen Haseler, *The Super-Rich*.

11. Redwood, *Stars and Strife*, p. 28.

12. The most that Britain can even begin to think about is to join with Mexico and Canada as members, with the USA, of the North American Free Trade Association.

Chapter 6: A Country Called 'Europe'

1. Interview with Jacques Delors, RTL, 17 November 1993.

2. Timothy Garton Ash, 'Is Britain European?', *Prospect*, February 2001.

3. Alan S. Milward, *The European Rescue of the Nation-State* (London, 1992).

4. Anthony D. Smith, *Nations and Nationalism in a Global Era* (London, 1995), p. 139.

5. Quotation from Marshall, *The Bank*, p. 350.

6. Nicholas Mayhew, *Sterling: The Rise and Fall of a Currency* (London, 1999), p. ix.

7. Roy Denman, 'Europe United By Its New Money', *International Herald Tribune*, 22 January 2002.

8. Andrew Duff, 'Towards a European Federal Society', in Kim Feus (ed.), *The EU Charter Of Fundamental Rights* (London, 2001), pp. 13–27.

9. Smith, *Nations and Nationalism in a Global Era*, p. 138.

10. Kenneth Minogue, in his elegant slim volume *Nationalism*, argues that the 'struggle' for independence is the 'centrepiece' in the formation of nation states'. Minogue, *Nationalism* (London, 1967), p. 27.

11. David Runciman, 'Invented Communities', *The London Review of Books*, vol. 23, no. 14 (1999).

12. The importance of a European idea of 'the other' was set out by Garton Ash in 'We Know What Europe Is For, But What Is It Against These Days?', *The Independent*, December 2001.

13. Jack Straw, 'In This New World, All Of Us Must Rethink Our Attitudes To Sovereignty', *The Independent*, 22 November 2001. On the effect of terrorism on common identity, see Barry Buzan, 'New Patterns of Global Security in the 21st Century', *International Affairs*, 67 (1991), p. 448.

14. For instance, the huge penetration of the televised national event of the coronation of Queen Elizabeth II in 1953, royal weddings and funerals and lowest-common-denominator sitcoms all helped create a continuing (and old-fashioned) sense of Englishness.

15. John Vinocur, *International Herald Tribune*, 29 May 2001.

16. *Financial Times*, 8–9 November 1997.

17. 'The Right Track', *Time*, 8 December 1997.

18. William Greider, *One World, Ready Or Not: The Manic Logic Of Global Capitalism* (New York, 1997).

19. Jim Hoagland, 'Needed, a Cooperation Agenda for America, Europe and Japan', *International Herald Tribune*, 12 October 1998.

20. Grant, *Delors*, p. 87.

21. For a powerful analysis and polemic about how mass tastes have overwhelmed and lowered standards in western societies, see George Walden, *A Career in the Masses* (London, 2001).

22. See Michael Young, *The Rise Of The Meritocracy*, paperback reprint (New York, 1994).

23. *International Herald Tribune*, 19 December 2003.

24. Fred Halliday, *Two Hours That Shook The World: September 11, 2001 – Causes and Consequences* (London, 2002).

25. The Amsterdam Treaty (1997) affirmed that the Union is 'founded on principles of liberty, democracy, respect for fundamental freedoms, and the rule of law' and provided for member states to be deprived of voting rights should these rights be abridged.

26. *The Observer*, 21 June 1998.

27. Mrs. Thatcher's quote is from a speech in 1994, quoted in *Collins Quotation Finder* (2001), p. 231.

28. For basic facts about the European Commission, see http://europa. eu.int/.

Chapter 7: Europe versus the USA

1. See Zbigniew Brzezinski, *The Grand Chessboard: American Primacy and Its Geostrategic Imperatives* (New York, 1997).

2. Ibid. p. 38.

3. Comparative GNP is tricky to calculate. It depends on which countries are included in Eurasia (I have included India) and on how high the dollar is at any given time. Brzezinski's calculation that Eurasia's GNP accounted for about 60 per cent of the world's GNP took place in the late 1990s. My calculation takes place in May 2003, after the dollar had fallen from its high point in the late 1990s.

4. Brzezinski, *The Grand Chessboard*, p. 35.

5. See Kagan, *Paradise and Power*, p. 61.

6. This is Kagan's description of the European approach to international problems; ibid. p. 3.

7. Brzezinski, *The Grand Chessboard*, p. 61.

8. See Michael Meacher, 'This War on Terrorism is Bogus', *The Guardian*, 6 September 2003. Meacher, a former British government minister, represented a widely held view in Europe that US foreign policy was sustained by an overblown threat culture. Ivo Daalder represented a similar widely held European view that 'for the United States, foreign

policy is first and foremost about threats – both traditional threats (including possible military or political subversion of US friends and allies by countries that are hostile to US interests) and new threats resulting from proliferation of weapons of mass destruction, the growing power of terrorist groups and other non-state actors, and the increasing vulnerability of US society to direct attack.' Ivo Daalder, 'Are the United States and Europe Heading For Divorce?', *International Affairs*, 77, 3 (2001), p. 559.

9. Robert Fisk, 'This Is Not A War On Terror. It's A Fight Against America's Enemies', *The Independent*, 25 September 2001.

10. See Paul Rich, 'European Security and the Resurgence of Radical Islam: The Issue of the Maghreb and Algeria', in Lisbeth Aggestam and Adrian Hyde Price (eds), *Security and Identity in Europe* (London, 2000), p. 230.

11. Buzan, 'New Patterns of Global Security in the 21st Century', p. 448.

12. See report in *The Guardian*, 6 October 2002.

13. Peter Rodman, *Drifting Apart? Trends in US-European Relations* (Washington, DC, 1999), p. 41.

14. F. Oz-Salzberger, 'Europe should step in – and look Israelis in the eye', *International Herald Tribune*, 29 March 2002.

15. Reported in Jeremy Rifkin, 'The US Must Follow Europe's Lead and Turn Its Back on Oil', *The Guardian*, 10 October 2002.

16. These figures are taken from US Bureau of Transportation Statistics, US Department of Energy, Energy Information Administration, *Monthly Energy Review*, November 2002. Also available at http://www.eia.doe.gov/mer.

17. See Bruno Coppieters, 'Between Europe and Asia: Security and Identity in Central Asia'. Coppieters argues that 'the EU has a greater stake than the US in Central Asia, given that it constitutes a major future consumer of energy products from the region', p. 209.

18. The experienced commentator in American-European affairs, William Pfaff, could write that 'it is widely believed in the region that the United States is actually planning a lasting security presence in a vast region extending [from the Balkans] to the oil rich countries of the Middle East and the Caspian Sea.' See William Pfaff, 'If NATO Quits The Balkans, Will the EU Step In?', *International Herald Tribune*, 8–9 September 2001.

19. See '2002 National Security Strategy of the United States of America', submitted to Congress, September 2002.

20. Figures from the World Development Indicators Database, World Bank, July 2002.

21. Gray quote in *Daily Express*, 11 September 1998, cited in Haseler, *The Super-Rich*, p. 36. Jeffrey Henderson goes further than Gray and has suggested that China may mutate into what he calls 'Market Stalinism' – 'a more thoroughly capitalist, but still authoritarian, economic and

political form, rather like South Korea between the early 1960s and the mid 1980s'. *The Guardian*, 13 January 1998, extracted from Grahame Thompson (ed.), *Economic Integration in the Asia-Pacific* (London, 1998).

22.   Quote from the American political thinker Michael Lind, *The Next American Nation: The New Nationalism and the Fourth American Revolution* (New York, 1995), p. 203.

Chapter 8: Goodbye, Columbus

1.   Bullock, *Ernest Bevin*, p. 526.
2.   Poll for the German Marshall Fund of the USA, *International Herald Tribune*, 4 September 2003.
3.   *The Guardian*, 5 March 2003.
4.   Poll results and quotation from German CDU MEP Elmar Brok, quoted in *International Herald Tribune*, 31 January 2003.
5.   Articles 21 and 27 of the Giscard draft written EU constitution.
6.   Joseph Nye's categories of 'soft' and 'hard' power, outlined in Nye, *Bound To Lead*, includes some uses of economic power within 'hard power' – because they are meant to change behaviour – although many subsequent commentaries about 'hard' and 'soft' power see economic power as 'soft' and military power as 'hard'.
7.   State Department official Strobe Talbot, quoted in Rodman, *Drifting Apart?*, p. 51.
8.   *Sunday Telegraph*, 17 June 2001.
9.   Rodman, *Drifting Apart?*, p. 35.
10.   At 2.4 per cent of GDP in 2000, the UK ranks only below special-case Greece on 4.9 per cent and France on 2.6 per cent. Figures for 2000 from *The Military Balance, 2001–2002*, International Institute for Strategic Studies, 2002.
11.   *Daily Mail*, 15 March 2002 (my emphasis).
12.   For one of the most comprehensive and detailed analyses of the St Malo agreement and the origins of the European Defence and Security System, see Ronan Fanning, 'Defence and Security', in Paul Gillespie (ed.), *Blair's Britain, England's Hope: A View From Ireland* (Dublin, 2000).
13.   Blair Press Conference, 8 March 1999. The relevant paragraph from the St Malo agreement read: 'In order for the European Union to take decisions and approve military action where the NATO Alliance as a whole is not engaged, the Union must be given appropriate structures and a capacity for analysis of situations, sources of intelligence and a capability for relevant strategic planning, without unnecessary duplication, taking account of the existing assets of the WEU and the evolution of its relations with the EU. In this regard the EU will also need to have recourse to suitable military means (European capabilities pre-

designated within NATO's European pillar or national or multinational European means outside the NATO framework).

14.   Gillespie, *Blair's Britain, England's Hope*, p. 225.

15.   Ibid. p. 220.

16.   Speech at the NATO conference to celebrate NATO's 50th anniversary, 1999, quoted in ibid. p. 219.

17.   Remarks, later withdrawn, by Richard Boucher at State Department Press Conference, 2 September 2003, reported in *International Herald Tribune*, 3 September 2003.

18.   Reported by German News Agency, http://www.dw-world.de/english, 7 May 2003.

19.   Quoted in *International Herald Tribune*, 17 October 2002.

20.   From Hilaire Belloc, in *Modern Traveller* (London, 1898), cited in Jay, *Oxford Dictionary (of Political Quotations)*, p. 31.

21.   *International Herald Tribune*, 18 October 2001.

22.   Quote reported in *International Herald Tribune*, 12 October 2001.

23.   See 'Schroeder Makes Anti-Bioterror Forces Available', *International Herald Tribune*, 18 October 2001.

24.   In 'Responsibility For Europe', SPD Policy Document issued for the November National Conference of the SPD on 30 April 2001.

25.   The strategy was formally adopted by EU Foreign Ministers in Brussels on 13 December 2003.

26.   All figures are from International Institute For Strategic Studies, *The Military Balance, 2001-2002* (London, 2001). Although the EU collectively is way out in front of any other power other than the USA (the *Military Balance* reckoning is that Russia spends $59 billion, China $41 billion, Japan $44 billion and India $14 billion), the EU's collective military budget, compared with all the other powers bar Japan, in no way reflects its collective economic strength.

27.   Ibid.

28.   Kennedy, *The Rise and Fall of the Great Powers*, p. 472.

29.   See Michael Alexander and Timothy Garden, 'The Arithmetic of Defence Policy', *International Affairs*, vol. 77, no. 3, July 2001. In this pioneering and informative article, the authors argued that 'unless European governments can find a way to get significantly better return for each unit of defence expenditures starting relatively soon, their ability, separately or collectively, to take substantial military action in defence of their interests is going to evaporate.' They suggest starkly that, unless such integration takes place, the nations of Europe might as well opt out of the military game altogether, as 'our forces will become unemployable in any remotely challenging environment.'

30.   IISS, *The Military Balance*.

31.   Data from Alexander and Garden, 'The Arithmetic of Defence Policy'.

32. John Keegan, 'Secret Defence Cuts That Labour Will Unveil After The Election', *Daily Telegraph*, 5 June 2001.

33. Quotes and report in *International Herald Tribune*, 27 March 2002. The EU decided in March 2002 to approve the Galileo project.

34. For discussion of the UK's intelligence dilemma, see Professor Clarke's testimony before the House of Commons Foreign Affairs Committee, 2 November 2001.

35. One of Europe's foremost federalist writers, John Pinder, argues that for the EU to possess an effective foreign and security policy it needs 'common instruments' removed from the grasp of national capitals – rather like the EU's external tariff or the euro (an instrument of power that belongs exclusively to the Union). The European Rapid Reaction Force is one such 'common instrument' as it has its own Military Committee and European Military Staff reporting to the ambassadorial-level Political and Security Committee of the EU. See John Pinder, *The European Union: A Very Short Introduction* (Oxford, 2001), p. 118. See Pinder for a clear exposition of the rules governing the CFSP, pp. 117–19.

36. The editors of *The Military Balance* (IISS) argue that 'the EU must acknowledge openly that the final operating capability can only be achieved at a much later date [than December 2003], say 2012… [although] it could be approached incrementally, with 2003 then becoming the target date for the ability to deploy two or three brigade-level formations.' *The Military Balance*, p. 291.

37. See House of Commons Defence Select Committee, 19 December 2001.

38. The Helsinki Communiqué announced that 'new political and military bodies and structures will be established within the Council' to enable the Union to carry out operations. Helsinki Communiqué, December 1999. Following the NATO 'Berlin Plus' agreement, the EU could have guaranteed access to SHAPE planning and the heavy NATO assets which the Europeans lacked. The December 2003 'troika' agreement, though, set up a process where EU operations could go ahead autonomously.

39. Frederick Bonnart, 'A Symbolic Step Towards Real EU Defence', *International Herald Tribune*, 23 December 2003.

40. *Financial Times*, 30 April 2001.

41. Paul Cornish and Geoffrey Edwards, 'Beyond The EU/NATO Dichotomy: The Beginnings of a European Strategic Culture', *International Affairs*, vol. 77, no. 3 (July 2001), p. 587.

42. Wesley K. Clark, American general and NATO commander during the Kosovo campaign. 'U.S. Actions Push the EU to Its Own Military Force', *International Herald Tribune*, 9–10 December 2000.

Index